D1336616

SELECTED PLAYS
OF
AUSTIN CLARKE

Irish Drama Selections

General Editors
Joseph Ronsley
Ann Saddlemyer

IRISH DRAMA SELECTIONS
ISSN 0260–7962

SELECTED PLAYS
OF
AUSTIN CLARKE

For Máire, le grá

Mary

Chosen and introduction by
Mary Shine Thompson

Irish Drama Selections: 14

First published in Great Britain in 2005
by Colin Smythe Limited, Gerrards Cross, Buckinghamshire SL9 8XA

British Library Cataloguing in Publication Data
A catalogue record for this book is available from the British Library

ISBN10:   0-86140-208-1
ISBN13:   978-0-86140-208-3

Distributed in North America by Oxford University Press
198 Madison Avenue, New York, NY 10016

Produced in Great Britain
Typeset by Pageset Ltd., High Wycombe, Buckinghamshire
Printed and bound by T.J. International Ltd., Padstow, Cornwall

CONTENTS

INTRODUCTION:

Austin Clarke's (1896–1974) literary reputation rests primarily upon his poetry published over a fifty-seven year period. Although his formative experiences in the Jesuit-run Belvedere College and University College Dublin resemble Joyce's in many respects, his apprentice poetry, written in the epic mode in the years after the 1916 Rising, earned him early recognition and comparison with W.B. Yeats. Yeats's model of poetic achievement simultaneously attracted and suppressed Clarke psychically, and the older poet's exclusion of his work from the Oxford Book of Modern Verse in 1936 did nothing to boost his confidence. Responding in part to Yeats's enmity, Clarke's Pilgrimage and Other Poems (1929) maps out as his poetic territory the historically verifiable, late medieval Celtic-Romanesque period, of which Yeats knew little. It became the backdrop to many of the verse plays he wrote in the 1940s. Particularly in his later poetry, after 1955, Clarke adopts a Swiftian stance, defending individuals' rights and expressing deep pessimism about public affairs, both ecclesiastical and secular. In old age he reverted to mythological subjects, treating them with an exuberant optimism that stands in marked contrast to the gloom that pervades his early epics.

Throughout his life he was plagued by depression, suffering at least one serious breakdown that led to his confinement in Swift's hospital, St Patrick's, for over a year, which became the topic of his long poem, *Mnemosyne Lay in Dust* (1966). His first marriage in 1920 was short-lived and probably unconsummated, and soon after University College Dublin terminated his employment as an assistant lecturer. This led to seventeen years in London as a literary journalist, and from 1940 he combined that career in Dublin with regular poetry programmes on Radio Eireann, the national airwave.

Clarke's interest in verse theatre was aroused by his visits to the Abbey Theatre when he was an undergraduate. The Abbey was still a poetic stronghold in those years before the 1916 Rising, and the heroic paganism, the gentleness and the cold, clear imagery of Yeats's poetic plays attracted him. He accepted Yeats's belief in verse drama's capacity to uncover 'that high, delicately organised soul of man and of action, that may not speak aloud if it do not speak verse'.[1] He took note of Yeats's use of ritual, his eschewal of the conventions of both realism and of the *pièce bien faite*, the well-made play. The stage properties of Yeats's plays seemed like symbols to him. 'I felt as if they were rather like the vessels and vestments of a religious service [...] All that mattered really was the play and the poetry and the theatre itself, well, it always seemed to me ideal for its poetic purpose – small and simple, perhaps austere, – and yet rich.' He resolved to write verse plays, but Yeats rejected his first, *The Son of Learning*, when he submitted it to the Abbey. Nonetheless, Terence Gray staged it successfully at the Cambridge Festival Theatre in 1927. While two of Clarke's verse plays (*The Son of Learning* and *Sister Eucharia*) were performed at the Gate Theatre in the 1930s, it was not until January 1942 that his work came to the attention of the Abbey, with *The Black Fast*.

By then social drama had come to dominate the national theatre and to supplant Yeats's aesthetic which was oriented towards the remote, the spiritual and the ideal. In the absence of other candidates, Clarke nominated himself Yeats's dramatic successor, and devoted his energies throughout the 1940s to reinstating verse drama, while redressing the imbalances he perceived in both the elder poet's plays and his theatre. Verse drama had enjoyed something of a mild resurgence of interest in Britain in the 1930s – the form was popular with Auden, Bottomley, Eliot, and others. In addition, verse-speaking technique had been developed by teachers Elsie Fogerty and Marjorie Gullan whom Clarke had encountered when he acted as adjudicator at the Festival of Verse-Speaking in Oxford, whose vice-presidents included Clifford Bax, John Binyon, Walter De La Mare and John Masefield. Many Irish writers, too, were attracted to the genre. Seumas O'Sullivan published verse plays in his *Dublin Magazine,* including Clarke's early works, and poet and playwright Padraic Fallon greeted the prospect of a verse-speaking movement as the most exciting moment in history. Eventually Clarke and Robert Farren, a poet employed by Radio Eireann, established the Dublin Verse-Speaking Society in December 1939, and it survived until the mid-1960s. From its inception it broadcast a weekly radio programme of poetry presented by Clarke, and so nurtured a ready audience for its verse-speaking. Its main purpose was, according to Clarke, not to broadcast poetry but to keep alive the Abbey literary tradition and to revive verse theatre. Radio was therefore a means to a theatrical end. The society had the additional attraction of providing a showcase for his own plays. It staged several in the Peacock Theatre, a smaller theatre within the Abbey complex, between 1941 and 1944, many of which Radio Eireann broadcast on later dates, including premiers of *The Flame*, *The Kiss* and *The Plot is Ready*.

Clarke set about cultivating the art of verse-speaking by gradually preparing his audience. His radio programmes served this didactic purpose, all the more necessary, in his opinion, because theatre audiences had degenerated into Calibans who would sit chuckling and guffawing in the stalls. He chose non-professional actors to perform his poetry, as Yeats had done, because he believed that actors kill the occasional performances of verse drama on the regular stage. He wanted to avoid both broad contrasts in tone and what he terms 'psychological inaudibility', the tendency to miss the nuance and suggestiveness of spoken phrases because of the customary practice of reading poetry silently. He proposed to counteract this 'inaudibility' by counselling his speakers to adopt a slower tempo and aimed at a quiet, intimate note.

He had roundly criticised Yeats both for his actors' method of intoning verse and for his failure to foster a receptive audience. He sought to avoid the mesmerism created by an emphasis on the metrical base, instead aspiring to a balance between meaning and emotion, imagery, movement and word-music. As the essay 'Verse-speaking and Verse Drama' (reproduced in this book) indicates, the presiding metaphor for his method is musical. The verse drama script is a musical score, the performance an orchestration, the interdependent rhythms of the various speaking parts 'seem, as if by invisible conducting, to set up a timing and spacing of their own.' In the spirit of Yeats he dismissed the imperative of commercial success. Ironically, the performances he directed usually played to full houses.

Among Clarke's professional collaborators was Ria Mooney, one-time Abbey actor and producer, whose contribution was almost as crucial as Robert Farren's. Out of that relationship evolved the Lyric Theatre, which was established in June 1944 and which employed professional actors for the main roles and members of the verse-speaking society for chorus and minor roles.

Its programmes proclaim that its main aim was 'to maintain the imaginative tradition of the Irish Theatre which the poets of the literary revival made famous'. Over seven years, until the Abbey was destroyed by fire in 1951, it staged plays biannually. Foremost among them were Clarke's and Yeats's plays, but also covered were the works of other Irish dramatists including Padraic Colum, Mary Devenport O'Neill, Donagh MacDonagh and George Fitzmaurice, and non-Irish, post-Yeats writers, notably Gordon Bottomley, Lawrence Binyon, T.S. Eliot, Archibald MacLeish and T. Sturge Moore.

Clarke's association with Ria Mooney honed his practical theatre skills. Their correspondence is replete with his practical suggestions regarding sets, costumes, and lighting, grouping and casting actors and the use of stage space. For Devenport O'Neill's *Bluebeard,* for example, he suggested the use of delicate spotlights in order to heighten the impact of Bluebeard. He also recommended that a rostrum be used as a set and that the window be narrow and high.[2] Writing on how he wanted his own *Black Fast* staged, his instructions were precise. He was concerned that the stage business be done properly, and stressed the need for rehearsal, as well as the use of music hall technique, claiming that the audience 'will not notice the dish moving unless their attention is drawn to it in a chaplinesque way: the dish moves an inch, the servant almost catches what is happening: it moves an inch again the moment his back is turned.'[3] He strove to avoid the faults of Yeats who, he believed, talked and wrote about a verse-speaking movement, but distanced himself from the practical aspect of rehearsal.

The first eleven of Clarke's plays, written between 1926 and 1953, are his best known, and were published in a single volume in 1963. In the late 1960s, Clarke was negotiating with Liam Miller of Dolmen Press with a view to publishing a volume that would include his unpublished plays. He withdrew one of these, *St Patrick's Purgatory,* after a disagreement with Miller. Five of the remainder were subsequently issued by Dolmen, two of them posthumously. *The Frenzy of Sweeney* had been completed by 1968 and had reached the stage of galley proofs before Clarke died. *St Patrick's Purgatory* had been completed and was with Dolmen also by 1968. *Bis in Nocte* remains unpublished. Clarke had drafted a play based on the experiences of Bishop John Butler (d. 1800) at the time of his death, a fragment of which appeared in the *Journal of the Butler Society* in 1974.

Among the plays included in this book are two not previously published or performed. The selection demonstrates that Clarke's contribution to drama is neither as limited nor as homogeneous as either his own critical work or the term 'verse drama' suggests. He has implied that he finds his subject matter and setting exclusively in the medieval period. Yeats, he observed, 'had only dealt with the Pagan and I was still left all the era of Christian legend and story'[4]. However, less than a dozen of the plays are so placed. The setting of *Sister Eucharia* is contemporary, although, as Clarke himself observed, religious orders had changed little since the medieval period. Effectively, therefore, the plays speak to Clarke's Ireland. In addition to the Celtic-Romanesque plays, he translated freely plays by the Spanish dramatists Miguel de Cervantes (1547–1616) and Pedro Calderon de la Barca (1600–1681) and from the French, works by Theodore De Banville (1823–1891). He adapted for stage Nathaniel Hawthorne's (1804–1864) story, 'Goodman Brown', under the title *The Impuritans,* and rewrote *A Deuce of Jacks,* a play by his one-time friend and later business manager of the Abbey Theatre, F.R. Higgins (1896–1941). The debt to the originals is minimal; rather, they launch Clarke's own imagination. The three *Kiss* plays are comedies in the style of the *Commedia del' Arte* and there are two plays for radio, *As the Crow Flies* and *The Viscount of Blarney,* the latter based on a Wexford folk tale.[5] *Liberty Lane: A Ballad Play of Dublin* is also an expression of the demotic folk tradition. The majority of the plays consist of one act, the most common form of modern verse play, but Clarke draws on a variety of forms. Among these are interludes, comedies, a pantomime (*The Plot Succeeds),* two three-act plays (*The Moment Next to Nothing* and *St Patrick's Purgatory),* and *The Frenzy of Sweeney,* described by Clarke as a lyrical play in four acts.

In his first play, *The Son of Learning,* a comedy based on the medieval tale, *Aislinge Meic Conglinne*[6], Clarke revitalises the caricature of the clownish Irishman. The high-spirited scholar is a gleeman or goliard, a juggler and confidence trickster, a poet-musician who exposes the Church's contempt for the minstrel. Clarke reverses the ending of the original story so that the student is not rewarded for curing King Cathal of his great hunger, in order to accentuate the tension between authority and the individual. *Black Fast* is based upon St Bede's account of a controversy about the correct date of Easter.[7] It too underlines the preposterous, comic pomposity of clerical concerns. The intense one-act play, *The Flame*, explores personal conflict between one individual, the novice who is prey to temptation, and the rigid dispensation of her religious order. Clarke notes that the flame of St Brigid 'was tended in Kildare for many centuries but the practice was ultimately condemned as superstitious by the Norman archbishop of Dublin. His action was probably due to a new ecclesiastical policy but this little play is sufficiently casuistical to comprise his point of view.'[8] The apparent miracles in this play (the flame does not die despite neglect) and in *Sister Eucharia* could have rational explanations. There is, however, no such ambivalent phenomenon in *As the Crow Flies*[9], one of the most successful plays. Here the veil of romance is torn away and the audience is confronted with a bleak vision of a recurring cycle of depravity and destruction. An eagle leaves her eaglets in the care of an ancient crow who initiates her quest after knowledge, only to discover that evil incarnate, in the shape of the same Crow, the disguised Hag of Dingle, resides in her nest, endangering her young. The eagle's mission takes her to the protean Fintan, the Salmon of Assaroe, who once took the forms of an eagle and a hawk, and who embodies the wisdom of ages. His knowledge of history prevents him from believing in Christian love. With Swiftian rage and despair he denounces the obstinacy, stupidity and violence of humanity as it is revealed in history, and declares that all are prey to disease and irrationality. That the innocent eaglets perish is evidence of that shape-changing, recurring certainty. Both this and the two *Kiss* plays in this selection have a contemporary resonance, in that they obliquely address the unspeakable horrors of the Second World War that raged as they were written. The harlequin of *The Second Kiss* is a projection of Pierrot's suppressed fears, his alter ego. *The Third Kiss* contains manifestations of evil, among them a priest obsessed with sexual temptation. It ends with the voyeuristic Harlequin ambivalently declaring that his wickedness 'is really not in earnest/Or is it?' Here an internal conflict is externalised dramatically.

   The Viscount of Blarney is best considered also as a psychological drama in which the defenceless servant Cauth is confronted by a succession of threats to her womanhood, represented in surreal, expressionist figures. *The Moment Next to Nothing* revives the narrative of Clarke's romance novel, *The Sun Dances at Easter* (1952).[10] *The Plot Succeeds* and *The Plot is Ready* are based respectively on 'The Conception of Mongan and His

Love for Dubh Lacha' and 'The Death of Muircertach Mac Erca'. The humour of the *The Plot Succeeds* revolves around the capacity of Mannanaun Mac Lir, the sea god, to transform himself, while *The Plot is Ready* pits Muriadach's wife against his fairy lover.[11] The conflict is resolved when the king goes to his death to purge himself of his sinfulness and Osna, the mistress, emerges somewhat equivocally as the victor.

The Frenzy of Sweeney is freely adapted from the middle Irish romance, *Buile Suibhne*.[12] The action is introduced and punctuated by tableaux in which Sweeney summarises events, sings panegyrics to nature and laments his condition. His well-documented lyricism is intensified in this version by the role the individual dirges, denunciations and rhapsodies play within the dramatic economy of the narrative. Sweeney simultaneously enacts many roles already familiar from Clarke's repertoire. He is the marginal figure who is living testimony to the consequences of conflict with ecclesiastical authority, represented in this case by St Ronán. He is the straying student with an acute lyrical sensibility, the ousted king, beyond the domain of either secular or church rule. Wild and mad, he begs comparison with those other deranged protagonists created by Clarke around the same period, Maurice Devane of *Mnemosyne Lay in Dust* and the eponymous Mis of 'The Healing of Mis'. Like them, he is a product of the literary imagination rather than a historically verifiable figure. The subject of Sweeney may have attracted Clarke for some of the same reasons that it appealed to Seamus Heaney a decade later. Sweeney's cultural affinity with the Madman of Britain (here named Caradoc), and his easy movement throughout the whole of Ireland become parables of ideal civil relations just as decades of strife were about to be unleashed.

St Patrick's Purgatory, the now inaccessible cave at the penitential island in Lough Derg, exercised the minds of many of Clarke's literary contemporaries including Denis Devlin, Patrick Kavanagh and Sean O Faolain. Clarke's source for his *St Patrick's Purgatory* was probably Denis Florence MacCarthy's translation of the original by Calderon.[13] However, no Irish contemporary has introduced into Lough Derg literature so evil a character as the lubricious adventurer Luis, among whose crimes are numbered rapacious incest, possible necrophilia and murderous intent. The story proceeds at a rapid pace. A ship led by a nobleman, Philip, carrying two Christian slaves, Luis and Patrick, is wrecked on Irish shores. The Irish king, Egerius, warms to Luis, who is personable despite his evil ways. He seduces and ultimately kills the king's daughter, Polonia. Meanwhile, Patrick is sold as a shepherd to a peasant and his wife, Lucy. She loves Philip, who is betrothed to Polonia, and he returns to Egerius's court after being discovered *in flagrante* with Lucy. Patrick raises Polonia from the dead, and Egerius and his retinue enter the island cave in Lough Derg, where the anger of the Almighty is apparent in its Dantesque horrors. Luis, maddened by a vision of death, also goes to Lough Derg, where he meets Polonia, now living as a hermit on its shores. She forgives him but he too enters the cave. Her sister Lesbia rules the kingdom of her father, Egerius, and she marries Philip. The play closes with Luis's entreaties to all to repent. It depicts sexual relationships governed not by romance but by pragmatic, political considerations, if not by lust, and (unusually for Clarke) the thrust of the tale is sympathetic to Catholic doctrine rather than sceptical of it. In *Two Interludes* and *Bis in Nocte,* in contrast, sexuality is treated as the stuff of bawdy, irreverent comedy. The subject of *Liberty Lane* is a traditional story about a trick played on Zozimus, *aka* Michael Moran, the nineteenth century balladeer who captured the imagination of W.B. Yeats. In his essay 'The Last Gleeman', Yeats compared Moran with Mac Conglinne, the subject of Clarke's first play, *The Son of Learning.* Clarke wrote *Liberty Lane.* which takes its tone from Yeats's essay, when he failed to get permission to adapt the ending of F.R. Higgins's *A Deuce of Jacks* (a play performed unsuccessfully in the Abbey Theatre in 1935), which treats of the same topic.

The few insights Clarke offers into his *modus operandi* for writing verse plays are mainly confined to comments on verse technique. In his early works, he claims that he determined to keep the speeches short until the interest of the audience had increased; then he allowed the poetry to expand in a lengthy speech. Later, however, he changed his approach, and used long speeches throughout, attempting to maintain interest with rapid action and variety. Clarke's fourth play, *The Black Fast*, is the first to contain even relatively protracted speeches and these are few. However, Cogitosus' twenty-two line defence of Colmcille, one of the few lengthy addresses, does not disrupt the flow. The rhetorical force of its cumulative argument carries along the listener. Less successful are the exchanges between Eithne and Ceasan in *The Moment Next to Nothing* (excluded from this selection), much of whose dialogue consists of verse paragraphs.

Clarke claims that he adopted the technical device of metre in preference to rhythm because the rhythm of free verse differs little from that of prose. In fact he imposes a metrical superstructure over the rhythms of prose, so creating tension between the stylised metrical norm and the occasionally opposing organisation compelled by meaning. He employs various patterns, although generally he favours the pentameter, because, he claimed, even in prose and speech the basic combination of five keeps reappearing. He distinguishes between stage speech and natural speech and asserts that the rhythm established by the latter can accelerate the tempo of the dialogue: 'stage speech only resembles natural speech and goes more easily, being set to definite patterns. The accented syllables are never followed by more than three unaccented syllables. Nonetheless, when rhythm takes control, the secondary stresses point the way, paragraphically, line beyond line.'[14]

At other times when speed is required he contrives to divide the metric line between two or even three speakers. The rhythm of *The Son of Learning* is very free, in line with the exuberance of the main protagonist and the robustness of the diction. It displeased Yeats when Clarke submitted it to the Abbey around 1926: he suggested that its natural rhythm was prose. *Liberty Lane* is also written in irregular blank verse, but peppered with ballads, rhymes and poems and containing what Clarke the 'wheel and bob stanza'. The metrical devices of *The Kiss* and *The Second Kiss* are, Clarke asserts, a natural counterpoint of ordinary verse forms and everyday speech. Both are written in rhyming couplets, but the latter is laced with trisyllabic, forced and imperfect rhyme, adding to the comic effect. *The Viscount* is in half-doggerel octosyllabics that accentuate Cauth's artlessness. *As the Crow Flies* is 'a half-hour of assonance, cross-rhyme, internal rhyme and off-accent harmonies'.[15] *The Plot Succeeds* is written in heroic couplets, apart from the prologue, but one of the rhyming words in each pair is disyllabic and only the first syllable of it is rhymed. Gaelic prosody suggested this pattern. Clarke challenges the assertion of Calderon's translator, MacCarthy, that to preserve the assonance and vowel rhyme of the original Spanish of *St Patrick's Purgatory* would be 'nearly impractical in English'[16]. Clarke retains the assonance in lengthy passages, so that several succeeding lines end with the same vowel sound. He varies this device by using perfect rhyme, or *rime riche*, or by adding or substituting internal rhyme. *The Frenzy of Sweeney* does not confine itself to the metrical pattern of the original – quatrains interspersed with prose narrative. It adopts a range of forms, metrical devices and lyric rhythms, and begins with a poem in verse paragraphs of alternating trimeters and tetrameters originally published in *The Cattledrive in Connaught* (1925), there entitled 'The Frenzy of Suibhne'.

What were Clarke's dramatic and theatrical priorities? His critical idiom is not analytical, and his writings on theatre in general avoid discussion on elements such as plot and character. As the essays on theatre included in this book suggest, he focuses on the production of sound, and on the relationship between poetry and speech, rather than between poetry and drama, leading him into discussion on such issues as 'correct' methods of verse-speaking. His plays and his theatre privilege the word, in the tradition of Irish drama, bringing to it the discipline and rigour of poetic norms. This is a flaw only if viewed through the restrictive lens of the naturalist theatre, and Clarke's dramatic language, form and central concerns react vehemently and self-consciously against naturalism, the orthodoxy in the Abbey of the mid-century. In *The Kiss* Pierrot summarises Clarke's position on realist conventions, especially as they had been applied in the Abbey when he exclaims 'I hate domestic dramas!' Often the movement is stylised, as in *The Flame*, or farcical, as in *The Son of Learning*. The plays variously incorporate dance routines, music, slapstick and other pantomimic elements. The characterisation, that includes speaking crows, eagles, the pierrots, lays down the gauntlet to verisimilitude. Puns and colloquialisms abound in the dialogue. The self-reflexive theatricality predates and finds its echo in *Waiting for Godot*, which was first not staged until 1953. In *The Second Kiss,* for example, Pierrot openly seeks a prompt, searches for the script, reads the stage directions, enacts them, suggests 'Let's be profound!' The energetic and ludic language reflects the abundance of food in *The Son of Learning*, a play that treats light-heartedly the subject of gluttony (and metaphorically, the theme of sexual appetite). The plays therefore are credible not in terms of their naturalistic representation of reality, but insofar as they interconnect with familiar images, myths and narratives and explore psychological states. With sensitive and imaginative staging and a mode of speaking appropriate to verse, they perform better than they read.

When Clarke set about establishing the Lyric Theatre Company, he had in mind not only the maintenance of high standards of performance, but also a more elevated purpose. He was intent on continuing the work of reforming the Irish national character undertaken by the early Abbey playwrights and in particular, by Yeats. This concern is evident in his characterisation. Clarke's dramatic heroes answer to their own conscience, not to any rule of law. They are often playful and irreverent and combine humour and finely tuned aesthetic sensibilities. As such they present alternatives to the restrictive models of identity idealised by the Irish Free State.

Clarke's recourse to the form of drama, and in particular, verse drama, is further evidence of his cultural nationalism. His early poetry (*The Vengeance of Fionn, The Fires of Baal, The Sword of the West*) had taken the public form of the epic, appropriate to its object of redefining national character in the image of the heroic. The theatre offered another public mode and arena adapted to the exploration of the emotions that shaped national life. Because of its ritual quality and associations, it had the capacity to stimulate an audience to pass from a state of indifference to a state of acute awareness. It aimed to ignite in its audience a collective, intense emotional reaction, an ambition shared also by the cultural nationalist. Verse drama held additional attractions. It implied a formality and discipline that amplified the *gravitas* necessary to a project with such exalted aims. It contradicted the illusion of reality and resisted naturalism: it both simplified and complicated ordinary experience. In addition, verse was memorable. Most importantly, Yeats had already established the tradition of verse drama as an integral genre of the Irish literary revival.

Clarke concedes that the forum for which Yeats wrote many of his plays, the literary drawing room, had vanished with the passing of the salons of the nineties, rendering their form unsuitable to his own contemporary needs, but inherent in Yeats's theatre he perceived intrinsic shortcomings. Among these were his over-reaction to the bustle of ordinary stage movement, his tendency towards lyrical monotone, the dramatic limitations of the plays themselves, and the fact that Yeats restricted his theatrical repertoire to his own plays. He also takes exception to the early Yeats's aestheticism, his tendency to purge his plays of the historical moment and prevailing dilemmas. In dramatic terms, he saw Yeats as an extremist who sacrificed theme and character development, confining his short lyric plays to symbolic figures for formal purity, ultimately seeking refuge in the exotic form of the

Noh. In particular he objected to what he perceived as Yeats's tendency to place a *cordon sanitaire* around poetry, to narrow its function. Clarke nurtured a romantic faith in the power of poetry. 'You can say anything in poetry [...] what we say is very often compressed into a quick succession of images and escapes the attention of the spotters who are sent to the theatres by the various religious bodies, to see if anything – heterodox had been said.'[17]

He blamed the failure of Yeats's theatre to remould the collective Irish consciousness partly on what he saw as his deliberate removal of poetry from the vital drama of good and evil and the exciting historic complications of Irish life, confining it instead to subjective and aesthetic domains. An additional weakness in his presentation of verse drama, Clarke believed, was the method of chanting adopted by Yeats's players: in his opinion emotion was suffocated by their elocutionary methods. Yeats was negligent too, in not educating his audiences. Lady Gregory, and, indeed, Yeats himself, had assumed the existence of an uncorrupted and imaginative audience trained to listen by its passion for oratory. Clarke was neither so presumptuous nor as optimistic.

Yeats's experience provided a blueprint of the pitfalls inherent in establishing a verse theatre. Yet the necessity of such a movement never seemed greater than in the late 1930s. Although the theatre did not fall within the ambit of the censor of literature in Ireland, an inhibiting moral and cultural climate prevailed that did nothing to encourage experimentation either in dramatic form or content. The Dublin Drama League, founded by Lennox Robinson in 1919 to introduce experimental drama to Dublin audiences, was now all but defunct, and there was no dramatic body devoted to innovation. The Gate Theatre, which continued the tradition of experimentation from its foundation in 1928, was opting for secure box-office choices and the Abbey, fallen into one of its periodic troughs, had lost all interest in verse plays, even in Yeats's own. Its productions were characterised mainly by unremitting caution and realism, in sharp contrast to the excitement and conflict which plays had generated at the turn of the century. Clarke believed that the Abbey's energies were devoted to a minor industry that spawned screaming, farcical kitchen comedies, with Peasant Quality as its primary criterion of dramatic worth. As he commented sardonically, 'The excellence of our bogland studies is undoubted, and the skill with which they are written is remarkable: but there are times when we weary of land-hungry farmers, policemen, prayerful old women, and the comic effect of the brogue.'[18] The concept of the ensemble theatre that had served the Abbey well was dissipating, and the exodus of actors to Hollywood had begun. Members of the Abbey board bickered and even publicly quarrelled, to the detriment of the management of the theatre. Money was scarce, and from 1945 much of it was channelled into the production of poor quality Irish-language pantomimes. Clarke regularly lambasted the Gaelic Abbey programmes, hyperbolically accusing them of the worst horrors of the age, and of turning heroic legends and themes into buffoonery. The final item in Clarke's acutely observed although overstated catalogue of theatrical woes was the absence of professional dramatic critics.

In such a climate, Clarke's initiative was significant. If he did not succeed in making verse drama a central part of the Abbey Theatre repertoire as he had hoped, the fault did not lie exclusively with his plays or his theatre company. In electing verse drama, he chose a platform of failure. While like Yeats he was always ambivalent about public acclaim and did not measure success in terms of box-office appeal, the commercial allure of verse drama is limited and therefore its attractiveness to a theatre with a limited budget. Furthermore, its conventions have never been fully accepted by modern theatre audiences. Given its presumption of an ideal linguistic domain, its roots in ritual and its links to the epic, its appeal is likely to be nostalgic. In practical terms, the Abbey fire of 1951 left Clarke without a venue and therefore unable to capitalise on the renewal of interest in verse drama in Britain. A complex of interacting factors, therefore, conspired both to conceal and to dilute the lasting impact of his efforts.

Appraisal of his plays, however, has to be set in the context of his theatre, the workshop within which many of them were developed. His contribution to drama extends beyond the boundaries of the role of playwright to include that of impresario, director and poet in the theatre and on radio. While his attention to poetic technique is meticulous, an acute awareness of speech rhythms, stage space, lighting, and a capacity to evoke a mood with sparse props match it. A considerable achievement of the Lyric Theatre Company was its rescue of Yeats's plays at a time when the Abbey had washed its hands of them. Two of them, *The Herne's Egg* and *The Death of Cuchulain*, remained neglected until the Lyric performed them. By staging these and *The Only Jealousy of Emer*, *Deirdre*, *The Countess Cathleen* (which had not found an audience in the seventeen years that preceded the Lyric production) and by broadcasting *The Green Helmet* on radio in the period immediately following Yeats's death, he saved them from obscurity. Colum's miracle play, *The Miracle of the Corn*, had languished in the Abbey since the early days of the literary revival until the Lyric disinterred it in 1948. It was the first company to stage Fitzmaurice's *The Dandy Dolls*; and it gave his *Magic Glasses* its first airing in thirty-three years in 1946.

Clarke's twenty-one dramas constitute the most significant collection of verse plays by an Irish playwright since Yeats, not only because of the seriousness of their intent but also because of their formal variety, their resistance to the successful stereotype of the Abbey play, and their subtle use of theatrical resources. No poet since has displayed so sustained an interest in marrying the form to native settings: Seamus Heaney's, Derek Mahon's and Brendan Kennelly's incursions into verse play, for example, consist of adaptations of Greek and French classics. Clarke's settings create a critical distance that enabled him explore the fault lines of the insular Ireland of the mid-century. His interrogation exposes the damage wrought on individuals by civil and ecclesiastical authoritarianism, a dominant preoccupation of his later poetry after *Ancient Lights*. Through sympathetic characterisation and the theatrical evocation of mood the plays avoid the charge of strident complaining often levelled against his later satirical verse. The plays evince, but are not limited by, his life-long resistance to institutionalised religion. They do not preclude the possibility of a supernatural presence in people's lives, although they deny their audience the consolation of either rational proof of or belief in it. Rather, the possibility that it exists hovers disquietingly on the verges of the narratives of several plays, among them *The Son of Learning*, *The Flame*, *Sister Eucharia* and *The Plot is Ready*. This possibility, both humbling and liberating, acts as a foil to the insidious persecution and perversion (particularly of sexual relations) that he believed was a dominant feature of the first half-century of the Irish state.

As vital as his intense epiphanic one-act plays are the light hearted, humorous ones. These attest not only to linguistic playfulness and pleasure, but also to a celebratory, exuberant, frankly physical mode of living. Their irreverence lampoons the piety and sterile frugality lauded as the ideals of the post-heroic

Free State. They suggest that Clarke's primary allegiance is to the individual self. However, their exploration of personal liberty acknowledges both an obligations to the community and a dissenting relationship with it – the hallmarks of the cultural nationalism of the literary revival. That he employs so traditional a dramatic form as the verse play, replete with heroic, ritual and nationalistic connotations, is further evidence of the complex tensions of his work. Its very form exemplifies that contest between the longing for unfettered individual expression and the recognition of the need for discipline and restraint. The plays extend and enrich the tradition established by Yeats as part of the literary revival, yet they absorb a range of contemporary theatrical trends, notably Gordon Bottomley's religio-historical emphasis, T.S. Eliot's so-called 'nervous rhythms' and the meta-theatrical self-consciousness of the absurdists. For fifty years Clarke devoted considerable energies to the theatre, and at his most successful combined dramatic economy to the pleasures of verse. His experimentalism and challenge to naturalism constitute a significant leaven in the unimaginative theatre of the mid-century.

Mary Shine Thompson

NOTES

1 W. B. Yeats, *Poems 1899–1905*, (London, 1905), pp. xi-xii.
2 Austin Clarke (hereafter AC) to Ria Mooney, Correspondence, Henry W. and Albert A. Berg Collection of English and American Literature, the New York Public Library, 9 May 1943.
3 AC to Mooney, Correspondence, Berg Collection, New York Library, n.d., probably early 1948. In the event, *The Black Fast* was withdrawn and replaced by another play. Nonetheless, the comment serves to illustrate AC's interest in staging.
4 AC, TS tape 6, TTR 14562, Harry Ransom Humanities Research Center, University of Texas, Austin, Texas, p. 24.
5 Patrick Kennedy, 'Cauth Morrissey Looking for Service', *Legendary Fictions of the Irish Celts* (London, 1866), pp. 158–163.
6 Kuno Meyer ed., *Aislinge Meic Conglinne: The Vision of Mac Conglinne A Middle Irish Wonder Tale* (London, 1892).
7 George T. Stokes, *Ireland and the Celtic Church* (London, 1886), pp. 149–165.
8 AC, *Collected Plays* (Dublin, 1963), p. 399.
9 The sources of *As the Crow* Flies are 'The Adventures of Léithin' and its folklore version 'The Comparison as to Age between the Four

Elders: namely, the Crow of Achill, the Great Eagle of Leac na bhFaol, the Blind Trout of Assaroe, and the Hag of Beare', Douglas Hyde, *Legends of Saints and Sinners* (Dublin, n.d. [1916]), pp. 40–62, and O. J. Bergin, R. Best, K. Meyer, J. G. O'Keefe, 'The Colloquy between Fintan and the Hawk of Achill', transcribed by Kuno Meyer, *Anecdota from Irish Manuscripts* Vol. 1 (Dublin, 1907).

[10] Its source is Lillian Duncan, 'The Fosterage of the Houses of the Two Methers' or '*Altram Tige Da Medar*' *Eriu* 11, (1932), pp. 184–225. Clarke also refers the reader to Máire MacNéill, 'The Legend of the False God's Daughter', *Journal of the Royal Society of Antiquaries of Ireland (*1949).

[11] *The Plot Succeeds* is adapted from V. E. Hull, ed., '*Compert Mongain ocus Serc Duibe Lacha do Mongán*', 'The Conception of Mongan and His Love for Dubh Lacha', 'An Incomplete Version of *Imram Brain* and Four Stories concerning Mongan *Zeitschrift fur Celtische Philologie* 18, pp. 409–424. The source of *The Plot is Ready* is T. P. Cross and C. H. Slover, 'The Death of Muircertach Mac Erca', *Ancient Irish Tales (*London, 1935), pp. 518–532.

[12] J. G. O'Keefe ed., *Buile Suibhne: The Frenzy of Sweeney, being the Adventures of Suibhne Geilt: A Middle Irish Romance, Irish Text Society* Vol. 13, (Dublin, 1913).

[13] Denis Florence MacCarthy (M'Carthy or Mac-Carthy) published at least two translations in the metre of the original, of *El Purgatorio de San Patricio*, in *Calderon's Dramas: The Wonder-working Magician, Life is a Dream, The Purgatory of St Patrick (*London 1887), pp. 235–377; and in *Dramas of Calderon, Tragic, Comic and Legendary*, Vol. 2 (London, 1853). Mac-Carthy (1887) contains notes on Calderon's source, Perez de Montalvan's *Vida y Purgatorio de San Patricio* (Madrid 1627), whose source was Thomas Messingham's *Floregium Insulae Sanctorum, seu Vitae et Actae Sanctorum Hibernae* (Paris 1624).

[14] AC, 'W. B. Yeats and Verse Drama', p. 26.

[15] AC, 'Why the 12.30 was Late', *The Irish Times (*7 Sep. 1957), p. 6.

[16] M'Carthy, Vol. 1 (1853), p. v.

[17] AC, TS Tape 6, Harry Ransom Humanities Research Center

[18] AC, 'Strange Enchantment', *The Irish Times* (21 Dec. 1946), p. 6.

The Son of Learning

A COMEDY IN THREE ACTS

to

George Moore

CHARACTERS

KING
ABBOT
SCHOLAR
WOMAN
DEMON
MONKS
LAY BROTHER
MENDICANTS
MILITARY

Period: THE MIDDLE AGES
Place: THE ABBEY OF CORC

ACT ONE

*The Guest-house; a large hall with arched walls, central door with
steps, doors to left and right leading to cloisters. In the gloom,
candles on the deal table light only the faces of the* BEGGARS, *some
of whom wear ragged Irish cloaks. The* RED BEGGAR *is lanky, tall,
with foxy hair and a patch over one eye. The* AMADAN, *or Natural,
has matted hair, in a glib, as behung as a bush over a holy well. A*
PILGRIM *crouches in the shadow by right door, with staff and scrip.
The* BEGGARS *are eating loudly and talking, but the Latin chanting
of the* MONKS *in the Chapel can be heard outside as the play
begins. The* BEGGARMEN *speak in a childlike sing-song.*

OLD BLIND MAN. Ssh! Holy men are praying for the
    King.
AMADAN (*jumping up*). Oh, oh, oh!
    My little milk-tooth is spilled, is spilled.
    There is
    A devil in the baker's heel.
ONE-LEGGED MAN.   Had I
    The heady buck-tooth that I weaned at
      Michaelmas
    In Cashel Fair when I was daring man
    And bucking horse, I'd bite.
ONE-ARMED MAN.   A lucky bit.
BLIND MAN. Ssh! Holy men are praying for the King.
BLACK BEGGAR.   Like buckets in
    The well of knowledge, hierarchies go
    Up and down.
ONE-ARMED MAN.   . . . I did:
    I seen you ducking in an empty barrel,
    A cockshot for the boys.
ONE-LEGGED MAN.   It was
    A stand-up fight, a roaring battle, tooth
    And toe-nail.
    (*They squabble.*)
BLIND MAN (*dreamily*). Their lovely prayers will cure the King.
RED BEGGAR. Oh, there was many a fine horsey fight

3

In the old days before the hunger came.

OTHERS. *In Bantry and Kilkenny town*
There's fine accommodation,
And feather beds are shaken down
For every occupation.
Oh, lashings of rich bragget,
Ripe buttermilk and beer,
With plenty for my faggot
And nothing for your dear.

OLD BLIND MAN. My curse upon you all,
I cannot say my beads.

RED BEGGAR.   Those were the days
For cadging the red pence until the King
Took bad and ate the people out of pot
And pocket.

ONE-LEGGED MAN.   I've seen publicans that had
An ale-bush at the fair grow lean again
As their own shutters.

AMADAN (*running from* PILGRIM). Oh, oh, oh!

OTHERS (*to* AMADAN). Grey droppings of a goose upon you.
Quit the man.
          (*to* PILGRIM). Was it a mortal sin
Behind a hedge put heaven in your mind
Or thinking?

ONE-LEGGED MAN. He is too pure and knowledgeable
To sup with rags and lazybones.

ONE-ARMED MAN.   On bran
And backward cabbage.

BLIND MAN.   The holy man is on
Retreat.

RED BEGGAR.   Aye, crops are black
And party men say that it is a woman's
Fault. I had a wife, oh, a fine shifty woman,
But windy o' nights. They say . . .
          (*He stops to pick a back tooth.*)

OLD BLIND MAN.   A lying pack
And great deceivers.

BLACK BEGGAR.   What was the name
The priest wet her with?

ONE-LEGGED MAN.   Ligach.

ONE-ARMED MAN. The daughter of Maeldune.

BLIND MAN.   An idle rip.

4

ONE-LEGGED MAN. It was a little apple that she sent
        The King.

AMADAN.   Give me a napple.
        A napple.

RED BEGGAR. 'Twas him, I say.

ONE-LEGGED MAN.   'Twas her.

RED BEGGAR (*rapidly by rote*). Her wicked brother when
        She was to wed the King of Cashel put
        A pagan spell into the pip that he
        Had learned from poets.

BLIND MAN.   God preserve us from them!

RED BEGGAR. The poor King ate the pippin and began to
        Swell.

BLIND MAN. God help us all!
        God help us!

RED BEGGAR.   There was a maggot in
        That apple.

AMADAN.   A napple in that worm.

RED BEGGAR.   It turned
        Into a demon and that demon made
        The poor King eat from fire to bed and back.

BLACK BEGGAR. Where is the demon?

AMADAN.   In his belly, fool.

RED BEGGAR. Now that I have my second wind, begod,
        I'll tell the tale or burst. Be quiet now.
        Oh, men, the King grew ravenous, roaring,
        Rampaging as a yellow lion. No food
        Could race his hunger. On the marriage day
        He gobbled up the banquet while the bride
        Was in the chapel.

OTHERS (*together*).   He was guttling in
        The kitchen.
                Scraping pan and crock.
                       His head
        Was in the pantry.

BLACK BEGGAR.   It was,
        For I was there.

RED BEGGAR.   She said she did not care, that
        She would marry him another day and
        Cure him.

BLIND MAN.   The hussy!

ONE-LEGGED MAN.   The King is hiding

Inside.

ONE-ARMED MAN.   She could not follow him
Here.

RED BEGGAR.   No, no.

He came here for the blessed cure.
They say a wandering scholar said between
Two public-houses that the poor King took
Four roasted boars, eight heifers on the jack,
A draining barrel and a sack of apples
To whet his royal appetite before
Each grace and yet that hungry demon howled
In him for more.

OTHERS.   It was Mac Conglinne
That made the rann.

He tied the knot upon
The tale.

They say he was
In Tirnanogue.

BLIND MAN.   A vagabond,
A rogue.

RED BEGGAR. They say he was in Hell, boys.
He went down by the black mouth of the Red Lake
And cheated the devil himself at a burning game
Of cards.

OTHERS.   The people say he knows
All tricks and magic.

OLD BLIND MAN. A wicked unbeliever,
A great deceiver.

OTHERS.   And he can dry a cow
With seven rhymes.

RED BEGGAR.   Oh, anybody could
Make poetry if he were lazy enough.
(*They make up this catch, each line in turn.*)
The king was growing thinner
For the demon ate his dinner
Of a thousand crubeens,
Pot of new beans,
Tripe and trotters,
Fish caught by otters,
Beef and sirloin,
Those we'd purloin.
A lake of milk, a sea of beer.

6

OLD BLIND MAN. *I'd swim in it and have no fear.*
ALL.   *We'd swim upon those tides of beer*
         And pray no shore was ever near.

                                        (*ad lib.*)
         (*A lupine howl is heard outside. They retreat in
terror.*)
AMADAN.   Oh, oh! The demon is the King.
OTHERS.   Maybe
He heard us talking of the food.
                            He roars
Because the King is fasting.
AMADAN.   I am glad
He is the right side of the King.
(*They creep back to table.*)
                         Oh, I
Could do with a demon or two if I had been
A king and well-to-do.
RED BEGGAR. Aye, but the demon gets
The food.
AMADAN.   Aye, but the King has got the taste
In his mouth, not in his guts; and what's in food
But the tasting, the sweetness, the juiciness of meat,
The sloppiness of custard, the sourness of green
      apple,
With crunching, munching, scrunching? Aye, it's all
Between brother tongue and gum. What is after
The taste but belching, roaring winds and a heart
On fire?
BLIND MAN.   What are you paring,
Boy?
AMADAN.   My nail.
OTHERS.   I smell.
                      Though I've but one eye,
I see
     Cheese.
               Cheese, the little grandson
Of milk.
           Where did you steal it?
AMADAN.   It was a tinker's wife
That gave it to me.
OTHERS.   You have stolen it
And must go to confession.

7

(*They quarrel over the rind while the* AMADAN *whinges.*)

RED BEGGAR.   Now give me the loaf,
      For once I was a carpenter.
      (*A* BEGGAR *throws the bread, which falls with a
      loud sound as a young* LAY BROTHER *enters from
      left.*)

LAY BROTHER.   Who threw that stone?

BEGGARS.   Nobody,
      Good Brother, nobody.

BROTHER.   Oh, *panis, panis,*
      Bread, blessed bread! Ungrateful mendicants,
      To waste good loaves out of our very oven,
      When there is hunger in the fields, to turn
      Your unblown noses up at this pure leaven,
      Though the King, the very lord of the land,
      Goes empty.
      (*A lupine howl outside.*)
      Get to bed now, Lazarites;
      To bed now, for the King is coming from his cell,
      Lest you offend his grace in sight, in hearing
      Or in smell.

BEGGARS.   Brother,
                 Good Brother!

BROTHER.   Go now.
      Go!
      (*All but the* PILGRIM *go to the flocks, hardly to be
      seen in the alcoves. To* PILGRIM.)
      Go!

BEGGARS.   There is no tick
      For him.

BROTHER (*to* AMADAN). Share with this man of sin.

AMADAN (*terrified*).   No, no!

BROTHER.   Share now.

AMADAN.   No, daddy. I saw . . .

BROTHER (*to* PILGRIM).   These strolling saints are
      A plague. Better than you have been thankful
      To pull a blanket.
      (*He takes out the candles and the moonlight shines
      through the leaky roof.*)

ONE-LEGGED MAN (*jumping up*). Oh, oh! the devil's in my doss.

ONE-ARMED MAN (*waving hands*). He has me in his clutches.

BLIND MAN. Can ye not bear this cross?

OTHERS. He's cured him of the crutches.

BLIND MAN (*hobbling out scratching himself*). A thousand devils
bite me.
They're hopping now to spite me.

OTHERS. Back, back, the King!
(*Dumb show: from right door or from the
auditorium, penitential procession of monks in cream
habits, with lit tapers: the* KING, *a tall, bulky, sinister
figure, cowled in black, his golden crown peeping out,
led by the* ABBOT. *The* KING *glides as by an invisible
compulsion towards the table, but is guided past by
the* ABBOT. *The* PILGRIM *follows with supplicating
gestures, but is waved back by the monks as they pass
out through left door.*)

BLIND MAN. His eyes were fire.

OTHERS. Poor King!
He stared
Upon the board.
The demon in him
Growled.
The palmer caught his habit.
He was
Begging.
He was stealing
Out.

OLD BLIND MAN. Sssh! Say your prayers and go to sleep.
(*Crepitus ventris. Sudden silence, gradually broken by
snoring. A loud knocking is heard at the central
door.*)

BEGGARS (*waking*). Bad luck to your
Black music!
Who is it that is pulling down the
House? Get up, Amadan!

AMADAN. No, no. It is
The tinker's wife.

OTHERS. Why did I suck those eggs?
Why did I whip the poultry into my bag? . . .
And milk the nannie? . . .
Skim the churn? . . .

RED BEGGAR (*uneasily*). It is
My wife. I know her fist.

BLIND MAN. Sssh!

9

Let on to be asleep upon the roost. (*Silence. The door is pushed openly slowly and the* SCHOLAR *stands on the top step in the moonlight. His clothes, thinned by skies, should suggest those of the wandering, medieval students of Europe, the vagi scholares goliardi seu bufones, as they were named by Church Councils, but with a racial or bardic touch. He acts all the time, obviously with an eye and ear for his immediate audience.*)

SCHOLAR.   If there is anybody in this house
Of holiness, awake or in his sleep,
My blessing on him. Rain has risen now
From the cold stone of music; there's no star
But can be found in water . . .
(*Stumbling down the steps, vehemently.*)
                      My sudden curse
Upon the threshold, on the journeyman,
The hammer and the chisel. Goban Saor
Fuddle the mason and the carpenter
Of the crooked plane and may they never hear
The harp again.
            I am half-famished, surely,
With the cold drizzle of the glen.
(*Searching around.*)
                        Nothing.
Nothing, nothing at all. I cannot smell
The shadow of a bacon rind. To-night
No rat would drip out of the black waters
Of Lee to this bare house.
                 My bones
Are sore; I will lie down upon a bed
Until an angel come.
(*Goes over to flocks.*)
               The beds are full,
But empty sleepers you will feast in dreams
As I to-night.
(*He sits on table and takes a cruit or small harp out of a sack. The* BEGGARS *sit up.*)
              Song,
We have borrowed the five lands and kept ourselves
Alive, and we have been cold bedfellows,
For all our years are Lent, yet we must fast

To-night that beggars may think their broken heads
Are bound with gold.
(*Tuning with a jack.*)
      Would I were in a turn of Kerry,
Eating blackberries out of my left hand.
(*He chants.*)
   Macgillicuddy of the Reeks,
My praise upon the hilly woody land
Where ruddy brambles are dark with feasting wings,
There in the grass the wind runs as a filly;
Could I sing as freely, it is I
   Would praise Macgillicuddy of the Reeks.
(*He walks about, muttering.*)
But I could swear as I came to the light,
Growing in wet bushes that the Red Swineherd
Had lost a pig to-night, for, by the smell,
The little monks were marrying fat bacon
And curly cabbage.
(*An old* LAY BROTHER *enters from the left with basket and bit of candle.*)

BROTHER. Who is it that is there?
SCHOLAR.   Frater dilectus,
Pax tecum.
BROTHER.   Oh, it is a Son of Learning.
Our Father Abbot thought he heard a row.
SCHOLAR. A row?
BROTHER. A cow? No, no, a breach of rule.
He sent me here, he did, with simple food
And silence, for this is a day of fast.
'Go, Brother Ruadan,' says he, 'for it
May be a sinner that has drink in heel,
Or storyteller; sure the air of night
Drives in queer soles. The King is meditating,'
Says he, 'and must not be disturbed.'
SCHOLAR.   The King?
BROTHER.   Yes, yes.
The King is fasting for a week
To vomit the green fiend of gluttony.
But come now, Son of Learning, to the refectory,
And put yourself before the fire and wash
Your feet. Supper is loud upon the spit,
And you shall eat.

11

My sight is turning grey.
Give me your gospel books.
(*He comes upon the harp.*)
Holy Saint Barra!
It is a poet!

SCHOLAR. Frater, I am a Son
Of Learning, and I have read in the book
Full of green dragons and of holy language
And red-gold cherubim. I can recite
The pious lives of Patric, Bridget, Maeve
And Nuadha of the Silver Hand.

BROTHER. No, no.
The Abbot had been bothered lately by
A school of poets. You must lie here
Until the bell of dawn.

SCHOLAR. I can amuse
The King with merry narration.

BROTHER. You must stay here.
This is your ration.

SCHOLAR (*takes up hunk and mutters*). The naked bread is blue
With cold.

BROTHER. Speak aloud, for I am soft of hearing.

SCHOLAR. This goodly bread is whiter than the flower
Of wheat. I think that it was ground
Within a golden quern.
(*Taking up cup of whey.*)
Poor cow, rest, rest in peace,
For you have eaten many a day since this
Was milked.
(*To* LAY BROTHER.)
The paschal richness of the grass
Is in this cup.
Good Brother, we will make
A song upon the fare.

BROTHER. O, I will call
The Abbot.

SCHOLAR. No, you'll stay, my Brother.

BROTHER. I
Must ring the Vesper.

SCHOLAR. You shall pray with me
And shout the Glorias.
(*Extemporizing to strings.*)

Were I in Clare of the ships,
Drinking with fishermen, I would not care,
Not I, not I, until the keg ran dry,
Or were I sailing on a windy morrow
By Tory, where the barefoot women work
And a man can take a bellyful of ease
Nor fear the rats of sorrow.
                              Were I backward
At a lake, when reeds were slipping their young
        shadows
Like black eels, I would take no care, not I,
Not I.
        But in Corc of the big-tongued bells
Where I put my foot in the coldness of day,
I will not eat the holey bread or drink
The parish whey.
(*He suddenly realizes that the* BROTHER *has stolen
out during the song.*)
                              Now that he is gone,
I might as well gnaw at the speckled dough
Myself, for I have had no scrap to eat
Since dawn but the grey berries at the Well
Of Loneliness.
(*He turns to table in time to catch the* PILGRIM, *who
has stolen out to snatch the food, roughly.*)
Robber, light-handed pilferer,
Plunderer of eggs beneath the clucking hen,
Poacher of woods and rivers, you'd take
The poet's bite. Oh, here's good money for song!
But I will fight you. Off with your stolen coat,
Your belt, if you're a man.
(*Cloak and cowl fall away from a slender, beautiful
young* WOMAN, *bright-haired and strange in the
moonlight.*)
                              A woman!
(BEGGARS *swarm out.*)
BEGGARS.   She's mine.
                    No, mine.
                    She's mine.
SCHOLAR (*driving them back*). Back, fleas and rags. You'd rob me,
                poachers of wood
            And river, red-handed pilferers, bagmen,

Would steal the phoenix on her fiery egg.
Back, or you shall pace by the cold seas
Of Tirnanogue this night.
(*He turns to her: in cajoling tones.*)
                              O Fairywoman,
What hill untroubled by the day
Or meddled dance has blessed this house? Are you
Etain, who washes in a basin of gold
With carven birds or that horsewoman, Niav,
Taking the fences of the sea? Are you
The wife of the musician, Craftine,
Who was unhappy when the holeheaded flute
Began to play and so is lost for ever
In the grass and cannot find her lover? Tell me,
For I have heard such music to-night, I fear
The waters work in my mind.
(*As he is about to sweep the cup and bread from the
board, she runs to stop him.*)

WOMAN.   Oh,
I am so hungry.

SCHOLAR.   I will call food
For you, the pure white bread and honeycomb
That drips the summer, dishes of rung silver,
A skin of wine the wearied sons of Tuireann
Drank in the south.

WOMAN.   You dream;
And what shall I do now in a hostel for
Men.

SCHOLAR.   I dream of the large ruddy fires
In a fairy house and of the beaching noise
In waves that dance as jugglers when they fling
White knives, that we are playing at the chess,
With Bishop, Knave and King upon the board,
For you are more beautiful than Deirdre or
Than Maeve.

WOMAN (*flattered*).   I think you praise a dream,
Or a woman that is dead.

SCHOLAR.   Have I not
Followed your bright heel on the road as a farmer
The price he will get at the big fair, even
To this house?

WOMAN.   I heard a little music

About the priory but when the bat-light stirred
The bushes, I was full of fear and I
Came in.
(*Weeps.*)

SCHOLAR.   I'll be an abbot
To-night and I've a trick or two of tongue
Will cure the King, for I have been acquainted
With that most famous juggler, Mannanaun,
Who runs from lordly fire to fire when he
Has wearied of the cold warrens of the wave
To mend the table for a farthing's worth
Of praise from men by pulling a supper, a hound
Or music from his pocket. He's the patron saint
Of merry rogues and fiddlers, trick o' the loop men,
Thimblemen and balladmen that gild
The fair and his devotions are the crowd,
For he looks on until the sun is red,
The tide turned and the drink and the horses are
        gone.

WOMAN.   These are but words.

SCHOLAR.   Have I not seen an angel,
Bright as the rainy bracken of a gap,
Last moon, because I had no supper? I will have
Excellent food brought down in tablecloths
From heaven.

WOMAN.   Want
Of food has made him dream.

SCHOLAR.   (*wildly*).   To-night I will
Entice the demon from the King that souls
May huddle in the hospice of Lough Derg.
I'll deal a merry pack of words will make
You Queen.

WOMAN (*surprised*).   Queen!

SCHOLAR.   And sanctify this house,
That foreheads will be thumbed with holy ashes
Again, big drovers stumbling as their curses,
Carters and men that lean with the old wheel
Outside the forge all day, will come like boys
Capping their way to Mass.
                      These beggarmen,
To double their spit, will have a barrel
Large as the turfstack of a parish priest

15

And full of . . .

RED BEGGAR. Beer!

(*They swarm out, crying "Where? Where?"*)

SCHOLAR. Come, all you rogues, make merry and rejoice,
Dance, rags and bones, for you shall feast to-night.

(BEGGARS *dance and caper in a ring with linked
hands around the* SCHOLAR *and the* GIRL, *singing.*)

> *Buttermilk and beistings*
> *Enough for seven feastings.*
> *Boiled green cabbage and white bacon,*
> *Everything that we can take on.*
> *Let the poet court her*
> *While we drink black porter.*

(*Ad lib.*)

(ABBOT *enters with monks; all run aside except the*
SCHOLAR, *who bows.*)

ABBOT.   Fellow, what is
This hullabaloo?

SCHOLAR.   Most Reverend Lord Abbot, I am a Son
Of Learning. I have read the holy book
Filled with green dragons, pious characters
And red-gold cherubim. I heard your praise
In Cashel of the kings, I can recite
The pious lives of Patric, Bridget, Maeve
And Nuadha of the Silver Hand.

MONKS.   He is a rogue!

SCHOLAR. Most Reverend Lord Abbot, I was filling
These simple ears with news of Barra, Saint
Of Corc.

LAY BROTHER. He made a satire on
The blessed food.

ABBOT.   Beggars at the pattern
Will sing this evil word and scandalize
The parishes.

SCHOLAR.   Holy Lord Abbot!

ABBOT.   Silence,
Fellow! You shall not mock the holy Church,
Nor me, her servant. I am a magistrate,
A man of law.

SCHOLAR.   My Lord, I came to cure
The King.

ABBOT.   He speaks against the King!

16

Let him be dipped into the river pool
At day-ring.

SCHOLAR.   I can make another satire
To raise a purple blister on your back
With little brethren.

ABBOT.   He threatens me!
Harper, you shall be whipped with more than
    rhymes,
For I have great power in the land.
(MONKS *discover the* WOMAN.)
                       A woman!
He has dared to bring his sin, his wench, his
    baggage,
His hedge companion here! Holy Saint Kevin,
Defend us!

SCHOLAR.   She is more beautiful than Deirdre,
Or the woman of the kindling town.

ABBOT.   He contradicts me!
Am I not a bishop? Have I not
A mitre, a golden crozier, a red carbuncle
On my finger? Have I not secular power?
Am I not a prince in my own right?

SCHOLAR.   Good Monk,
Good Monk, before your crook was jewelled,
Columcille opened the heavy door of praise
For us. My mind has broken fast in schools
Beyond the Shannon where the saints live. I
Have read so bright a book that kings
Warred for the lettered dragons and the gold.
Harper I am, now, a rogue for merriment,
A ballad-maker, a juggler at the fair
Of gaping, a wandering scholar in the glens,
With rain and hunger stitching in my bones,
But I'll not praise your Lenten bread nor drink
The parish whey . . .

ABBOT.   The law
Of Church in land has made the mind of man,
That is the troubled body of the soul,
Obedient, but the holy order, work
And prayer, the mortar of this house, are mocked
To-night. It may be that the demon in
Our King has turned a bad mouth from the road

17

To be a rod. Bring all these simple guests
To sleep in the cells – there is corruption here –
And send the woman to a convent. Let
This man count up his sins upon the hour
And pray. There is a cross upon the Hill
Of Ravens where the bones of all malefactors
Are chained, for, when the breath has suffered,
    heaven
Has mercy. I will try this wicked man
Within my court to-morrow.
(MONK *locks central door. The guests, menacing the*
SCHOLAR, *are hurried out. He turns to the* WOMAN,
who walks past in disdain. AMADAN *comes to the*
crestfallen culprit.)

AMADAN.   Frater, pax
Tecum.
(SCHOLAR *alone. He tries all the doors and sits down*
in an attitude of despair. After some time the 'Dies
Irae, Dies Illa' is heard faintly without as the curtain
falls.)

CURTAIN

ACT TWO

Scene: The Refectory: central door with steps. Door on left to Pantry. Door on right. A high carved armchair in front of a Lectern on which there is an illuminated book, to centre. A blazing wood-fire on hearth to left. Bright candlesticks on long table. A lean LAY BROTHER *is setting the table in indifferent fashion, humming a hymn in a taciturn tone. A very fat* LAY BROTHER *bounces in from Larder or Pantry with dishes piled to his third chin.*

FAT BROTHER (*bustling*).   Hurry
      Now! Hurry, Brother Dove! The holy candles
      Have been put out. Here are more platters.
THIN BROTHER.   I
      Am at my share, but you are jumpier than
      A pot-lid even at your *Paters*.
FAT BROTHER (*expansively*).   Had you
      To sweat, to toil before the blaze, to toast,
      To roast, to boil, to broil, to baste, to braze,
      To stew, to simmer, to grill to the very spill
      O' the spit . . .
THIN BROTHER (*sharply*).   And have I not to peel, to scrape.
      To mince, to grind, to pluck, to singe, to draw
      The guts o' the fowl, to crumble, season, truss
      And skewer?
FAT BROTHER.   To carve?
THIN BROTHER.   To carry?
FAT BROTHER.   Ladle?
THIN BROTHER.   Slice
      And portion?
FAT BROTHER.   Pour?
THIN BROTHER.   And sing the Grace?
FAT BROTHER.   Hand me
      That breadknife.
      (*They work. Conciliatory*):
            Brother Dove,
      I have another recipe for soup.

19

A pinch of . . .
(*Whispers*).

               mug of . . .

(*Whispers*).

                       and a tablespoon

Of . . .

(*Whispers*).

THIN BROTHER. Hum.

FAT BROTHER.   Shake and slowly stir
And put to sleep upon a little hob
Until the thickening gold comes up again.

THIN BROTHER (*laying table*). For Brother Goldsmith . . .
      Joiner . . .

                             Sacristan . . .

(*Harp outside.*)
There's that wirepuller again.

FAT BROTHER.   A handy man.
Oh, Brother, when I was in smaller shoes
I, too, could pick a tune or two between
My teeth.

THIN BROTHER. I'll say a prayer.

FAT BROTHER.   How is the King?

THIN BROTHER (*snapping*).   Better.

FAT BROTHER.   The Father Carpenter was saying
That they have blessed him with a bucketful
Of water from the holy wells of Croom
And Templemore.

THIN BROTHER.   Hum.

FAT BROTHER.   He was saying they
Have brought the King up to the silver shrine,
And he has kissed the relics, one by one,
Of Jarleth, Canice and the sainted daughters
Of Einan, rung the little bell that came
To Declan.

THIN BROTHER (*impatiently*). The board is laid.

FAT BROTHER (*expansively*).   O Brother Dove,
I love to hear all day of miracles,
Small children cured of ringworm, milk in cow
Again, devotions at the blind man's well
And every parish cross; for knees are feet
When a great pope is walking through the land
With bell and cope. They say that Bridget pegged

> Her saintly linen on a beam of sun
> To dry . . .
>> Poor Brethren, I hammered out
> A bung, for, as you say, their swallows are
> On fire with plain-chant, parching matins, nones
> And lauds . . .

THIN BROTHER (*interrupting*). The holy can . . .

FAT BROTHER (*eagerly*).   Yes, holy canticles.

THIN BROTHER (*interrupting*). The holy candles have been capped.

FAT BROTHER.   You prate
> Too much. Go, Brother Dove, and bring the pail
> Of soup in.
> (*A crash and commotion outside. Crossing himself.*)
>> Brother, Brother, what is that now?

THIN BROTHER. Alas, it must be that the heady scholar
> Has broken down the door.
> (*The* KING *rushes in followed by the supplicating* ABBOT *and* MONKS *carrying the royal cowl and habit: he charges to the table. He is tall and corpulent, clothed in red and gold.*)

KING (*roaring*). I'll fast no more,
> No more, for I am starven, starven! I
> Am drenched with holy water, bruised and sore
> With kneeling down, half-moidered with your prayers
> And penitential psalms. Where is the supper?
> Is it carven?

ABBOT.   Calm, calm your troubled soul,
> O noble King.

KING.   I'll meditate no more.
> As I was nodding in the nave, I heard
> An angel plucking up his harp and dreamed
> My mouth was appled in a mighty pie.

ABBOT. The frightened demon like a wild doorkeeper
> Runs between ear and eye.

KING.   I tell ye, hunger
> Is roaring in my belly now.

ABBOT.   Resume.
> O King, spiritual exercises.

KING.   I
> Am starven. I could eat the . . . rafters. Bring me
> The larder.

ABBOT (*aside*).   We must deceive the demon

By venial guile.
(*To* KING.)
                              Such Lenten food as ours
Is not befitting for so great a king
As Cathal More. Our diet is but . . .
(*Considering.*)
                                                    Simples . . .
Garlic . . . green cresses from the river . . . when
In season . . . a little bread . . . water . . . a pick
Of meat on Feastdays.

KING.   Bring, bring me in your supper,
All, all of it, even if it be the bones
And gravy of a goose or some poor stew
Reheated in the pot. I will eat all
Your suppers. You shall fast for me to-night.

ABBOT (*aside*). The Tempter speaks.
(*Harp outside.*)

KING.   Am I in Cashel again?
You have a harper hidden in the house.
Oh, I'll have music too.

ABBOT.   High King, it is
A vagabond whose grey bed is the wood,
An idle clerk that mocks the Church, I have
Condemned him.

KING.   Bring him in, for I will salt
My supper with his music.

ABBOT.   Let us pray.
KING. Bring, bring the harper.
(*Two* MONKS *are reluctantly sent.*)
                              Hasten now
And carry in the crockery.

ABBOT.   O King,
Repent. We have implored you not to break
The holy edge of fast, for public prayer
Will cast the demon out. Oh, do not let
This man of sin . . .
(SCHOLAR *brought in.*)

SCHOLAR.   Most reverend
Archbishop, I am a Son of Learning. I
Have read a pious book . . .
(*Seeing the* KING.)
                              O mighty King

22

Of Munster, grandson of the noble Fingan,
Lord of the Southern Half, I can retell
The deeds of your forefathers from the Flood
In fourteen hundred verses.

ABBOT. Vanitas.
The King is going to prayers.

SCHOLAR (*to* KING). I can amuse
You – for no doubt you are about to sup –
With merry tales of how the Daghda ate
Too much or how the wanton women made
Cuchullin blush again.
(KING *beams.*)

ABBOT. Secular stories
Are most unsuitable. The King is on
Retreat.

SCHOLAR. I have more edifying tales,
How Maravaun called dinner down from Heaven
To entertain King Guairë, how Saint Cieran
Rebuked a wench.
(KING *glooms.*)

ABBOT. No doubt you have a poem
Upon the Deadly Sins.

SCHOLAR. On Simony
And how an abbot fell by pride.

ABBOT (*anxiously*). Perhaps
An edifying vision.

KING (*gloomily*). Visions! I
Have had enough of them.

SCHOLAR. I made a lesson
Upon the supper I have had.

KING (*hopefully*). On victuals?
Go on. I love the marrow of sweet words.

SCHOLAR. Praise to the guesting house, the generous house
Of Corc, the pail of ready washing there.
The big-tongued fire that dried my shriven feet.
Two brothers shook out linen for a meal
And it was whiter than the tablecloth
That Peter saw the angels letting down
From heaven. In a blaze of wax they served
The platters, dishes, saucers and tureens.
Appetite steamed in them.

KING (*impatiently*). And what was on

23

Each plate?

SCHOLAR (*slowly*).   O Savour of all savours!
Brown roasted beef, basted upon the spit
With lavish honey and the large white salt
From drying-pans, choice mutton that was suckled
Upon green tits of grass, a crock of gravy
In which the fattened geese could swim again
And poultry in the egg, parsley and sauce,
Green cabbage boiling with a juicy ham
Crumbled with meal; whole puddings, speckled
        puddings,
Fat puddings with their little puddings, sweet litter
O' the pig, loud celery.

KING (*excitedly*).   I crunch!
I crunch!

SCHOLAR.   Salmon too fat for leaping
And freckled trout.

KING (*wildly*).   More, more!

SCHOLAR.   Mustard
And red-eyed pepper; from their shaken woods,
Ripe hazel-nuts to waken teeth, custard,
Big steamy dumplings.

KING (*ecstatically*).   Dumplings!

SCHOLAR.   Hashed
With red apples!

KING (*eagerly*).   And had you milk, for I
Love milk!

SCHOLAR.   All the white brewing of the cow.

KING.   Her new milk?

SCHOLAR.   Skim milk?

KING.   Old milk?

SCHOLAR.   Buttermilk.

KING.   And fat milk?

SCHOLAR.   Lean milk.

KING.   Yellow bubbling milk?

SCHOLAR. Her curd milk.

KING.   Whey milk?

SCHOLAR.   Cream milk.

KING.   Double milk?

SCHOLAR. Aye, calving milk that blobs and blubbers down
The gullet till the first gulp cries to the last:
'Stop, cur, for my doggedness, I swear,

24

O speckled mongrel, that if you come down
I will come up, for there's no share for two
Such dogs as us in this dark puppery,'

KING.   I'll buy that cow!
(*He claps* SCHOLAR *on back.*)

ABBOT.   Our holy rule is mocked
To-night.

KING.   Gillie of song, where is this food?

SCHOLAR.   I smell it here.

MONKS.   He is a rogue. There is
A hunger in the fields.

KING.   Bring in the spit.
My grinders ache.

ABBOT.   It is a sin to break
The fast.

MONKS.   He has put spells upon the King.

SCHOLAR.   Master,
I am inspired to work a miracle,
If you but eat and drink your fill and do
My bidding.

KING (*heartily*).   That I will.
(*Sits down.*)

SCHOLAR.   The Abbot said
There is a barrel of white-hooded ale
Here. Send for Brother Ale.

KING (*roars*).   Bring in
The beer!

MONKS.   He lies.

SCHOLAR.   O King, lend me your torc
Of gold that I may hold authority
Above the monks of Corc.
(*The* KING *puts his golden collar around him
joyfully.*)

SCHOLAR (*to* MONKS, *with airs of authority*). Put on
The royal cowl and habit.

ABBOT (*pleased*).   Learned Scholar,
We shall obey you.
(ABBOT *and* MONKS *do, despite royal protests.*)

SCHOLAR.   Come, bind the King.
(*The* KING *jumps up with indignant exclamations.*)

MONKS.   He raves,
He raves.

25

SCHOLAR (*snatching cords from the waists of* ABBOT *and* BURSAR *and slipping the* ABBOT'S *keys into his pocket*). Come, bind the King!

KING (*pompously*).   I am
          The King!

SCHOLAR.   O Branch of power, I put a spell
          In these poor cords that have not swaddled food
          Since they were spun. You gave a kingly word
          To do my say.

KING (*apologetically*).   I have heard tell that blacksmiths,
          Red women, poets and the like can work
          Queer spells. Do it.
          (*They bind the* KING *in the high chair, directly in front of Lectern.*)

SCHOLAR.   Out, Brothers, to your fast;
          Hurry, Lord Abbot, to your stool, for I
          Must exorcise the demon.
          (*Confusion.* MONKS *cast lingering looks as the* LAY BROTHERS *carry in steaming dishes. Having driven them out, the* SCHOLAR *juggles with the stolen keys and, sitting down, eats ravenously, talking between mouthfuls.*)

KING (*cheerfully*).   That looks to me
          Good Kerry mutton. Carve the dinner, carve,
          For I am starving! Come, unbind my arms.
          Gillie of song, make haste!

SCHOLAR.   Soon, soon. The spell
          Is working in the wool.

KING.   You gobble up
          My share, my grief.

SCHOLAR.   O King, the beef
          Is beautiful, crisp, done as I desire.
          My blessing on the spit, the charcoal fire,
          The luscious grease.

KING.   Release me, for my mouth
          Is thawing.

SCHOLAR.   But the meat is yet too hot
          For your royal demon.

KING.   I have diabetes.

SCHOLAR. That is heretical.
          (*Eating.*)   O simple bacon,
          Milky and fatter than rich honeycomb,

The dumpling . . .

KING.   I will hear no more. You've drunk
Three pots of ale!

SCHOLAR.   Come, I will drown
Your demon in a holy well of wine.
The monks have claret in a cellar, cold
As the flagstone of Hell.

KING (*calling*).   Wine, bring me wine!
(BROTHERS *bring wine. The* SCHOLAR *takes wine
half-way and drives them back, capering.*)

SCHOLAR.   Wine, red noisy wine,
More beaded than the Abbot. Oh, it danced
Out of its little skin.
(*Drinking.*)
And litany,
O litany, it fills my throat with rhyme.

KING.   For God's sake, Poet, stop! Give me a cup
Of wine, nay, half a cup to wash the lime
Out of my mouth, a drop, a little drop
Out of the lees.

SCHOLAR (*capering*).   O wine, red litany wine,
To fit any head.

KING.   Scholar, I will give you
Green pasture lands, a herd of lowing heifers,
A silent wife . . .

SCHOLAR.   Better to me the noisy wine,
The scolding wine.

KING.   Then, I will have you flogged.

SCHOLAR (*mocking*). Oh, oh, I will be cudgelled in a wood
Of blackthorns, beaten in a tanner's yard
And pounded by the miller. Ready your mouth,
For I will give you wine.
(*He holds the cup to the* KING'S *mouth, then slowly
withdraws and drinks. The* KING *splutters with rage
while he recites*):

> *Summer delights the scholar
>   With knowledge and reason:
> Who is happy in hedgerow
>   Or meadow as he is?*

> *Paying no dues to the parish,
>   He argues in logic*

27

> *And has no care of cattle*
> *But a satchel and a stick.*
>
> *The showery air grows softer,*
> *He profits by his ploughland,*
> *For the share of the schoolmen*
> *Is a pen in hand.*
>
> *When mid-day hides the reaping,*
> *He sleeps by a river*
> *Or comes to the stone plain*
> *Where the saints live.*
>
> *But in winter by the big fires,*
> *The ignorant hear his fiddle*
> *And he battles on the chessboard*
> *As the land lords bid him.*

                    My mind was in the cup. I know
A fairywoman that shall come to sup
With us. I am in heart, in love, with this
Most notable lady.
(*He turns a somersault.*)

KING.   A woman?
SCHOLAR.   Yes.
KING.   They have
A woman hidden in this house. Oh, how
I am deceived!
SCHOLAR.   Now you will see her.
KING.   There is
             No food for her.
SCHOLAR (*at central door*).   She shall complete the cure.
KING.   Stop, stop! There is no food for her!
    (*The* KING, *alone, talking to himself.*)
    If I had married Ligach,
    The daughter of Maeldune, I would be full
    Of bacon. She has droves in every wood.
    But I will say my prayers:
    (*Raising his eyes, in pious tones.*)
                    O . . .
    (*The* DEMON *tempts him.*)
                         cabbage, boiled.
    With bacon, thy butter green as peasoup . . .
    (*Bewildered.*)

28

Thoughts
Have tripped my words and I must say an act
Of nutrition.
(*Bowing his head, in contrite tone. Through . . .*
(The DEMON *tempts him.)*   *my dumpling. Through.*
My dumpling. Through my most suety dumpling.
(Despairing.)   'I cannot tell'
My puddings, count the mutton-juicy, thick
And yellow-fatted, gravy-dripping joints.
(*His lips smack themselves as in a fit. The candles burn*
dimly and in the half-darkness his cowled figure
suggests demonic possession.)

THIN BROTHER (*putting in his head from the Larder*). They're
        gone. A draught has sickened the light.

FAT BROTHER (*cautiously putting his head in*).   Oh, save
        My soup.

THIN BROTHER (*entering*). I'll not. I have to scrub,
        To rub, to tub, to drub, to rinse, to wring,
        To mangle, steep and scour, to wet, to whet,
        To whiten, blow on, polish.

FAT BROTHER (*waving him backwards towards the table*). Have I
        not
        To make, to bake, to roll, to thicken, thin,
        To flour, to sour, to grate, to wait, to pan
        And handle in the oven?
        (*A lupine growl.*)

BOTH BROTHERS (*terrified*). The Demon!
                            The Demon!

(*They retreat into the Larder.*)

CURTAIN

ACT THREE

Scene: The same as in Act Two, a few minutes later. The Refectory is bright again. The cowled head of the KING *is bowed and he appears to slumber. The* BEGGARS *can be heard approaching in the corridors outside. They enter by central door singing a catch.*

RED BEGGAR.   *Upon Lough Ale we sailed at rise o' day.*
OTHERS.   *And golden were the waves O.*
RED BEGGAR.   *But when we turned the boat into a cup*
                  They ran so high, we did not get a sup,
                  For none of us could blow the froth away.
OTHERS.   *Oh, none of us could blow the froth away.*
RED BEGGAR (*standing with his back to the fire*). It's a fine life to
        beg the miles, to quit
        A scolding wife and shake a single shirt
        In holy houses.
RED BEGGAR (*uneasily*).   Will the lucky Son
        Of Learning come back?
OLD MAN.   A wicked unbeliever?
        A great deceiver.
RED BEGGAR.   Oh, he has conjugated
        In Clare and women love a wordy man,
        I heard them say Mac Conglinne himself,
        Discoursing with Queen Maeve behind a bush,
        Would coax her, like the she-moon, on her back.
        But, theologians, what has two-legged man
        To pair with woman's tongue? Consider that
        Poor wagging piece of flesh: all day it runs
        That has no shin: being brought to bed, it is
        But livelier: it is the fiery branch
        Of wickedness . . .
        (*While he is talking, the others have crowded around the table and have begun to quarrel violently over the food. The* RED BEGGARMAN *drives them back angrily, imitating the* SCHOLAR'S *tone.*)
        Stop, rogues and ragmen, broachers of wooded wine,
        Would steal the meaning from the Testament,

30

The hairy cross upon a donkey's back.
I am the first man here.
(*Pleased with his prowess, he fills and lifts a jug of ale.*)

Well, here's luck, boys!

AMADAN (*peering around the Lectern and seeing the* KING'S *cowl*).
Oh!
The Abbot's in the chair.

RED BEGGAR (*hastily putting down the untouched jug.*)

Holy Mother!

He'll excommunicate us all!
(*They rush towards the central door as the* SCHOLAR *enters.*)

SCHOLAR. Run, all you mouths, make merry in the larder,
And if head turns, the cure is drinking harder.
(*As they disappear into the Larder by the left door, the two* LAY BROTHERS *bounce across the stage and out by the opposite door. The* WOMAN *appears on the central doorstep, shading her eyes, and the* SCHOLAR *stands before her.*)

SCHOLAR (*proudly*). Lady,
Though you have laughed at me, I rule this house,
And you shall dine, for I have turned your wishes
Into meat, into wine, into plentiful dishes.

WOMAN (*surprised*). But where is Father Abbot?

SCHOLAR. At his beads —
A worthy habit.

WOMAN. And where is the King?

SCHOLAR. Asleep, for he has eaten far too much.

KING. Ligach, Ligach!

WOMAN (*running to him*). Cathal, I have come
For you, now.

KING. Ligach, I have had no supper.

WOMAN. Lift me upon your lap again.
(*amazed.*) The monks
Have tied you up!

KING (*nodding at* SCHOLAR). He ate my beef. He did.

WOMAN (*sharply*). Unbind the King!

SCHOLAR (*mysteriously*). There's magic in that wool
That I have learned on hills where mighty Fionn
Still sucks his thumb for wisdom when the hounds
Are flatter than the hare.

WOMAN. Untie him!

SCHOLAR. Touch
But a loop and from that royal mouth a demon
Will leap in fire.

WOMAN (*trying the cords*). The knot is blacker now.
(*She runs for a breadknife.*)

SCHOLAR (*mockingly*). Lady, he does not love you now. His eyes
Eat up the table.

WOMAN (*in a huff*). Little Cathal, I
Have hurried by house and bush with pilgrims that
Took ship and women sided on their nags;
Last night, when music went round at a merry
Fair, packmen tumbled from a fiery tent
And plucked my holy frock to bless them . . . I
Was full of fear . . . I ran into the dark
And came to water thinning in the light
And called until the ferryman came out
On sleepy oars and for your sake I hid
With evil men. And, Cathal, do you love
Me?

KING. I am starving, starving!

WOMAN. But you look
So well!

KING (*crossly*). I'm not. I'm thinner than a shadow
Hung out to dry.

WOMAN. But Cathal . . .

KING. I am starving!
I have not had a drink since I came here.

WOMAN. Is it all, is it all you have to say
To me?

KING. Beg him, implore him, if you love me,
To pass that barrel.

WOMAN (*in rising temper*). Black hedges pluck me
Again and strong arms saddle me upon
A horse before I kneel now. Am I not
The daughter of great acres? Gamble and wink
With the rude soldiers on a cloak until
The candle swim, acquaint the stablemen,
The potboys and the cooks of Cashel, for
I am deceived again, again.

SCHOLAR (*mocking*). A health!
A health to a loving pair!

KING.   I am deceived,
She does not care.

WOMAN.   You do not care.

KING.   I am
Deceived and I may die.

WOMAN (*scornfully*).   And have you not
Abandoned me? Did you not leave me at
The altar foot? Oh, now let matchmakers
Put hedge to field and pair the board and blanket.
For I must house my face in shame and girls —
Before they have pinched the last decade of
Their penance – laugh at me and sun becomes
My enemy. Oh, you are fat!

KING.   Fat?

WOMAN.   And oh,
I hate you, for there is a baldy spot
Lighting your crown!

KING (*indignantly*).   I never heard that like
Before!

WOMAN (*sidling up to the* SCHOLAR). This young man is my fancy
          now.

SCHOLAR (*drinking*). And this is mine.

WOMAN (*in pretended distress to* SCHOLAR). Oh, what will I do?
I will unlock my hair, I'll weep so. For
I think you do not love me any longer.
But an hour, less than a tallow, and your words
Are dark.

SCHOLAR.   Poor thought must lag when fancy doubles
Back. You were proud.

WOMAN.   I was afraid.

SCHOLAR.   I know,
I know. You follow summer.

WOMAN (*wringing her hands*).   Oh, he won't
Believe me and I will not dine. He does
Not care for me and I am nothing but
A rhyme that pleases best when it is new.

SCHOLAR.   You hid in a house of men and are you not
The daughter of Maeldune?

WOMAN.   Believe me now,
Believe me, for you are swift, merry and own
A mouth of honey. Are you not the dealer
Of magic in this house to-night? Am I

Spun of such common wool that I could love
An empty king when you pulled music in
The middling wood?

SCHOLAR. I fill a hidden ear
That has no drum.

WOMAN (*mysteriously*). Look in my eyes and tell
What seems is not, if by another logic
Reason can know itself.

SCHOLAR (*he gazes silently; following a new fancy*). O
Fairywoman,
I see all clearly now. You are not Ligach,
The daughter of Maeldune? You put a cloud
Upon my mind, a spell upon the King,
That he should hear and see a mortal woman,
But you are lofty, apple-skinned and dance
In the dark grass?

WOMAN (*mysteriously*). My name grows in the woods.

SCHOLAR (*wheedling*). Are you Queen Aoibhill,
Who makes a yearly circuit for the silk
Of cattle, taxing the farmers by the Shannon
That she may have good wine?

WOMAN. I hold
My court where years have been.

SCHOLAR. I know, I know.
For I have heard an earful of good stories
About you when the fire was low.

WOMAN (*alluringly*). Cure, cure
The King and we will hurry to those glens
Of softness where the dews are heavier
Than blackberries and hid too well in grass,
Come on the stony hills, though days have broken
The last grey crop: and leaving the dim blue steps
Of Burren while the little airs of twilight
Take footing, rest in a big house beside
The waves.

SCHOLAR (*enthusiastically*). I know a bay where blacksmiths are
binding
The cartwheel twice upon the stone with fire
And cold. There as the tide the blowing sails
Have dropped and hands that rowed with blessed
Brendan
Unload the chasubles from boats; nobles

    Hurry with women, whose red lips are cut
    By the salt dark, into a lighted house
    To talk, to dance: and when fire thickens the roof,
    White clergy bless their mirth in Latin, for
    Their grace is such – a couple every night
    Is married and with candles, music, they
    Prepare those innocent delights.

WOMAN (*coaxing*).   Oh, cure
    The King and we will hurry west to know
    Those companies that never sinned and whisper
    Together as we go.

SCHOLAR (*shocked*).   We must be married
    First.

WOMAN (*indignantly*). Am I immodest in the look
    Or tongue?

SCHOLAR.   Lady, you are more beautiful
    Than the bright-sided women that caress
    A hermit in his dreams and turn his bed
    Of rock to down: but what is sin to man,
    Even in the thinking, matrimony
    Makes virtue and his duty.

WOMAN (*flattered*).   And am I
    So fair?

SCHOLAR.   So fair we must be wed. A bishop
    Will join us when the wax is glittering
    In Cormac's Chapel. Our indulgence shall
    Be lawful.

WOMAN.   Oh, I have begun to dream
    Of my own marriage day, now.

SCHOLAR.   There would be
    No sin if troubled lovers could be married
    As quickly as confessed; for, to be good
    Is to have pleasure freely. There is laughter
    And dancing half the night, coming and going,
    After a marriage, a crowd at food and cards,
    A merry crowd at drink: when man and bride
    Stop whispering at the last fiery lap
    O' the candle, and knowing the ring is blessed
    By prayer, are sporting shyly in the dark
    Like . . . twopence in a beggar's pocket.

WOMAN.   I
    Will dream no more, because your learned words

  Surmount the altar step, where woman must
  Remain.
KING (*waking*).   I starve! I starve!
WOMAN (*to* SCHOLAR).   Let us be happy
  And eat together.
  (*They sit down at table.*)
KING.   No, No! You shall not dare!
  That is my supper.
SCHOLAR.   Here is white bread,
  O Fairywoman.
WOMAN.   Full of season, here,
  Black honey that I love.
KING.   Oh, this is treason!
  It is my food.
SCHOLAR (*to* WOMAN). Dumpling?
KING.   I'll marry for
  A mouthful. I will give a hundred acres
  For half that loaf.
  (*The* WOMAN *hesitates but the* SCHOLAR *leads her
  away.*)
SCHOLAR.   Come, Queen, away from him,
  And pledge me in a cup.
WOMAN (*smiling at* KING). And we shall mock
  The King who ate too much.
  (*The* SCHOLAR *empties the cup.*)
SCHOLAR (*slightly swaying*). You have deceived me!
WOMAN (*uneasily*). No, No!
SCHOLAR.   Are you not Cliodhna,
  Who was a woman and is now a wave?
WOMAN (*relieved*). Men that have carved my head upon the
   prow
  May tell.
SCHOLAR (*sternly*). If any tide can call you up,
  Dance, dance before I turn.
  (*To humour him, she moves slowly to the harp as in
  an antique dance. The* BEGGARS *come in with bones
  and mugs.*)
BEGGARS.   A strapping girl!
  A lovely pair!
      They are so young
  And her so fair.
  (*She dances before the* KING.)

KING.   Huh! Fairywoman! I will never make you
                My queen. Jig, for I know another one
                That will not let me starve.

WOMAN (*stopping*).   I know her, too.
                It is that Lasarina. And she has
                Red hair. She cannot dance so.
                (*She whirls faster.*)

KING.   Rossie! Shameless
                Woman!
                (*She runs laughingly to the* SCHOLAR *and kisses him.*)

SCHOLAR (*staggering back*). But where am I?
                Is this the house of Con? After a night
                Of wind, there is work for the wheelwright.

WOMAN (*disturbed*).   You are
                In Corc. You love me.

SCHOLAR (*slightly fuddled*).   But I am a cleric
                Then. I have been in minor orders. I
                Remember. Blessings on the fisherman
                Who smuggled in the wine! You have deceived
                Me!

WOMAN.   No, no!

SCHOLAR.   Where is my little sister, the harp?

WOMAN (*despairing*). He will forget to cure the King.

SCHOLAR.   Beggars,
                Strip me a deck of cards.
                (*He reels forward, rapt, to the front.* WOMAN *sidles to
                the* KING *and during the song slips on to his regal
                lap.*)

SCHOLAR.   *Had I the diamonds in plenty, I would stake*
                *My pocket on kings that walked out with Queen
                    Maeve*
                Or wager the acre that no man digs in Connaught,
                *And after the drinking, I would cross my soul,
                    there,*
                At the bare stations of the Red Lake.

WOMAN (*to King*). I love your baldy spot!

SCHOLAR.   *They gave me hearts as my share of the dealing,*
                *But the head that I love is not red and it is not
                    black,*
                *And I thought of the three that went over the
                    water*
                And the earth they had when they brought

Deirdre back:
For who break their money on a card that is
foolish
May find the woman in the pack.

RED BEGGAR. A little ewe between two rams!

SCHOLAR. *Patric came, without harm, out of Hell . . .*
A beggar nailed the black ace on the board.
I flung the game to the floor. I rose from their
cursing,
And paler than a sword, I saw, before me,
The face for which a kingdom fell.

(*As the song closes, the* WOMAN *comes to him.*)

WOMAN. Fancy is sharp upon the busy stone
Of wishing, but your merry say can change
To wine, food, fire and pleasure. I would now
Sweet mouth was turned to bitter tongue again,
The purple stole put by, the napkin shut,
For you can never cure the King.

SCHOLAR (*indignantly*). I can.
But who has heard the pot boil over when
The fuel was green? A passion in his demon
And his imagination must release him,
For prayer and fasting are desire again.
He fed on richer thought and he is full.
But since true argument attends the eye
And hearing, I must do a trick or three

BEGGARS. The conjurers despise.

(*To Beggars.*)

Give me a ladle, boys.

BEGGARS (*accusing Old Blind Man*). He tuk it.

OLD MAN (*indignantly*). God forgive them! I
Am deaf and dumb!

(*The* BEGGARS *search him and produce forks and*
spoons from his pockets while he protests. The
AMADAN *with a howl runs forward clasping his*
stomach.)

BEGGARS. He ate too much.

AMADAN. Diabolus in ventre meo est!

SCHOLAR (*politely*). Potes ructare?

AMADAN. Non possum.

(*The* SCHOLAR *makes conjuring passes and as the*
AMADAN *opens his mouth in astonishment, he draws*

38

slowly from it a ridiculously large ladle. They laugh.
The AMADAN *hides in terror.)*

SCHOLAR (*filling the ladle with food*). Lady, your hand must fill
   the King.

WOMAN (*approaching the* KING *with the ladle, in playful*
   nervousness).   Cathal,
   Open your mouth and shut your eyes and see
   What I shall give you.
   (*The* KING *immediately does so*).

RED BEGGAR (*making for the Larder*). Boys, the demon will
   jump out.
   (*The* SCHOLAR *steadies himself with a long drink and*
   blows out all the candles slowly except one, so that the
   Refectory is in ruddy firelight. As the WOMAN *holds*
   the ladle to the KING'S *mouth, the* SCHOLAR,
   whispering and laughing behind her, draws her back
   slowly by the waist.)

DEMON (*in a terrible ventriloquent voice inside the* KING.)
   That was a foolish trick, Mac Conglinne.
   I heard you whispering. You know that I
   Am starving in the King.
   (WOMAN *screams, drops ladle and flies.*)

MAC CONGLINNE.   A juggler's trick!
   Imagination in the vat has brought
   Up sound and bubble.
   (*He fills the ladle again and holds it cautiously under*
   the KING'S *nose.*)

MAC CONGLINNE.   Demon,
   Here is a larger bite dripping with honey
   And juice to dream on.

DEMON (*ventriloquently, as* MAC CONGLINNE *slowly withdraws*
   the big spoon). My hunger
   Is terrible and I will wait no longer.
   I will come up before it is too late,
   And you have emptied every cup and plate.

MAC CONGLINNE (*gabbling in broken Latin*). Vade retro, vade
   retro, sathane . . . in nom . . . ejicient.
   Obmutesce . . . exi, daemonia . . . ab eo . . . et . . .
   cetera . . . exi . . . ab . . .
   (*He leaps backward, knocking over the last candle.*
   Black out. A rumbling of thunder outside. A blaze on
   hearth. Wild burst of harp music outside, diminishing

39

with distance. Lights approach slowly in corridor outside and the WOMAN *is seen against the central door in an attitude of despair.*)

WOMAN.   Oh, oh, oh! The King
Is dead and I shall never be a Queen.
(MILITARY *rush in with battle-axes,* MONKS *with lights,* BEGGARS *from Larder. The high chair and dishes are overthrown. Confusion.*)

SOLDIERS (*shaking off the rain*).   By Hell!
The storm was bucketed. We ran for shelter.

MONKS.   Oh, oh! The Demon!
Run for the holy water!
                          We saw the Demon!
He sat upon the bell tower.
                                    His eyes
Were flaming red.
                    He clanged his wings.
                                          He flew
Away.

SOLDIERS.   By Hell! The clap of rain
Came up again. We never saw the Demon.

BEGGARS.   He had big horns.
                          And crooked
Hoofs.
          A tail.
                A fiery fork.
                          He knew
The Scholar's name.

RED BEGGAR.   Why wouldn't he?
I knew it was Mac Conglinne himself.

SOLDIERS.   By Hell! Where is the King?

OTHERS.   Alas! The King
Is carried off!
(*The* KING *rises majestically from behind the Lectern in his royal clothes. They draw back.*)

WOMAN (*running to him*).   Cathal!

KING.   My Ligach! I am cured. I have been ill, Dear.
I have been in a dream, a terrible dream.
Forgive the wicked words that I have said.
(*Withdrawing.*)
                                          But I
Remember . . . that clerk . . .

40

LIGACH. No, no! I was but desperate
With love for you and I was wild and foolish
Because you were so ill. And oh, let us
Be married now.
(*They embrace.* ABBOT *enters with rest of community.*
LIGACH *withdraws.*)

KING. Most Reverend Lord Abbot, I am cured,
Cured by your prayers and holy offices,
And I shall give this pious monastery
Green pasturelands and golden candlesticks.

ABBOT. O noble King!

KING. A hundred cows, a cart of frankincense.

MONKS. O generous King!

ABBOT. Saint Barra
Be praised! Our solemn prayers are heard and fast
Has cured the King. Let hymns be chanted. Light
Thanksgiving wax. Ahem. I had forgotten,
The Demon hurries with the unbeliever.
Let us remember him in private prayer!
It may be that those fiery claws will drop
The Poet into Purgatory.

LAY BROTHERS (*coming from table*). Alas!
He did not leave a bone upon the board:
He ate them all.

ABBOT (*seeing* LIGACH). What is this . . . this woman
Doing here?

KING. It is Ligach, the daughter
Of Maeldune.

ABBOT (*bowing*). Most noble lady!

KING. Good Abbot, you
Shall marry us with book and candle, for
The night is growing late.

ABBOT. We shall
Obey our King.

BEGGARS. A noble Queen!
A lovely pair!
He is so grand
And her so fair.
(KING *and* LIGACH *hold hands before the* ABBOT. *A
procession is formed.* KING *suddenly feels his neck.*)

KING. Where is my collar?
My golden collar? It is worth a kingdom.

41

ABBOT.   Great King, you gave it to that Scholar!

KING (*resigned*). Is melted now.   It
                (*The procession of chanting* MONKS, MILITARY *and*
                MENDICANTS *passes out through central door. The*
                RED BEGGARMAN *and the* AMADAN *linger behind.*)

RED BEGGAR (*stretching himself comfortably at the fire*). Put on a
                tree.

AMADAN.   Red Muireadach, that tree has not been planted.

RED BEGGAR. They say in Bantry that you are no fool.

AMADAN.   My grandfather was never late for school.

RED BEGGAR. By my own wits I fill my mortal sack.

AMADAN.   But I, more wisely, live upon the lack.

RED BEGGAR. I recommend this house for noble welcome.
                (*Young* LAY BROTHER *enters.*)

LAY BROTHER (*sternly*). Beggars, have you not heard the blessed
                bell? Come!
                The candles have been lit and you are last.
                (*Both get up reluctantly and come forward.*)

RED BEGGAR. When beggarmen can feast —

AMADAN.   their betters fast.

RED BEGGAR. When youth is fire —

AMADAN.   old men can warm their shins.

RED BEGGAR. There's but one party wins —

AMADAN.   respect and power.

RED BEGGAR. Be slow in thought —

BOTH (*together*).   for who can tell the ball
                That brings the best of jugglers to his fall?

CURTAIN

The Flame

A PLAY IN ONE ACT

to

SEAMUS O'SULLIVAN

CHARACTERS

NUN
NOVICE
ABBESS
SISTERS OF THE COMMUNITY

Scene: INTERIOR – THE 'HOUSE OF FIRE' AT KILDARE

THE FLAME

As the curtain rises, the stage is in complete darkness and nothing can be seen but the gold flame of St. Brigid, remote and calm. A sound of unending prayer, a murmuring of many voices, metrical and monotonous, is heard below. The murmurings become a single murmur as the light gradually rises and the stage becomes clear. The scene is conventionalized but by builded glooms and sectional light, the massiveness of the early cyclopean architecture is suggested: this house of an older century remains unchanged though a new fashion prevails in ecclesiastical art, as indicated by the Celtic-Romanesque manner of the play. There is a low entrance, on right, well forward, with broad lintel and inclined jambs; a similar entrance, left side, set well back. The walls are plain; in centre, at back, wide steps lead up to the oratory or shrine, which is in the form of a deep and lofty recess; the lamp of the saint is sunken but the flame is represented by a screen or transparency of pure golden light. A settle is on right: a vessel of oil on step.

An aged NUN, *robed in white and heavily hooded, so that her face remains concealed during the scene, is kneeling on steps at right. A young* NOVICE, *in bluish grey and lightly veiled, is kneeling opposite her: the* NOVICE'*s dress should be slightly secularized to indicate her state of mind. The aged* NUN *is motionless, with joined hands: and the monotonous murmur of her prayer is still heard. The* NOVICE *is glancing around nervously, restlessly, her hands working. Twice she is about to speak, twice she fails. Suddenly from outside, there is a harsh, vibrant stroke of a bell, as though an hour were marked, and the* NOVICE *starts to her feet.*

NOVICE.   Sister,
      I cannot pray to-night.
      (NUN *points to shrine with averting hands.*)
                    No. No. I cannot
      Pray.
      (*She runs aside in shadow.*)
NUN (*slowly rising*). What is it, child?
      Why have you left the flame again?
NOVICE (*at a distance*). I cannot pray, I cannot pray.

45

NUN (*coming down*).   Temptation
          Can strike between the fingers and the font.
          (*To herself as she peers around.*)
          Had not the carvers seen, while storm broke
          On rubble and cut stone, a fiery serpent
          Tongue-tied beneath the tall unfinished Cross
          Of Flann?
          (*Alarmed.*)
                              Attracta, Attracta!
NOVICE (*nervously, coming into light*).   I
          Am here.
NUN.   Where? Where?
          (*Groping.*)
                                        Come closer, for my sight
          Has but this flame to lean upon.
                                        Come closer
          Now.
NOVICE (*obstinately*). I am here.
NUN (*catching her arm*).   What mortal cold
          Has shaken you?
                              Why have you left the flame
          Again?
NOVICE (*trembling*). I could not pray.
          I could not pray.
NUN.   The soul is found in crook
          Of knee and neck.
NOVICE.   I bowed three times.
          I could not pray.
NUN (*meaningly*).   Attracta, you have veiled
          A secret. Tell it to me now.
          (*She whispers to* NOVICE.)
NOVICE (*shrinking back*).   No, no.
          I told that in confession.
          (*Looking fearfully to door on left.*)
                                                            Listen!
          Sh-sh. Listen!
          (*She runs to left entrance.*)
NUN.   What do you hear?
NOVICE (*puzzled and uneasy, coming back*). Nothing, and yet
          I know that Mother Abbess walks alone
          At night.
          (*Mysteriously.*)

46

THE FLAME

Once she stood by the Chapel door,
Pale as the shadows that fled across the Curragh,
For thaw outran the wind and the last snow
Was spirited away – nor did she stir
An icy foot, though I saw veil and fold
Escaping.

NUN (*reprovingly*). She is holier than us.
But idle thought is an unknotted thread
Forgetful of the needle.

Bless your face

And do not speak.

NOVICE.   But O it is the silence,
The silence that I fear and when you talk to
Me – why is it that I feel good again
If it is wrong to speak?
(NUN *shakes her head and moves to steps silently*.)

NOVICE (*pleading*.)   Stay but a little,
Stay with me; I am full of fear
To-night.
(NUN *beckons silently from shrine*.)

Help me a little, help

Me; when I bow my head to pray, I seem
Much smaller than I am – in this great, lonely
Light.

NUN (*pointing to shrine*). Attracta, Attracta,
If you have told all in confession, kneel
Before the flame again.

Remember long ago

Saint Brigid, wrapped in her dark mantle, drew
The holy spark from heaven on a night
When she had fasted and the builders lay
Asleep beneath their ladders.

NOVICE.   But I am
Afraid.

NUN.   Has not that flame been raised
To try the patience of our Order? Think
Of them who stayed the beam for centuries
With precious oil, as we do now, and kneel
If you have told all in confession.
(*The* NUN *kneels on step murmuring*.)

NOVICE (*with averting hands*).   Ah!
I fear the ancient flame.

(*Wildly to herself.*)

                                              What can

I do?

(*Calling.*)

        Sister.

(*Desperately.*)

               I have told

                                                      A line.

NUN (*coming forward, shocked*). A lie!

NOVICE (*retracting*).   It was a dream—

NUN.   A dream?

NOVICE.   - that troubled me.

NUN.   When, when?

NOVICE.   Last night.

NUN (*sitting down on settle and drawing the* NOVICE *to her, eagerly*).

        Now tell me, tell me. Have you dreamed
        Of that tormented spirit who must stem
        A boat of ice against the fiery falls
        Of Purgatory? Have you seen the beast
        That children fear? Brindled with green or blue,
        He banks his mighty head; but when they lie –
        Crinkling his hide and turning inside out
        So angrily that he is pawed and spotted
        With purple, ribbed in black and red, he sinks
        Into the night again, for he was stabled
        Beneath the Flood.

NOVICE.   No, Sister; no, dear Sister.
        I dreamed that I was walking in the garden
        Along a pathway summer had made less
        And the great oaks had gathered all their leaves
        So close, I wondered how the ivy found
        A branch.
                Then, halfway in the wood, I saw
        A fair-knee'd youth that had been trumpet-blown
        Among those leaves and would escape them
        On golden elbows but he was betrayed
        And buckled by the anger of his hair –
        Great hair that glittered like the tightened strings
        When the long nails of the harp-player live
        In the dark clef and the pale.

NUN (*reassuringly*).   You dreamed
        Of Absalom, the son of David, for

I told you but last week how he was in vain
Of every tress that had been pegged with gold,
And then I said: 'A novice, when her head
Is shaven, is not troubled as those women
Who knuckle their own foreheads nightly, spit
And rag their hair into so many knobs,
They search the pillow for poor sleep, catching
The day with curls.'
(*While the* NUN *is speaking, the* NOVICE *has been
glancing around uneasily. She interrupts.*)

NOVICE.   But I dreamed more.
NUN.   Tell me.
NOVICE. On the stone benches by the hedgerow
The nuns were sitting quietly together,
So quietly I thought that they were praying
Because the evening was so fair.
                         I looked up
And O the sun was but this holy flame.
(*Pointing to shrine.*)
No lamp seemed there – but when the metal-workers
Have chaliced a great jewel, is the shape
Not conquered by the light?
NUN.   That was a good dream.
What do you fear?
NOVICE. O then my foot struck chill
Too deep for spade and as I fled, lustres
Of freezing rain were in the air … I saw
Behind the black grid of the sky, that flame
Grow dim.
NUN.   O horrible!
NOVICE.   I ran
To call the nuns, for they sat in the churchyard
So quietly I thought that they were praying
For that young man who died among the trees.
I cried 'Attracta, poor Attracta is
Afraid.' But as I plucked at them between
The tombs, they shook with my own shivers and all,
All, suddenly, fell to dust.
NUN.   O horrible!
NOVICE.   I did not sleep again.
NUN.   Great Brigid, pray
For her to-night –

NOVICE (*wildly*).   I do not want to grow
  So old.

NUN.   - And save her from temptation.

NOVICE.   Never
  To look across Kildare in sun and know
  The far flocks move along the mountain slope
  Before soft cries that drive them until grass
  Is hushed with cloud.
  (*Sound of rising wind outside.*)

NUN.   Winter has camped upon
  The Curragh now. The sea is waked far inland
  And the bright estuaries of the day
  Are flooded. Chill can strike from every door.
  Pray, pray, when fever strips the young.

NOVICE (*childishly*).   I'll run from every ill
  So happily along the cold grey flags
  The clergy will not hear at all and, if
  They do, must think that I am running on
  Bare toes.

NUN.   Pray quickly, for that is
  The dancing evil. Think of Lassara.
  (NOVICE *crouches on step, the* NUN *bending over
  her.*)

NOVICE (*in terror*). Ah, ah! The dancing nun! Do not tell me
  Of her or I will dream again.

NUN (*in a frenzy of aged asceticism*). Ugh! She had little shoes
  That danced her to a sin. 'Confession-box!'
  She cried, and clapped a red-hot coal within
  Her heels. She cobbled them, she chilblain'd them,
  And as she jigged the cinder, sang: 'Burn, burn
  To bone and make me pure again, that I
  May hobble into heaven.'

NOVICE.   Ah, you frighten,
  You pinch me!

NUN.   What do you know of the shame
  That virgins fly from?

NOVICE.   But I tremble, pant!

NUN. Impurity of thought and act.

NOVICE (*weeping*).   Fear is
  A mad bird i' my throat.

NUN (*prostrating herself before shrine*). Saint Brigid, I
  Am old. These lids that time has picked and glassed

>   With glues are overtaken by the hands
>   They once despised. The silver lattice has
>   Been closed; the blessed figures I have seen
>   Are smaller than the minims in the Mass-book
>   Now.

NOVICE (*timidly touching the* NUN's *robe*). Sister.

NUN.   When I nod at night, the flame
>   Seems but a spark.

NOVICE (*contritely*).   Rest, rest.
>   I have been bad, but I will get the oil
>   And serve the lamp.
>   (*She leads the* NUN *to the settle, lifts the beaker
>   carefully and approaches the shrine.*)

NUN (*pleased*).   My prayer is heard.

NOVICE (*hesitating on step, her hand shaking*). No, no, I cannot.
>   (*Tearfully.*)   See, I cannot.
>   (*She replaces the vessel and runs to* NUN.)

NUN (*kindly*).   You
>   Are tempted and I know that you have veiled
>   A secret.
>   (*Drawing* NOVICE *to her.*)
>   Tell me all.

NOVICE.   I will. I will.
>   Because it is not wrong.
>   (*Confiding in a low eager voice, as she undoes her
>   veil.*)
>   I know it is not wrong,
>   For it has grown so shiny in the moonlight
>   Yet it is not like the moon; and not a soul
>   Can tell how I have treasured, tempered with
>   My happy tears and measured it upon
>   My fingers in the night until it weighed
>   So quickly, the bright balance of my hands
>   Could hold no more.
>   (*She rises and flings back her veil; a cymbal clash is
>   heard and her head is seen armoured with new half-
>   grown hair in abundant curls and rings that reflect
>   metallically the light from the shrine. Unveiled, she
>   acts her thoughts, her gestures become rhythmic;
>   singing tones are heard in her voice.*)

NOVICE.   Look. Look. Am I
>   Not beautiful now?

NUN (*disturbed*).   Who is shining there?
          What voice is that I hear?
NOVICE (*rapt*).   Curl beyond curl,
          They climb in falling and I shake them out
          To ripple and ring, because I have no comb
          To burnish what my fingers will uncrown
          At night. But see how they are turned and curved
          As capitals upon a page of gold
          And dragon-red from which the choristers
          Are reading. O I could be happy in
          A house where armies have been kept, had I
          A topheavy pin of fine bronze, a comb
          To stay me, to hold me from ripple and ring.
NUN (*coming forward, horror-stricken*).   Ah! Ah!
          Attracta. It is evil, evil. When
          The King of Heaven leaves his tent with cheek
          Of flame and bright-topped hand, to count
          His captives; pale in their far camp the saints
          Await ...
NOVICE (*moving back from her grasp frantically*).   No. No.
          It is not wrong, not wrong, though I have dreamed
          Of Absalom who galloped under leaves
          Nor shall I fear the branches when my own
          Are longer than those tresses that unhorsed
          Him.
          (*There is a sudden harsh clangour of iron handbells
          in the passage outside; represented by rapid beating of
          a gong. The* NOVICE *runs aside veiling her head.*)
BOTH.   Mother Abbess!
          (*The clangour becomes maddening; for we hear, as well
          as see through the distorted imagination of the* NOVICE.
          The sounds cease abruptly and the ABBESS *appears, at
          doorway, right. She enters, swiftly, silently, followed by
          SISTERS, from left and right doorways. All are habited
          in white and heavily hooded: and their faces are hidden
          during the scene, for they wear the face-veil, which is
          attached to the bandeau on the forehead and is of fine
          net. The actions and steps of the SISTERS are drilled.
          Two by two, they come forward and bow before the
          shrine: at the side of which the ABBESS stands. They
          take their places along the side walls, left and right. The
          ABBESS comes forward, alone, bows before the shrine*

*and remains in silent prayer. At last she turns and
comes to front. The stage is now brighter.*

ABBESS (*to aged* NUN, *sternly*). Sister,

     Why have you left the flame? Is this your place?

NUN.   The Novice was afraid.

ABBESS.   Why did you not

    Remain?

NUN.   She could not pray.

ABBESS.   Was not bowed gaze,

    The calm of counted hours, enough?

NUN (*humbly*).   If I have failed, forgive me.

ABBESS (*to* NOVICE).   Attracta,

    Why have you wearied Sister who is bowed
    In years as a dim candle by a cowl?
    Did I not send you here to kneel, to mind
    The precious oil? Have you been troublesome
    Of tongue again?

        Why are you fidgeting
    And fingering your veil? Come here.
    (*The* NOVICE *hesitates.*)
    Obey me.
    (*She pounces and pulls back the* NOVICE*'s veil. There
    is a cymbal clash, as the bright metallic halo of her
    head is disclosed. The* SISTERS *point rigid right hands
    towards the* NOVICE, *with a low 'Ah, Ah!' of horror.*)
      Saints above!
    (*Checking herself and the* SISTERS.)
         What holy show
    Is this? Has vanity made vow, mocked rule?
    Is wanton curl and clip our fashion? Veil –
    The secret lodging?
    (*A silent pause.*)
    (*To aged* NUN.)
        Did you know this?

NUN.   The girl is ignorant . . .

ABBESS.   Did you know this?

NUN.   Aye. Aye.

    I groped, I guessed – but slowly.

ABBESS.   Why

    Did you not tell me now?

NUN.   The girl is young . . . She . . .

ABBESS (*interrupting*). Are women not unchurched

By scandal of bare head? Has not Saint Paul
Written that demons strike their fiery tents
And hasten to such hair?
(*Sharply to aged* NUN.)
                                        Sister, I
Will speak with you again . . .
NOVICE (*interrupting, excitedly*).   No. No.
            It was my fault, my fault.
ABBESS.   How dare you,
Have you unlearned obedience and respect?
(*To others, aside.*)
These curls must now be cut.
(*She beckons a* SISTER, *instructs and sends her out.
She beckons two other* SISTERS *to come and stand on
each side of her. During the questioning of the*
NOVICE, *the* ABBESS *consults them. She speaks in a
conversational tone.*)
                                        Attracta, stand
Here. Do not be afraid, but tell me what
Has troubled you at night.
                              Have you
Been at confession?
(NOVICE *nods.*)
                    Speak.
NOVICE.   Mother, I
            Have.
ABBESS.   You promised me you would
            Be good.
NOVICE.   Yes, Mother.
ABBESS.   Have you tried?
NOVICE.   I have.
ABBESS.   But when dark comes, your mind is bright, and you
            Forget this house?
NOVICE.   Yes, Mother.
ABBESS (*softly*).   I think
            You were afraid to tell me.
NOVICE.   I have been
            Afraid.
ABBESS (*consulting* SISTER *on right*). You told a sister you had
                        visions?
NOVICE (*startled, hesitating*).   I did.
ABBESS.   And that these visions made you glad.

54

NOVICE. Yes, Mother.

ABBESS (*consulting* SISTER *on left*). And I think ... you sing
                yourself
      To sleep ... but very softly.

NOVICE (*hesitating*). Yes.

ABBESS. You know these dreams are good?

NOVICE (*earnestly*). I know,
      I know, that they are good.

ABBESS (*consulting* SISTER *quietly*). Sister forgot
      To cut your hair upon Saint Declan's eve.
      You did not tell her?
      (*The* NOVICE *remains silent.*)
      (*Consulting* SISTER.) Did you not say
      The month before ... that you were ill?
      (*The* NOVICE *remains silent.*)
      (*Soothingly.*) But do not be afraid.
      You could not pray
      To-night?

NOVICE. No, Mother.

ABBESS. But you tried?

NOVICE. Yes, Mother.

ABBESS. When you close your eyes
      You seem in light.

NOVICE (*eagerly*). I do. I do.

ABBESS. And then
      The vision comes again?

NOVICE (*happily*). Yes, Yes.

ABBESS. Now close
      Your eyes, Attracta, think and tell us what
      You see and hear.
      (*The* NOVICE *pauses and begins to speak at first in a
      low tranced voice – then excitedly and male
      murmuring as of distant crowds is heard without.*)

NOVICE. Faintly as in the dreams
      Of Fionnuala on the wave, before
      She was baptized, a stir of music comes
      At dark.
          O then I see a house where heads are
      Bare; ruddied with impatient light, tall men
      Come in, storm at their heels, for they have sailed
      All day from the black soundings of the north
      Beyond the gleam of sand – and laughing, they

Unharness the fierce tackle of the voyage
To shout and make up stories of themselves
And stir so noisily around the blaze
Of coal, I think that keels are grounding on
The very doorstep.

ABBESS.   And what are they like –
These men you see?

NOVICE (*dreamily*). They are not like the red Apostles in
The book. They are not like those saints who cross
The ocean with bright tonsure.

ABBESS (*to others*).   Sound and stir
Of Ireland, glitter of assemblies, fill
Her mind.

NOVICE.   Each man is stronger than the big oar
Three monks must bend to pull; and women run
With welcoming hands – they are dressed in green
Or blue and they have drawn their long hair back
To show a pale sweet crown: they twiddle rings,
They laugh, they look, for every man's their glass,
And they are talking all the time as though
It were not wrong.

ABBESS.   And you would like to be
With them?

NOVICE.   Yes. Yes. Nor would I care at all
If any woman spoke too loud or laughed
As though an arm were round her, had I sat
Awhile, favoured on the great bench beside
The fire.

(*The murmur and music fade away.*)

ABBESS.   And so you let those curls grow,
Attracta?

NOVICE.   Yes, Mother.

ABBESS.   Come now and listen
To me. (*Patiently.*) The saints in their bright colleges
Are tempted when they pray. There is an eye
That keeps a mock in every mind, though sound
And sight be out. You have seen vanity
Whose food at first is delicate, whose beds
Are soft. But vanity grows violent
With flattery and quarrel, hating them
Whose hands are only raised to bless.

(*The* SISTER *who has been sent out, returns with a*

knife, the ABBESS *motions her to keep back.*)
(*To* NOVICE.)   Kneel down,
Offer these fallen locks before the flame
And rise in peace.
(*The* ABBESS *takes the knife and approaches.*)
                                        Come,
Attracta.

NOVICE (*with a startled glance of realization*). No. No. I will not
          (*Running to a* SISTER.)   Sister, you were kind
And spoke to me at lesson time. Please help me
Now.
(*The* SISTER *remains motionless.*)
(*Running to a second* SISTER.)
          Sister, the evening that I fell,
You lifted me with little words. O help
Me, now.
(*The second* SISTER *remains motionless.*)
(*Running to a third* SISTER.)
          Sister, you never spoke,
For you were always quiet, but you smiled
At me one day and O at night I dreamed
Of you.
(*She waits with outstretched hands. The* SISTER *starts
but remains silent.*)
(*To* ABBESS, *tearfully.*)
          Reverend Mother, pity me,
No soul can tell how I have treasured them
And moon has tempered. Happy I at day
Though head had ached in veil, to think that brow
Went brighter.
(*Dashing back her tears.*)
                    I confess, all, all . . . I'd wake
Early – I thought – when they were longer, see
Light battling, loose them – so – with wielded head
To shine along my shoulder and bared arm.

ABBESS.   Girl, rid yourself
Of vanity. Kneel down.

NOVICE (*her voice harsh with self-will*). No. No. I won't.
          (*A murmur of horror from the Community.*)

ABBESS (*coming forward with knife*).   Obey me.

NOVICE (*moving back with a half-scream, guarding her hair – and
in a strange voice*). Back, back, Mother Abbess. Do

Not touch them. Do not look at me with those
Unlidded eyes . . . All night the cold flags try
To hide your footsteps . . . Where the thorn is sharper
You kneel . . . But in the snow and rain you sigh
Like those who have been in their graves. Back, back
And do not touch them.

SISTERS. She is possessed! She is Possessed!

ABBESS. Hold, hold her.
I must cut down that spirit in her hair
Lest it grow mighty; for demoniacs
Break chain, rushing like the ear-blinded droves,
To their destruction.

(SISTERS *come forward, timidly hold the* NOVICE. *As the* ABBESS *approaches, she struggles and screams, but her cries are lessened by the loud ringing of handbells. Or the action here may be silent and conventionalized. At the same time the flame begins to sink to an angry red glow and the stage fills with shadows.*)

ABBESS (*in alarm*). The flame is sinking. Pray, Pray.

(*In consternation the* SISTERS *retreat to the walls, hide their hands in their sleeves and bow, murmuring in prayer. The* NOVICE *remains, alone in the middle of the stage.*)

NOVICE (*strangely*). See how they join great sleeves
And mourn within their hoods, for they have found
The son of David now. They cut him down
Among the convent oaks, they severed each
Thin strand his hanging body had uncurled
And left the bright grain quivering. See how
They join great sleeves and mourn in heavy hood.
(*The flame is dimmer.*)

ABBESS. Evil spirits hide
The flame from us.
Pray, Pray aloud.

(*The* SISTERS *raise their joined hands, lift their heads and the murmuring rises, quicker and on a higher note. The tranced girl remains in an attitude of listening, she smiles and gestures.*)

NOVICE. I hear them coming,

For it is darkfall now. Men leave the deck
And laughing women have unbridled their
Own tresses . . .
     But they stop, they bow,
And some of them are carrying the pall
Of that young man who died upon a tree.
And listen, listen, they are praying . . . They
Repent. Black and white clergy have put on
The purple stole and candles will be lighted
In sad procession.

ABBESS (*loudly*).   Ring the evil back.
 (*The harsh exorcising bells are struck again. The
 clangour ceases abruptly: as in silence all watch the
 NOVICE who comes slowly to front, and, going on her
 knees, speaks in a clear, simple voice, her face uplifted.*)

NOVICE.   Holy Brigid, save
Me from the flame, for I am full of fear
Because there is a great pain in my head
That makes my body small. Hide me with pity,
Hide me in your blue mantle that was spread
By miracle until it covered half
The plain and I will find a fold there, warm
As bed in winter and too far for dream.
O hide, hide poor Attracta in your mantle
Now.
 (*During her prayer the flame disappears and for a few
 moments lovely hues of blue seem to interweave
 themselves in the air with a rustling sound, as though
 the holy mantle were descending, enfolding and
 enwrapping her until there is complete darkness. The
 measured grieving of the Community can be heard.
 Tapers are brought in hurriedly, and now, as the stage
 becomes half-lit, the pale faces of the crowding
 SISTERS are seen, human, agitated. Their gestures are
 gentle, graceful, for we see them as they really are.*

 *The SISTERS withdraw to their places, again, at side
 walls and, lying at the foot of the shrine, can be seen
 the veiled form of the NOVICE, strangely still.*

 Several SISTERS hasten forward to steps.)

SISTERS (*at steps*). Her brow is calm and cold. She breathes.
 So quietly –
     We cannot hear.

Her sleep
Is stronger than our hands.
(*The* ABBESS *bends over the comatose girl.*)
ABBESS (*moved*).　　　　　　There is no evil left; and she will wake
Again.
(*She veils the girl's face again:* SISTERS *lift and bear
her out, by doorway, left, while others pray.*)
SISTERS (*on right*). Mother, we fear the darkness –
SISTERS (*on left*).　　　　　　　　What have we heard,
What have we seen.
SISTERS (*on right*).　　　　　　Mother, we fear the darkness.
SISTERS (*on left*).　　　　　　Where is the flame we served?
What punishment
Have we deserved?
SISTERS (*on right*).　　　　　　Mother, we fear the darkness.
(*The aged* NUN *comes forward with uplifted hand.*)
NUN.　　　　I am the oldest. Let me speak.
Had not that blessed flame been raised
To try the patience of our Order, night
And day?
ALL.　　　　Yes: night and day.
NUN.　　　　　　　　　　I can remember how
At darkfall – and it must be sixty years
Ago – we trembled in this house . . . But they
Are dead . . . all dead . . . who prayed with me
　　　that night . . .
(*Her mind wandering.*)
And sometimes, lately, when your hoods are lifted
I think those Sisters have come back again.
(*A pause.*)
What was I saying to you? . . .
. . . We trembled for a great storm rang
And trampled in the convent. Every door
Was living. Evil spirits beat themselves
Against the shrine. They rose . . . it sank. We
　　　prayed . . .
It shone. And all that night with frantic robes
We fought among those climbing winds to keep
The lamp in oil.
ABBESS.　　　　　　　Remember us.
We do not understand.
SISTERS.　　　　　　Remember us.

                        We do not understand.
NUN.   Those spirits came to-night
                        In guile, tempting the young with vanity,
                        Plying the old with sleep.
                        (*Breaking down.*)
                                            . . . And we forgot
                        The duty of the flame.
A SISTER (*lifting the vessel carefully, from step*). It is the truth,
                        Here is the oil. The lamp has not been filled.
                        (*A general murmur of consternation.*)
ALL.   The lamp has not been filled.
A SISTER (*from the shrine*). A miracle!
ALL.   A miracle!
SISTERS (*from shrine*).   Deep in the lamp
                        The spark that Brigid drew from Heaven
                        Lives, lives!
ALL (*joyfully echoing*).   Lives, lives!
                        (*The* ABBESS *comes to shrine.*)
ABBESS.   A miracle!
                        The holy spark is bright.
                        (*Renewed murmurs of joy.*)
                        (*Admonishing*).   Do not rejoice
                        So soon.
                                    Have we not doubted?
SISTERS.   We have doubted!
ABBESS.   Did we not fear?
SISTERS.   We feared.
ABBESS.   Our faith was weak.
SISTERS.   Our faith was weak.
                        (*All bow as the* ABBESS *takes the vessel and ascends
                        to shrine; she returns, places the empty vessel on steps.
                        Very slow action.*)
ABBESS.   Let us pray.
                        (*The* SISTERS *all come forward and kneel across stage,
                        facing the shrine. The* ABBESS *kneels on steps. As they
                        pray, the flame slowly rises, the tapers are extinguished
                        one by one, and the rest of the stage darkens. The sound
                        of unending prayer, murmuring of many voices is heard
                        and only the gold flame can be seen, remote and calm.*)

CURTAIN

Black Fast

A POETIC FARCE IN ONE ACT

CHARACTERS

In the order of their appearance:

BLACK FAST

The seventh century controversy over the exact date of Easter had its lighter moments according to the Venerable Bede. The culinary complications in this play were suggested by some pages of his ecclesiastical history. But the episcopal challenge used in the play has been taken from a debate between an Ulster saint and a Munster saint on this vexed subject of Easter observance. The scene is the judgment-hall of CONNAL MORE *in Ulster. On the right, dais and two chairs of state. Entrances, front, right and left. At the back, through a lofty doorway formed by two transverse curtains, can be seen part of the supper room and the long table. The judgment-hall is partly in shadow; the supper room is cheerful with lighting. A man* SERVANT *comes in, left, carrying a large basket-dish piled high with apples. He crosses the stage with great care and places the dish in the centre of the table. He puts out his hand to re-arrange the king-apple at the top, then hesitates, as if he were afraid even to touch it. He moves the dish a little, stands back, moves it again, stands back to admire. The light seems to become intensified around those magnificent apples. Pleased with himself, the servant turns to cross the stage. Immediately the dish moves mysteriously along the table and disappears from sight. The* STEWARD *comes in, right, carrying a small dish. He sees the empty table, lays down the dish on dais and calls after the* SERVANT *in great excitement.*

STEWARD.   Where are the apples?
        Where are the apples from Armagh?
SERVANT (*outside*).   Upon
        The table.
STEWARD (*running and bringing him back*). Where did you put
        them?
        Where did you put them? Twenty times I told you
        To keep your mortal breath from them,
        To carry in that dish as if it were
        Your soul.
        (*With emotion.*)
        Frecklings of honey in their shadow!

65

The last in the winter loft! I polished them
As a special treat for Connal More himself.
My darlings brought the summer back: they bore
The branch away!
(*desperately.*)   Tell me the truth. You let
One fall . . . two . . . three . . . or half a dozen, hid
Their bruises in an overall?

SERVANT.   I swear
I didn't let a single apple fall.
I put them all on the table.

STEWARD (*sarcastically, turning and pointing to table*). My sweet
        ones turned
To cookers, peeled, pipped, pied themselves or soured
Into a stew!

SERVANT (*running to table*). They're gone!
They're gone!
(*Searches, then looks up towards heaven and comes
back in alarm*). It is a miracle!

STEWARD.   Aye, somebody has cut the apron string
And they have tumbled into the next world
That saints may pick them up in Paradise!
Tell that to Connal More when he is asking:
(*grimly.*)
'Where are my favourite apples from the sunyards
Of ecclesiastical Armagh?'

SERVANT.   It is a warning,
A warning from above.
                      Major, I've seen
Strange things before my time that put the fear
Of God in me. Last year I saw a saint
Darken the sky with his stick, crackle a rock
As quickly as a rotten hazel-nut
And put a swollen river back to bed again.
This is a warning, a terrible warning to those
Who break the fast.

STEWARD (*mocking*).   Abstain from apples, twice
A day, before and after . . .

SERVANT (*earnestly*).   You forget
The big joints sitting up before the fire now,
The stirabout soup, the boilers and the rounders
Of crusty ham. Is this the way to keep
The fast?

STEWARD. The seven weeks
    Of Lent are passed.
SERVANT. Our mistress says that this is Lent,
    According to the scholars from the south.
STEWARD (*indignantly*). I say that our own clergy ought to know.
    They celebrated Easter a month ago.
SERVANT. Major, those scholars must be right.
    Heaven is warning us to-night.
STEWARD (*excitedly*). This house
    Has been distracted by religion, late
    And early. The Ri says this . . . his wife says that . . .
    And everybody quarrels at the grace
    Before the fry skips off the fire. The milk
    Won't yield, the dashing butter is afraid
    To turn. The cooks are scalding their own tears
    In suet puddings, they lard the leeks, they skewer
    The sausages. Both high and low complain:
    'Who put the mutton fat into the pot
    The fish was cooking in?' 'Who saw my ham?'
    'Who boiled the cabbage with that sinful bacon?'
    The wind of indigestion bangs the door,
    And when the salmon smokes upon the grill,
    The spiced beef turns to penitential ashes.
    Enough of this.
    (*With determination, as an idea occurs to him.*)
       I'll show you miracles.
    (*Taking up the dish.*)
    Here, put this dish of chitterlings
    On the table.
SERVANT. . . . and see an angry messenger
    From the Almighty snatch it up in smoke, while
    Board and joining roar in a single draught
    Down to the water butts! Upon my soul,
    I won't!
STEWARD.   I'll do it, then, myself.
SERVANT (*edging away*). Come back!
    Come back!
    (*The* STEWARD *places the dish on the table, walks
    back with heavy steps to left exit, then creeps back to
    the transverse, bringing the unwilling* SERVANT *with
    him. A hand is seen stretching towards the dish. The*
    STEWARD *pounces and drags forward a girl servant.*)

STEWARD.   Here is your miracle!

SERVANT (*catching her*).   You think
           That you can steal the breath out of my body
           And take my living from me while my back
           Is turned!

STEWARD.   Where are those apples?
           Where are those apples?

GIRL.   Let me go!
           (*Struggling.*)   ah . . .
                                Let me
           Go now!

STEWARD.   Hold her tight!
           (*She escapes.*)

SERVANT (*discomfited*).   They learn that double trick
           Struggling with stableboys until they snap
           Their blessed scapulars.

GIRL.   I'll tell
           My mistress on you both. She ordered me
           To take those apples from the table.

STEWARD.   Wait
           Until the master hears of that.

GIRL.   What right
           Has he, my mistress says, to break the fast
           And eat those apples for dessert to-night?

STEWARD.   The seven weeks of Lent are passed.

GIRL.   They're not.
           This is a day of total abstinence
           According to the scholars from the south.

STEWARD.   Can you stand there and have the impudence
           To doubt my word before it leaves my mouth
           And contradict what our own clergy tells us?

GIRL.   My mistress says . . .

STEWARD.   *My mistress says . . .*
           Will you deny the Lenten pastoral
           In which our Bishop, speaking from the altar,
           Denounced all women who have shortened skirt
           And petticoat . . .

SERVANT.   . . . till every tuck becomes
           A sin.

STEWARD.   They listen to new doctrines, he
           Declared . . .

SERVANT.   . . . and all respect for modesty

Is gone.

STEWARD.   Where are those apples now?

GIRL (*saucily*).   Find out!

        (They seize her again.)

        Help! Help!

SERVANT (*triumphantly*). I've got a couple of big apples.

STEWARD (*anxiously*). Be careful with them.

GIRL.   Stop. Those aren't
        apples!

        (CONNAL MORE *has come in. At the same time the
        hall becomes brighter though the change to normal
        lighting is imperceptible.)*

CONNAL (*loudly*). What shameful immorality is this?

        (servants retreat respectfully)

STEWARD (*breathlessly*). She took the apples, sir, the apples from
        Armagh.

GIRL (*frightened but sullen*). My mistress ordered me.

CONNAL.   I'll see to this.

        (BLANAID FAIRNAPE, *his wife, has come in.)*

BLANAID.   Yes, Connal,
        I told the girl to take them.

CONNAL (*dismissing servants and turning to her angrily*). What do
        you mean
        By giving orders to your women servants
        To steal the courses from my table?

BLANAID.   Connal
        For three weeks now or more, on every fish-day,
        You have deliberately mortified me,
        Sitting behind a roast with noisy fellows
        Who eat their way into your favour, calling
        Your carvers in with swear-words, honeying
        The champion's portion, hurrying each mouthful
        With toppings of sweet ale. You clap late hours
        Together, devouring, drinking, till every hiccough
        And story is a shout.

CONNAL.   Can anybody say
        I do not practise my religion? All
        Through Lent, I kept the days of abstinence,
        Both black and white. I made my Easter duty
        And that is more than you have done. When I
        Was fasting, you ate meat. You picked a wing
        Of devilled chicken twice upon Ash Wednesday.

69

    You scandalised my cook and made him heat
    The grill again.

BLANAID.   I said repeatedly
    It was an ordinary Wednesday. You
    Began the Lent a month too soon.

CONNAL.   I tell you
    That Easter's come and gone.

BLANAID.   This is a fast day.

CONNAL.   I say that it is not.

BLANAID.   It *is* a fast day
    And what is more, you think of other ways
    To shame me in this house, humiliate
    My feelings and distract me from devotions.
    You treat me worse than any common woman,
    Start quarrelling when we retire to rest,
    And in the small hours waken up the baby.

CONNAL.   It is your duty to obey me.

BLANAID.   Not
    In Lent.

CONNAL.   That is untrue.

BLANAID.   Then tell me why
    Are weddings never held in the holy season?

CONNAL.   I say that Lent is over. Our
    Own clergy ought to know. Year in, year out,
    Our fathers, our grandfathers, all observed
    One date. Am I to resurrect their dust,
    Scribble the altar book with this new ink
    You have a fancy for?

BLANAID.   Romanus says
    Our clergy are in error, that we should follow
    The calendar of Gregory.

CONNAL.   Put back
    The sun a month, melt down the moon for wax
    And stick a newer wick in it! I say
    These converts are the curse of Ireland.

BLANAID (*leaving*).   Say
    Your worst. Romanus and his company
    Are coming here to-night and rigid fast
    Must be observed while they are present.

CONNAL (*calling after her*).   I
    Refuse to fast.
              I do not want them here.

70

BLANAID (*at door*). Remember what I say now. Rigid fast
Must be observed by everyone to-night.
(*She goes out, left, leaving* CONNAL *speechless with
anger.* MAHAN, *his advisor, comes in, right.*)

MAHAN. Saint Cummian and his deputation are here.

CONNAL. O tell them I am busy.
I cannot see them.
(*Confusion outside. The Abbot-Bishop, carrying his
pastoral staff, enters rapidly with his monks. They are
in white robes.*)

CUMMIAN. Connal More, I have come
To warn you solemnly and for the last time
That these disturbers, these strangers from the south
Must not be heard in any diocese
Within my jurisdiction. Caillin who called
An angel to his flinty pillow, Gillabocht,
Who heard at night the people talking in heaven,
Were my own ancestors and these poor veins
(*Holding out left hand.*)
More knotted than the roundstone of their graves
Are scored with chalks of pain. But I remember
My uncles and grand-uncles held the crook
In true humility, inheriting
The harvest charities, the unwritten dues
And rentals of this land. Have I not kept
The simple from themselves, firmly denounced
The sins of immorality and pride
In every pastoral? On Easter Sunday
I mentioned from the altar foolish women
Who dig up beauty from the very clay,
Redden their lips, unbar the modest stitch
At neck and ankle that the eye may find
A short-cut to false Edens. Now these strangers,
These unfrocked clergy, who have sent loose tongues
Ahead of them, are coming here to unbury
Our past and, with a wicked doctrine, spread
Dissension through the countryside, upset
Authority of church and state.

CONNAL. What can
I do? You know it was my wife
Invited them.

CUMMIAN. You have authority

71

And in all lawful matters she must obey
Her husband.

CONNAL (*excitedly*). Nothing is sacred to her now
Since she became a theologian! Early
And late she quarrels with my fonder wishes.
She sends the servants to remove the dishes
From my own board, expostulates in bed . . .
Father, she makes a mock of matrimony
And scorns the sanctity of family life.

CUMMIAN. This is what happens
When women listen to the Adversary,
Borrow bad tongue and open every satchel.
But Connal More, you have yourself to blame.
I warned you solemnly two months ago
And now I warn you solemnly again
That these disturbers from the south, these strangers
Must not be heard in any diocese
Of mine.

CONNAL (*helplessly*). What can I say, your Holiness?
My wife insists.

CUMMIAN. Then I
Must do my duty.
(*To monks.*)
Put on my cope, please.

CONNAL. What are you going to do?

CUMMIAN. Place all
This household under interdiction.

CONNAL (*angrily*). You
Would dare to threaten me.

CUMMIAN (*to his coadjutor*). The handbell, quick.

MAHAN (*aside*). He is in earnest, Con. Remember how
Your second cousin was cursed right, left and centre,
For pitching a psalter into the lake. His shirt
Blew off and, springing from her cheeky bed,
His wife ran to the door and saw him pelting
Along the tree tops. After that, he had
To beg his daily bread from passing crows
That pitied him.

CONNAL (*angrily*). Well, let him do his damnedest!

CUMMIAN (*to monks*). The breviary!

MAHAN (*aside*). You know that scratching stone
At Inishmore, the one the spotted heifers like

72

The best.

CONNAL (*uneasily*).   I do.

MAHAN.   Men say
It is your grandfather, the pagan one,
That he was turned to granite by a saint
When he refused a site for a new church there.

CONNAL.   Stop, Cummian!

                    I give in.

(*To Mahan.*)

                    Call up my men.

                                        Bar every door.

(*Confused sound of happy voices outside.* BLANAID
comes in with ROMANUS *and his monks. The
Munster monks are dressed in blue or black robs.*)

BLANAID (*sweetly*).   Dearest,
Romanus and his monks have come, hasty
As angels and indeed, much earlier
Than we expected. But their holy news
Can scarcely wait. They carry information
And spiritual benefits for all.
How can we welcome them enough?

ROMANUS.   Connal,
We thank you for this hospitality.
Your noble wife has told me in her letters
Of your anxiety to promulgate
The truth in Ulster.

CONNAL.   You are welcome. Just now
I was in consultation with my soul-friend,
My spiritual adviser –
(*Quickly presenting him.*)
                    Most Reverend
Lord Bishop Cummian.
(ROMANUS *and* CUMMIAN *bow stiffly to one another.*)

ROMANUS (*to* CONNAL, *smiling*).   I must explain
The meaning of this sudden visitation.
I have obtained, in fact, a dispensation
To travel even on a day of fast.

CUMMIAN (*sternly*).   This is a feast day, sir.

ROMANUS (*politely*).   I fear
That you are misinformed. It is
A fast day.

ULSTER MONKS.   No, a feast day . . .

MUNSTER MONKS. A fast day . . .

ULSTER MONKS. A feast day . . .

(*The two parties of monks approach each other and begin to argue excitedly.*)

CUMMIAN (*to his monks*). Come back, have you forgotten all respect?

All discipline of foot and mouth?

Connal,

I warned you. Now I will pronounce
A challenge.

CONNAL (*startled*). A challenge?

ALL (*echoing*). A challenge!

CUMMIAN. Yes,

A challenge to the strangers in our midst.

(*Slowly.*)

Let two books, one of the old order, another of the new, be cast into the fire and let us see which of them will escape the flame.

(*He pauses but there is silence. He continues, with a smile.*)

Or, if you have no books, let two monks, one of yours and another of mine, be shut up in the same house. Then let the house be set on fire and we shall see which of them will escape the flame.

(*The Munster monks look at one another anxiously.*)

AN ULSTER MONK (*rapt*). O Father, let me go into the flame
Again to see the terrors of the past,
The trumpet-scattered armies of Canaan,
The iron pits, war prisoners, polishing
The brasses of the Moloch . . .

ANOTHER. No, it is

My turn.

ANOTHER. No, mine!

CUMMIAN (*in a firm but kindly tone*). Be patient.

(*Addressing his opponent.*)

If

You fear the flame,

(*Impressively.*)

then, let us go to the grave of a deceased monk and raise him up to life and he will tell us which order we ought to observe in the celebration of Easter.

CONNAL (*good-humouredly*). That is a sporting proposition. I

Will gamble on my Battle Book, Romanus,
Or if you wish, wager my capuchin
Will not be fried before his time.

ROMANUS (*quietly*).   What
Is the name of the little hill we passed
Above the holy well?

BLANAID.   Slieve Corry.

ROMANUS.   Thank you,
Lady.
            I have no doubt that, Heaven willing,
Cummian could rock that hillside with his staff,
Such is his holiness, his practical
Renown. So how could I, a simple schoolman,
A humble servant of the Lord, compete
With him in wonder-working? Rather let us
Discuss the matter quietly. Connal,
Your judgment is respected far and wide.
Your word is law. Attend each argument.
Detect each fallacy. We are your books.
Decide among us like that Emperor,
The famous Constantine, and so restore
The faithful to one service.

CONNAL (*flattered, consulting his wife*). I agree.
And furthermore I am prepared to stake
My supper on the scholarship of Ulster.
Will you support me, Cummian?
(*The Abbot-Bishop hesitates, consults senior monks,
yields to their urgings.*)

CUMMIAN.   I will.

CONNAL.   Then choose your two word-champions.

ROMANUS.   I, myself,
Will speak.

CUMMIAN (*consulting seniors*).   We choose
Our classic scholar, Cogitosus.

OTHERS.   Yes,
Yes, Cogitosus.

CONNAL (*briskly, giving orders*).   Set the supper.
                                                Lay places
For all.
            Ignorant fish and joint must come
To trial.
(*With some ceremony,* CONNAL MORE *and his wife*

75

take their places on the dais. Men and women of the household assemble. The monks group themselves, left, right. Trumpets outside. During this scene servants place dishes on table for supper.

CONNAL.   The conference may now begin.
We call on Cogitosus.
(*Monks bring forward* COGITOSUS, *a tall, lean man, slightly greying around the tonsure and obviously absent-minded. He begins to speak, as if he were unconscious of his surroundings and lived in the spacious past which he evokes but gradually his voice changes and quickens as he becomes aware of the suave opponent facing him.*)

COGITOSUS.   White-robed Patric
Preached to our people by the lake-shores, bright
With baptism and when the branch at evening
Became a tent and berries seemed larger than
The birds that pick them now, he sat among
His new disciples, listening with a smile
To ancient stories of Oisin, but heard
None greater than his own.

                     The glens sprang up
With gospelling until the faith had come
To rest. How often in her old age, Brigid,
Herdswoman of heaven, gazed across her plain
In happiness: for praise found residence
In gold that ran the river, mortar made
With milk. The churchmen called on architects
To marry broad and slender, take by sleight
The crooked from the straight. O not from plan
Or parchment but by the holy rule of thumb
The tower was capped, the arch was sprung!

                       Who cupped
The inner sacrament with scope of chasings
That angels had foreseen? Who multiplied
The letterings of books? Go ask the bell-ringers
Of Cluanbeg, eye-straining copyists
Beyond the Shannon reed-beds. Ask the child –
Who hides the night-spark on the hearth? Who makes
The glad sun dance on Easter morning? Simple
Or wise will tell you all. For we maintain
The gospel truth that the Evangelist,

John o' the Holy Bosom, propagated
Among the deacons and the presbyters
Of Asia Minor.
(*A murmur of admiration from the northern monks.*)
               And shall we extinguish
The Pentecostal fire, huddle together
Within a lower story, shaken by street-noise
Of cities, ancient in their wickedness,
Where countryfolk lose faith?

ROMANUS.   Will you deny
What all men practise now in Rome? In Gaul?
In Greece? . . . Dispute in Antioch? . . . Or come
Again to Carthage? In the Libyan desert –
Where noon is falsifying, the very plants
Stuckful o' pins and needles – contemplatives
Pick out the opposites of thought, distinguish
The substance from reality. The truth
Is voiced in solitude, in Lower Egypt,
In Alexandria. Your nettled hermits
Assume, no doubt, that God Almighty rests
On the Old Law. Borrow these eyes that saw
Last year the wonders of the New. Beyond
The isle of Golden John, our pilgrim ship
Was stopped by darkness on Good Friday. All
Could see the alp that opens into flame
At the Third Hour. Believe me, I have sponged
From this poor body, this passing dust, the pock
Of cinders flying from the lower regions
Where the lost souls are tortured.
(*Murmurs of astonishment.*)

BLANAID.   And you saw
The wonders of the Holy Land, too?

ROMANUS.   Lady,
I did, for I was in Jerusalem
At the last annual fair. Crowds basketed
The Gate of David, stalls were everywhere,
The cattle backed against the shuttered sills,
The prices rose and fell. And, saving your presence,
Those streets are never staled with donkey dung
Or camel drench, for when the fair is over –
A sudden clap of cloud comes down to cleanse
The cobbles. I sheltered from that miracle,

I heard it pass the arches of a bridge,
Roar from the rocky gutters, vanish down
The valley of Jehosophat.

COGITOSUS.   Come
To your point.

CONNAL (*intervening*).   This is most interesting.
And did you see Mount Olivet?

ROMANUS.   I did.
And Brother Diuma was with me.
(*Indicating a monk.*)

                                    We climbed
The rocky pathway to the last basilica
Of all. We saw the sacred circle of air
No roofing stone can vault. We stood in fear
And trembling there for the gigantic lamp
Swung back, the pulleys creaked and we ran with
     others
To pray in the portico, cried out and our sleeves
Were plucked apart by the miraculous blast
That passes on the Night of the Ascension.
And many other things I saw, showing
The active Hand of God . . .

                                    But who will dare
To contradict what is decreed by councils,
Deny what is believed by all the faithful
From Palestine to Rome?

COGITOSUS (*drily*).   We have a saying
That those who go to Rome might well have stayed
At home.

ULSTER MONKS (*excitedly*).   And why did Patric bring to Ireland
The relics of the apostles?

                                    The bones
Of Stephen . . .

                         Martin . . .

                                    and the other martyrs?
(CUMMIAN *silences them with a gesture.*)

ROMANUS.   Will you deny
That Peter, preaching in the capital,
Reckoned his candle from the waxing moon
Upon the fifteenth night, the seventeenth,
The twenty-first, according as the Lord's Day
Occurred?

78

COGITOSUS. I say that John began
His midnight fast upon the fourteenth moon
But did not calculate the Easter date
Beyond the twentieth. Will you admit
That he ignored the Lord's Day in that sum?
ROMANUS. Of course.
COGITOSUS. And yet he was the favourite
Disciple?
ROMANUS. Granted but he paid respect
To the Mosaic Law. And what of Paul?
Did he not practise circumcision, shave
His head at Corinth, go up to the temple
With gum and spice for fear of giving scandal?
COGITOSUS. A clever quibble, friend.
But I will stand within your camp. Do you
Approve of Anatolius?
ROMANUS. Truly,
A learned father . . .
COGITOSUS. Most respected?
ROMANUS. Yes . . .
COGITOSUS. Completely orthodox?
ROMANUS. Agreed.
COGITOSUS. And yet,
He calculated Easter in his writings,
As we do here.
ROMANUS. I have you by the horn
Of that dilemma, for he reckoned twice
According to the old Egyptian figures,
Acknowledging the fourteenth risen moon
To be the fifteenth in our calendar.
MUNSTER MONKS. He tosses on our bull!
He is impaled!
COGITOSUS. Repudiate my premises.
ROMANUS. Will you
Deny the cycle of Vitruvius
By which we reckon from the Flood?
COGITOSUS (*scornfully*). Unflatten
The earth, revolve it round the sun! Unfix
Creation's date!
ROMANUS. Not only that, I hear
You sometimes reckon from the thirteenth moon . . .
COGITOSUS. That is untrue . . .

79

ROMANUS. . . . . forget the Older Law,
Despise the New.
ULSTER MONKS. That is untrue.
We count
The fourteenth to the twentieth moon.
MUNSTER MONKS. We count
The fifteenth to the twenty-first.
COGITOSUS. I say
That Ambrose, Cyril . . .
ROMANUS. Dionysius
Exiguus . . .
OMNES. The fourteenth . . .
fifteenth moon
The twentieth . . .
the twenty-first moon . . .
(*Complete confusion and noise of argument.*)
CONNAL (*rising and clapping his hands*). Order!
Order!
This house
Has been distracted by religion, night
And day. I cannot sleep in any comfort
Until this matter has been solved. I will
Acknowledge, Brethren, that accuracy
Is everything. It keeps the soul and body
In space and time, directs the mineral
And plant, upholds the double heavens. I
Respect theology. I do not think
That we can make the soul into a parcel
And tie it up with simple heart-string, save
Ourselves by common ignorance.
(*Suddenly addressing the auditorium.*)
But some
Among our audience grow restless . . .
(*A loud cough from auditorium.*)
. . . sound
The chest as if they were at church.
So now
Let Cogitosus give his final speech,
Our guest reply – and let them both be brief.
Why need I fast in public here? And if
I should decide this is a feast day
(*Indicating with some relish, the laden supper table.*)

                                            – must
The mutton roast be spoiled?

COGITOSUS.   I have but little more
To say. Three hundred years have come and gone
Since Columcille drew the breath of life,
Moving among the mysteries of earth
As we do now, the patron of our hopes
Beyond the grave. Three hundred years, Brethren,
We have observed his strict monastic rule
Within the north. His word of mouth maintains
The islands where he sang the matins. Nettle
And briar remember how he lived. Shall we
Forget when the poor husbandmen can tell
His blessing on the buckle strap and women
His prayer that protects the churn? The books
Of his biographers attest in full
The wonders he performed. The night he died
The coasts were shining, invisible messengers
Were heard at every crossroad. Shall we say
This man who talked with angels in his sleep
And penned the painful gospel in his cell
Too near to heaven, could not calculate
Exactly from the changes of the moon
The true date of the Resurrection?

ROMANUS.   Many
Who have worked wonders, Cogitosus, shown up
The vanities of air, will not be recognised
Upon the Judgment Day. I have no doubt
This elder you praise,
                         this . . .
(*One of his monks prompts.*)
                           Columcille . . .
                                 thank you . . .

This holy Columcille lived in truth
According to the knowledge of his time
But fear you have not proved your point. I will
Explain once more.

CUMMIAN.   He has insulted us!

ULSTER MONKS. Attacked our faith!

CUMMIAN.   We will not stay
Another minute. Connal More, I warned you.
And now I place your household out of bounds.

Come, brethren.

(*He walks out, followed by his monks. General confusion.*)

CONNAL (*gloomily*). This is the frypan!

BLANAID. Give
The verdict for Romanus now.

CONNAL (*listening, in alarm*). What's that?
What's that?

(*A distant rumbling is heard. Lights dim, complete black-out in supper room, nearer rumbling of thunder, clattering of dishes and plates. Lights up. The table is seen to be completely bare.*)

ROMANUS. A miracle!

OMNES (*in awe*). A miracle!

BLANAID. The joints have disappeared.

CONNAL. The very plates are gone.

ROMANUS. Yes, they are gone,
Connal.
(*Solemnly pointing upward.*)
This is a warning from above,
A terrible warning to all unbelievers
Who scorn our holy fast. Proclaim the truth
Before we kneel in prayer.

CONNAL (*rising*). I here proclaim
This is . . .
(*Distant rumble.*)

BLANAID (*prompting*). a fast day.

MAHAN (*rushing in*). Stop! It is a feast day.

CONNAL. What do you mean?

MAHAN. Another miracle!

CONNAL. Another miracle?

MAHAN. I saw with my own eyes
Your dishes streaming through the air!

CONNAL (*amazed*). Where did
They go?

MAHAN. Down to the monastery.
(*General astonishment.*)
Our monks
Are laying them on their table.

ROMANUS. A sign
Of Evil. Powers of wickedness have come.
Let us all pray.

82

CONNAL(*indignantly*).   Why should the Devil dish up
         Late dinner for my venerable Bishop?
         I say that you are wrong.

BLANAID.   Were it my last day
         On earth I would maintain it is a fast day.

CONNAL (*turning to her*). You mean a feast day

BLANAID.   . . . a fast day . . .

CONNAL.   . . . a feast day . . .

BLANAID.   . . . a fast day . . .

         (*The wrangling voices of* CONNAL *and his wife are
         lost in the general confusion and noise of argument as
         the curtain falls.*)

CURTAIN

The Kiss

A LIGHT COMEDY IN ONE ACT

After the French
of
Théodore de Banville

CHARACTERS

PIERROT
UIRGEAL

Time: A SUNNY MORNING LAST MAY
Place: A WOOD NEAR CLONSILLA

THE KISS

As the curtain rises, the wood is still in shadow. But the morning sunlight has reached one spot, just in front of the mossy trunk of a fallen tree, left, downstage. Imagine birds are twittering but cease as UIRGEAL *comes on, right. She is wrapped in a ragged cloak with a heavy hood and drags herself as if under the weight of centuries.*

UIRGEAL. Why must I hobble, shudder with old age,
Wrinkle the raindropped pools in tiny rage,
Bedraggle the spine of the bramble rose,
When by the very whiteness of the clothes
He wears and their big buttons, I can tell
Pierrot will surely break the wicked spell
That keeps me old? What is the only cure
For me? The first kiss of his life, so pure
He has not dared to dream of that first kiss,
And if I steal what he will never miss
Until he looks for it, no tongue will blame
My meanness, so I can escape from shame
And anguish. I have only half an hour
Or less to save my being from the power
Of evil. First touch of mortal innocence
Belongs, all say, to spirit, not to sense.
I'll catch him by that sweetness of the heart
Before his senses have had time to start
From me. But will he pity my distress?
How can his young eye know my ugliness
Is only skin deep?
(*Peering round.*)
                              Now I see him run
Between the ivy shadows and the sun.
I'm frightened, frightened to the wings.
(*Going right.*)
                                        I'll hide
A moment, watch those lips that have not lied
As yet to any girl.

87

(*She conceals herself among the trees.* PIERROT *enters,*
carrying a luncheon basket. He is young and ingenuous.)

PIERROT (*to audience*). What's in the basket?
That is your question, and before you ask it,
I'll answer everything. But let me take
My luncheon out.
(*Suiting rhythmic action to word.*)
First, an old-fashioned cake.
What are the specks? You've guessed it – caraway.
Some muscatels,
a cake knife,
corkscrew, –
– Pray
Excuse the tissue paper and the twine –
Together with a bottle of light wine,
For when I drink, I love to see the grape.
A napkin –
I can wrap it round the nape.
Two little glasses, one inside the other
For company.
You ask why do I bother?
Well, anything can happen in a wood
Like this.
(UIRGEAL *appears from behind a tree, but is unseen*
by PIERROT.)

UIRGEAL (*aside*). My Pierrot, when dare I intrude?
PIERROT. I'll pick a nosegay, while the dew is wet
On lily o' the valley, violet.
UIRGEAL (*aside*). My favourites!
PIERROT. But first, in case of theft,
I'll hide my luncheon basket in a cleft
Among the oaks or – safe as sound – under
A rock that has been shattered by the thunder.
(*He runs out, left.*)
UIRGEAL (*appearing for a moment*). I must be brave, and take him
by surprise.
(PIERROT *comes back, brushing his sleeve.*)
PIERROT. This is a spot for laughter not for sighs.
Had I a sweet companion, dark or blonde,
I would not care if only she were fond
Of me and very brave and when she flung
Her arms around me I would hold my tongue,

Though I could gossip on this heavenly morning
With the devil himself, in spite of every warning.
(*Catching sight of* UIRGEAL *stooping on right.*)
I see a country girl beside that stream,
Her cheeks, no doubt, beetroot and double cream.
She stoops to gather twigs. When she turns round,
I may be disappointed.
                  H'mm.
                        Confound
It! Why, her nose is tippling with her chin,
The poor old creature – and her ancient skin
Is tougher than a taproot.
(UIRGEAL *approaches slowly.*)
                          I must talk
To her. She may be ill, can scarcely walk,
A centenarian. She must have known
The years of peace. I wish I were alone
Eating my seed-cake, cracking my bottle of wine,
For who could call that one a Columbine?
(*As* UIRGEAL *totters,* PIERROT *runs to her.*)

PIERROT.   Pray, madam, take my arm.
UIRGEAL.   You are polite,
Sir, I am faint. I have not had a bite
Of food for days.

PIERROT.   Come, Madam, you must rest
Upon this moss. I'll bring you cake, fruit, best
Of all, a glass of wine.
(*He runs off.*)

UIRGEAL.   His kiss is mine.
(PIERROT *returns with basket and busies himself.*)

PIERROT.   Now eat and drink,
                    I'll sit upon the grass,
Elbow the early sun and take a glass
With you.
(*A pause.*)
(*Making conversation.*)
          This wine is not so bad.
                        Another slice
Of seed-cake?

UIRGEAL.   No, thank you.
PIERROT.   Weather has been nice.
(UIRGEAL *nods.*)

I hope that you are better now.

UIRGEAL.   I feel
The centuries are going back. I reel
With hope since I have had some food to eat.
Dear child, how fortunate it was to meet
You in the sunshine. Picnics are so few
Now.
    What's your name?

PIERROT.   Pierrot.

UIRGEAL.   What do you do
For a living?

PIERROT (*getting up*). Nothing much, I fear, delight
In momentary fancies, dress in white.

UIRGEAL. May-blossom in the hedge! Yes, white is pretty
And suits the country better than the city,
My Pierrot.

PIERROT (*shyly*). White looks well on me, I think.
(UIRGEAL *sways as she rises to her feet.*)
But what is wrong? You're faint. More wine.
              Please drink
It.

UIRGEAL. No. No. I am trembling. I am chill,
But there is something that can save me still,
(*Hobbling into the shadows.*)
Something that I am ashamed to ask of you.

PIERROT (*puzzled but polite*). If I have got it, it is yours.

UIRGEAL.   I knew
That you would save me.

PIERROT.   But what is it? Tell
Me, have I got it?

UIRGEAL (*solemnly*). Swear by book and bell
To give it to me first.

PIERROT (*gallantly*).   Madam, I bare
My head to Heaven. May I go in black
And all salute the serge, if I take back
My word. But tell me, is it far or near?
I'll race your wish and bring it to you here.
The electric clock upon my mantlepiece?
It's yours. A gigue from Italy or Greece?
I'll dance it. Sign a cheque . . . without a blot?
Snatch the last sovereign from the melting pot?

UIRGEAL. I only want a moment. Swear to give it.

PIERROT. It's yours, although I never can relive it.
By my own sister, the snow, and my brother, the swan,
I shall be happier when it is gone!

UIRGEAL (*clutching him*). Then give it to me quick.

PIERROT. How?

UIRGEAL. In a kiss.

PIERROT (*withdrawing, aside*). Her eye is catching fire . . . her tongue's a-hiss.

UIRGEAL (*pleading*). What only takes a moment will not hurt you.

PIERROT (*coming downstage, to himself*). This strange old woman has alarmed my virtue.
My heart is jumping. I can feel it dash,
(A frightened swallow at the window sash).
Must my first joy be broken on the wing?
Disgust unsparkle the engagement ring?
But no, I must be kind as I am pure
And this good deed will help me to endure
What's horrible. Horatio held a span
Across the Tiber. Am I not a man
And why should I be so afraid of her?
Scævola, scorning agonies of fire,
Branded his own right hand. Did Theseus blench
When he went down to Hell for all the stench
Of sulphur?

UIRGEAL (*calling*). Dear.

PIERROT (*aside, wavering over his oath*). Did heaven hear me swear?

UIRGEAL. Dearest.

PIERROT (*without turning*). What?

UIRGEAL. Kiss me.

PIERROT. I . . . I . . .

UIRGEAL. Kiss me.

PIERROT (*running to her, with sudden determination*). There!
(*The moment he kisses her, the stage becomes fully lit and* UIRGEAL *is transformed into a young girl. Still masked, she appears as the ideal Columbine of his thoughts.* PIERROT *is overcome with wonder and delight.*)

PIERROT. Heaven and earth! Is there a catechism
Of kissing? Are the gay tints in the prism
Pure science or the lingerie of light?

	Were our First Arts and peaceful Ovid right?

Were our First Arts and peaceful Ovid right?
Can lap of water, flame, trees, money, snore
Of bull, conceal the shape that we adore?
And do we wake or dream, when we lie down?
Love is a proper, though a common noun,
So let *me* be the gentle verb to *live*
And rule *you* in the sweet accusative.
Plural or singular, can I decline
Your loveliness, if you are Columbine?

UIRGEAL. No. No. I am a creature of the air
Light as your syllables. Why should I care
Whether you see me only in the shape
Of Columbine or not? I can escape –
A poet loved me once when he was young
And foolish. He spent half his time among
The woods with me. In fact we were engaged.
But he grew famous and the more he aged,
He dealt in rags and bones, in dirty delph,
Then seized and tried to make me like himself.
I am most grateful, Pierrot, for you gave me
Quite willingly the one thing that could save me
From fate.

PIERROT. But is there something else you need?

UIRGEAL. No. Thank you. Thank you very much indeed.
(*Leaving.*)
And now, goodbye.

PIERROT (*calling after her*). Madam, you've dropped a glove,
I think.

UIRGEAL (*turning*). What do you mean?

PIERROT. I am in love
With light of hand.

UIRGEAL. I do not understand.

PIERROT (*sarcastically*). All property is sacred in this land.
When patriots can pick the public purse
But not the private pocket, what is worse
Than petty larceny? To rob mere pence
And not a bank increases the offense.
If company directors are promoted
For fraudulence and deputies have voted
Large pensions for possession of a rifle.
It is indictable to steal a trifle.
Your takings are too modest, Madam . . . Miss . . .

UIRGEAL (*indignantly*). In that case, I will give you back your
kiss.

PIERROT. One kiss to set my heart and mind at rest!
Lady, however business men invest
Some fraction of their total, they insist
On quick returns. Would the industrialist
Compete, when he can have monopoly
Of tariffs and unship the Irish sea?
The poor ratepayers groan, are apprehensive?
Dam every river, make their light expensive!
Charity fund and social service bless
Obedient rollers of the printing press
Until the Constitution shakes with laughter.
What did I say? This country makes me dafter
Than my own heart. I touch a floating mine.

UIRGEAL. What do you want?

PIERROT.   All, all, my Columbine.

UIRGEAL. If love were fancy, given for the asking
How could I hope to please you?

PIERROT.   By unmasking.

UIRGEAL. You want too much.

PIERROT.   And what do you suppose is
The reason of your own metempsychosis?
If one plain kiss return you to the sky,
Dare we in one another's arms be shy?
Whisper to me of all that whiteness none
Have been but airmen, flying past the sun
Through icicles, before the lever drops
The high explosive, whiteness that never stops,
Whiteness from which the moon is shining back,
Although the clouded skies we know – are black
With horror.

UIRGEAL.   In a happier, peaceful time
We'll talk of love.

PIERROT.   Say I were past my prime,
Grown old, what kiss could make a younger man
Of me? Let us be happy while we can,
Wander among the woods, do what we please.
The sun is most discreet among these trees
And never goes too far lest hidden flowers,
That show their paleness at unearthly hours
And fear the day, might come to any harm.

So be my Columbine and take my arm,
Where none can see us, you shall pay that debt
With lily o' the valley, violet.

UIRGEAL (*moved*). I think you love me, Pierrot.

PIERROT.   Dare I tell
How much I do?

UIRGEAL.   Let us be sensible.

PIERROT.   Of course.

UIRGEAL.   What is my nature, Pierrot? Light
And innocence, perhaps love at first sight.
But mortal longings are the deathward flight
Of midges towards the dusk – and must I sigh
For transitory pleasures, learn to die
When all my sisters are content to be?
Only the adolescent mind can see
By that forgotten faith men dare not name
Since they inherit consciousness of shame.
Pierrot, those first impressions cannot last,
This blazing universe goes much too fast
And men exchange so soon the startling presence
Of all the heavenly bodies for sad lessons
In dualism.

PIERROT.   Spiritual change
Is more important. Do you fear the strange?
Despise the marvellous experience.
Of life upon this earth, spirit and sense?
You were engaged once. Love can bring all nearer
The farther that it seems and men hold dearer
What they must lose too quickly.

UIRGEAL.   Though you tempt
Me, Pierrot, with your thoughts, I am exempt.

PIERROT.   Not from my love. This fire-clay world's not yet
A cinder track.

UIRGEAL.   But, Pierrot, you forget
One thing.

PIERROT.   What is it? Let me know the worst.

UIRGEAL.   Morality. We must be married first,
If I am to be yours.

PIERROT.   Then be my wife.

UIRGEAL.   You really mean it?

PIERROT.   Darling, share my life.

UIRGEAL (*pleased*). That would be very charming, Pierrot.

94

PIERROT.   I would
                 Purchase a caravan of painted plywood,
                 All weather white, with cupboard, pantry, shelves,
                 A tiny sitting-room just for ourselves.
                 With innocent amusements we would pass
                 The summer, chaining daisies in the grass.

UIRGEAL.   I'd wash your white clothes by a river's edge
                 And hang your pantaloons –

PIERROT.   upon a hedge?

UIRGEAL.   I would not send them to a common laundry.

PIERROT.   They'd dance in sun there. Could my brother swan dry
                 His wings as quickly?

UIRGEAL.   We would both be white –

PIERROT.   As our reflections –

UIRGEAL.   white as the distant sight
                 Of snow –

PIERROT.   in April –

UIRGEAL.   white as avalanches
                 That veil the Alps.

PIERROT.   At midnight, barely conscious
                 With pleasure, dream how all that whiteness stole
                 Around the globe once –

UIRGEAL.   lingers at the Pole –

PIERROT.   And on the heads of the Academicians,

UIRGEAL.   In Paris,

PIERROT.   London,

UIRGEAL.   make as quick decisions.

PIERROT.   And have a villa,

UIRGEAL.   vegetables,

PIERROT.   fence.

UIRGEAL.   Large family –

PIERROT.   regardless of expense.

UIRGEAL.   A gardenful of columbines

PIERROT.   – and pierrots.

UIRGEAL.   We'd teach them Irish.

PIERROT.   Tell them of the heroes –

UIRGEAL.   Of Easter Week.

PIERROT.   My heart is beating fast.
                 Say, say you love me.

UIRGEAL.   Yes, I do.

PIERROT.   At last!
                 We are as good as married, darling. Kiss

Me.

UIRGEAL (*withdrawing*). But there must be something more than
　　　　　　this?

PIERROT. 　　You mean?

UIRGEAL. 　　　　　　O nothing in a wrong or sly sense.
　　　　　　Something, I think, they call a special licence.

PIERROT. 　　I have a fountain pen, if it will write.
　　　　　　(*Produces one and shakes it.*)
　　　　　　It does.
　　　　　　(*Takes out a small diary and starts to scribble on a
　　　　　　page.*)
　　　　　　Our marriage lines in black and white.

UIRGEAL. 　　Not that. Some person in a domino
　　　　　　Performs the marriage service, people throw
　　　　　　Confetti at us afterwards and drink
　　　　　　Our health in noisy glasses.

PIERROT. 　　　　　　　　　　　　Let me think.
　　　　　　(*Going aside.*)
　　　　　　Is this a question of Ne Temere?
　　　　　　Mixed marriages with the ephemerae
　　　　　　So serious, when those who live on air
　　　　　　Can find the finches nesting everywhere?
　　　　　　(*Coming back.*)
　　　　　　Dear, in these woods where strangers do not stray
　　　　　　Only the birds can give a bride away.
　　　　　　The blackbird is their senior. He will bless
　　　　　　Our happy union if you murmur 'yes'!

UIRGEAL. 　　But is that ceremony recognised?

PIERROT. 　　Of course, it is, dear; no one is surprised
　　　　　　By what can happen nowadays.
　　　　　　(*Eagerly.*)
　　　　　　　　　　　　　　　　　Consent!

UIRGEAL. 　　I do.

PIERROT. 　　　Then let us marry –
　　　　　　(*Aside.*)　　　　　　as in Lent!
　　　　　　(*He leads her to the tree trunk, goes down on one
　　　　　　knee.*)
　　　　　　Dear, if in fancy I have made too free,
　　　　　　Forgot the long wars of the apple tree,
　　　　　　What harm have hasty lovers ever done
　　　　　　Who only want to be alone with one
　　　　　　Another? Has not every young man tried

To find the woman taken from his side?
UIRGEAL.   You speak so strangely, Pierrot.
PIERROT (*jumping up*).   I will dare
        To call our witnesses out of the air.
        (*We imagine we hear the singing of birds.*)
        They've come already.
UIRGEAL.   I can hear the dotes!
PIERROT.   They bob, flip, hop it.
UIRGEAL.   Dash off little notes.
PIERROT.   Congratulate us on our private wedding.
UIRGEAL (*alarmed*). But what has happened to me?
PIERROT.   You are shedding
        A tear for the first time. Take off your mask
        That I may catch it.
UIRGEAL.   Pierrot, do not ask
        So soon. I only hear finch, sparrow, linnet.
PIERROT.   The blackbird will be here at any minute.
        Look! Wagtail, pipit, yellowhammer, perch
        On branches. Show me all your beauty.
UIRGEAL.   Search
        The wood first, Pierrot. Somebody might pass.
PIERROT.   The wood is empty.
UIRGEAL.   Try the meadow grass.
PIERROT (*aside*). But can I dare to let her out of sight?
UIRGEAL.   Go. Go.
        (PIERROT *runs off.*)
        (*Alone, unmasking.*)
        I wonder am I doing right
        To marry him? It is no harm to flirt in
        The sunshine for a while. But am I certain
        I love him? Must I weep . . . weep . . . come to earth?
        How can I tell the facts of life are worth
        Acquiring? I must weigh the pros and cons.
        For if his nearest relatives are swans
        He may be flighty, have too much in common
        With them. What shall I do? They say a woman
        Can never be too careful. I refuse
        To give my hand. No. No. I love him, choose
        All the responsibilities of life.
        Yes, Yes. I love him. I will be his wife.
        (*Quickly masking herself as she hears his step
        returning.*)

PIERROT.   We're quite alone, dear. Come into the shade.
                  (*A sound of distant spirit voices.*)
UIRGEAL (*alarmed*). What's that?
PIERROT.   The blackbird. Do not be afraid.
UIRGEAL.   No. No. I hear my sisters calling.
PIERROT.   Stay
                  With me. I love you, Columbine.
UIRGEAL (*wavering*).   Delay
                  Is dangerous.
PIERROT.   I will not let you go.
SPIRIT VOICES (*off*). Uirgeal!
                              Uirgeal!
UIRGEAL.   They call me.
PIERROT.   Now I know
                  Your name, Uirgeal, I love you more.
UIRGEAL.   They miss
                  Me.
                  (*Running to him with a sob.*)
                  Darling, I must give you back your kiss.
                  (*She kisses him quickly and as she disappears through
                  the wood turns for a moment.*)
                  Goodbye.
PIERROT (*running and looking up*). She's gone.
                  (*Craning.*)
                                        She's smaller than a fly
                  Now.
                  (*Coming downstage.*)
                          Gone . . . and that first tear was scarcely dry.
                  (*Desperately.*)
                  I will destroy myself with such a stir
                  And upshot, she will know I follow her.
                  (*Knowingly.*)
                  There's bound to be an ammunition dump
                  Within this wood. My friends will hear the bump
                  And guess at last that Pierrot is no more.
                  (*Considering.*)
                  But firearms are illegal now. A door
                  Should shut more quietly.
                  (*Looking round and selecting a tree.*)
                                        and so I'll choose
                  That tree instead, if I can find a noose,
                  Cast off my holiday clothes for the circus clown

Who tickles village better now than town.
(*Sadly.*)
But who will wash them by the river's edge,
Hang them unseen upon as white a hedge
In Maytime?
(*Firmly.*)
       No. I'll keep them, brace the sleeves
Into a lover's knot among the leaves.
(*Begins to take off his jacket, then pauses reflectively.*)
But let me think. This may be serious
For when the brainpan is delirious,
The mind repents of all that it has been.
Man finds no comedy in the unseen.
What shall I do?
(*Slowly.*)
       To be or not to be? . . .
(*Takes out a large claspknife and feels the blade.*)
This pocket knife is stronger than a tree,
And since all human shadows fear the dark,
(*With a sudden smile of relief.*)
I'll carve her name and mine upon the bark.
(*He goes over to the tree and begins to trace and cut
the initial letter U as the curtain slowly descends.*)

CURTAIN

As The Crow Flies

A LYRIC PLAY FOR THE AIR

CHARACTERS

FATHER VIRGILIUS
BROTHER MANUS
BROTHER AENGUS
THE EAGLE OF KNOCK
HER EAGLETS
THE CROW OF ACHILL
THE STAG OF LEITERLONE
THE BLACKBIRD OF DERRYCAIRN
THE SALMON OF ASSAROE

SCENE ONE

An evening in late summer, on the Shannon, in the seventh century.
A boat, in which there are two monks, is moored in a creek.

MANUS (*softly*). Father Virgilius . . .
                                   Father
                 Virgilius . . .
VIRGILIUS (*waking*). God bless us all. I must
                 Have nodded again. My head was in the sun . . .
                 My eyes are gilded by it.
                 (*Happily*)
                                   Brother Manus
                 The best of spirits came upon this journey
                 With us to-day.
MANUS.   Father, I am uneasy
                 Now. We've been resting on our oars too long
                 And Brother Aengus is still away.
VIRGILIUS.   We've time
                 Enough upon our hands. We can be back
                 At Clonmacnoise before the midnight bell rings.
MANUS.   But you don't know the Shannon, Father. This boat-
                         load
                 Of rushes will be heavier than our faults
                 The more we pull against it. Brother Aengus
                 Should never have gone into the forest
                 Alone.
VIRGILIUS.   God will protect him.
MANUS (*obstinately*). But why did you let him go?
VIRGILIUS.   Because he is
                 young.
                 And the young see but the eye in every bolt
                 That keeps them from the meaning of Creation.
                 Yes, they want all that breathing space
                 Before bird, beast or reptile had been named
                 And pain started the first rib.
MANUS.   But, Father . . .
VIRGILIUS (*good humouredly*). I know too well what you are

103

going to say,
Manus. For twenty years you've chased the raindrops
From Clonmacnoise with crossbeam, patches, gluepot.
Whenever we dare to sneeze, you give a nail
Another rap and heal us with your hammer;
And if our old bones creak too much in church,
You hurry up the rungs to mend a joint
Or clap a comfortable cap of stone
About our chilling pates.

MANUS (*pleased, puzzled*).   That's true.
But why did Father Abbot send me out
To cut him rushes in the wilderness?

VIRGILIUS (*quietly*). Perhaps he sent you here
To learn the mercy of the elements.

MANUS.   Well, maybe so.

VIRGILIUS.   Do take
Another look at those gigantic reeds.
Whoever saw green toppings half their size
On any roof? They might have been cut down
To floor the heel of Finn. The very Salmon
Of Knowledge mentioned by the storytellers
Could scarcely jump their height.

MANUS.   I do not like
The look of them. They are unlucky, Father.

VIRGILIUS. Well, then, we'll bless them in the shed
And sacristan will dip a few for me
When he has fired our own fasciculi.
Good soul, he hates to see me annotating
A manuscript at night. But they will strengthen
My hand and dry my ageing eyes . . .

MANUS.   Pardon
Me, Father. I see big clouds upon the hob.
We should be gone.

VIRGILIUS. Call Aengus. He is sure
To hear you from that rock there.

MANUS.   I will.
(*At a distance*)
                                        Aengus!
Aengus!
          There's no reply.

VIRGILIUS.   Call, call again.

MANUS.   Aengus!

104

Aengus!

(*A far shout*)

MANUS (*coming back*).   Thank Heaven he is safe.
But why is he waving to us? Something
Has happened.

(*Running steps*)

What is it, Aengus?

AENGUS (*breathlessly*).   The cave, Father
Virgilius, the cave!

MANUS (*impatiently*).   What cave?

VIRGILIUS.   Brother
Has been uneasy at your absence.

AENGUS.   Forgive
Me, Father, if I have been late.

The forest
Was dark as Doom. I groped from age to age,
Among the knottings of each century;
And then my eyes were opened
So suddenly by Heaven, it seemed their dust
Had risen and this everlasting body
Was glorified. Humbly I prayed, I ran . . .
My habit tripped me on a chiselled step
Beneath a cliff . . . and I saw the cave.
Father, a hermit must have lived there all
His life, it was so full of thought.
I could not catch up on my breath again
Because I was too happy with my spirit
In that heart-beaten solitude.

MANUS (*drily*).   You heard
No stir of beetle, bird or beast?

AENGUS.   No stir.
No stir.

MANUS.   I told you, Father. Every creature
Is hiding from the sky.

VIRGILIUS.   Brother
Is troubled, Aengus . . . fears a storm. So let
Us go.

(*They get into the boat.*)

AENGUS.   I'll take the other oar.

MANUS.   We must be cautious with that heavy load
Of cuttings.

Are you ready?

105

AENGUS. Yes, yes. I
Am ready.
Pull now . . .
One . . . two
One . . . two
One . . . two.
(*The voices and splash of oars recede and only the quiet river is heard. Gradually the dipping of the oars is heard again, then stops suddenly.*)

MANUS. Listen! Listen!

VIRGILIUS. What is it?

MANUS. The wilderness
Is stirring.
(*A faint sound of wind.*)

AENGUS. And look, look at the forest.

MANUS. We must turn back before the furl squall
Strikes down.
(*The wind rises.*)
There, there it is!

VIRGILIUS. What shall we do?

AENGUS. I know, I know, Father Virgilius.
Take shelter in the holy cave.
(*Their voices are swept away by the sudden storm which rages with ever-increasing fury.*)

106

SCENE TWO

Inside the cave.

AENGUS (*from the cave*). Father, can you hear
                Me?
VIRGILIUS (*below*).   Yes.
AENGUS.   Give me your hand. I'll help you up
           Into the cave.
VIRGILIUS (*panting*).   Bless you, my pupil. That climb
           Was heavier than my years. Heaven be thanked
           That we are safe at last.
           (*Anxiously.*)
                      But where is Manus?
MANUS.   Beside you, snug as your own Latin books
           At Clonmacnoise.
VIRGILIUS.   God sent us to this cave.
AENGUS.   And Father, the rock is dry.
MANUS.   A bad night, surely
           For lath and latch. Can you remember, Father,
           So sudden a storm?
VIRGILIUS.   I can remember the Night
           Of the Big Wind and that was fifty years
           Ago, the very week that I had passed
           My first examination. The Shannon rose
           Three times and locked us in the chapel. Blocks
           Of mortar fell and the foundations moved
           Beneath our knees. Those hours come back to me
           Again. We prayed together, sang in turn
           The greater psalms and all that night in dread
           We heard the roar of waters multiplying
           As if God called His creatures from the deep
           But in the morning, happy youngsters paddled
           The trout, indoors, with dish or pannikin, caught
           Our dinner in the refectory and went
           To class by boat. Thanksgiving services
           Were held at ebb. But never have I known
           So bad a night as this.

A VOICE (*outside*).   *Never have*
          I known so bad a night.
MANUS (*alarmed*).   What's that? Who spoke?
VIRGILIUS.   Nobody.
MANUS.   Listen. Listen!
ANOTHER VOICE.   *Never have*
          I known so bad a night.
MANUS.   I hear the voices
          Of demons talking.
OTHER VOICES.   *Never have we known*
          So bad a night.
          (*Peal of thunder.*)
AENGUS.   Father, are you near me?
VIRGILIUS.   Yes, yes.
AENGUS.   I crouched behind a chink of rock,
          And clearly in that flash of lightning saw
          A demon bird with eyes of glassy fire.
VIRGILIUS.   Where?
MANUS.   Where?
AENGUS.   Sitting upon the cliff top.
MANUS.   We
          Are lost.
AENGUS.   Father, Father, I am afraid.
VIRGILIUS (*calmly*).   And yet
          Aengus, you want to be a hermit.
                                        God
          Has let us hear the voices of the fallen.
          His pleasure is revealed by miracle.
          Kneel down, kneel down. The three of us will pray
          Together.
          (*They murmur in prayer as the storm rises again.*)

SCENE THREE

In the eagle's nest.

EAGLETS.   Mother, mother, something wicked,
             Something cold is in our nest.
             Catch it and kill it, kill it quickly!
EAGLE.   Come under my wing and try to rest.
EAGLETS.   Mother, mother, can you hear us?
EAGLE.   Yes, yes, my children.
EAGLETS.   Are you near us?
EAGLE.   What is it children?
EAGLETS.   Something wicked,
             Something cold is in our nest.
             Catch it and kill it, kill it quickly!
EAGLE.   Rain is drenching every stick
             And stone we own. Keep close together
             With every feather.
EAGLETS.   But the thing
             That freezes underneath your wing
             Is shivering. It must be sick.
             Catch and kill it!
AN EAGLET.   Kill it quick!
CROW.   Don't be frightened, little chick,
             Because your mother doesn't know.
             (*Chuckling.*)
             I am a crow, a poor old crow.
EAGLE.   What do you want?
CROW.   You are annoyed,
             Eagle. But feel me, now! Destroyed
             I am this night, blown helterskelter.
             Give me an inch, a pinch of shelter.
             I am so weak, I can hardly speak,
             So very cold, I cannot build
             A nest: and this big wind that filled
             My wingbones blew me into the trees,
             For the first time in centuries.
EAGLE.   Where do you live?

CROW.   I hop and pop
Into a hole before I drop,
As best I can on my bad leg.
And I am baldy as the egg
That hatched me out, so long ago
I cannot count.

EAGLETS.   But has she known
So bad a night, mother, so bad
A night as this one?

CROW.   Clouds that shadow
The Shannon dripped into the nest
I used to have. The sudden west
Would come at day with flap of waters.
But I was strong as my own daughters,
Though they were greedy of claw and craw.
I kept the air. One time I saw
The tree-tops bending back to snap
Their joints below. From pit and trap
The wild pigs came up with a bound,
Then hurried, grunting, underground
Again. Eels glided on the flood
With grassgreen skin through every wood.
The holy man who lived alone
Upon an island, threw no stone
At birds but fed them every morning,
Was carried off without a warning.

EAGLE.   What did he do?

CROW.   He gave a screech,
Clutching at reeds beyond his reach
And vanished down a mighty hole
Among the waters. Salmon pole
And netting took the river races
And after, came pale floating faces
And painted timber, cattle trussed
In their own muscles.
                              Another night
When no house in the glen had light
But hers, I flew from salt and shingle
And foam to see the Hag of Dingle.

EAGLE.   For what?

CROW.   I was her messenger
That time. Every two-hundredth year

110

In storm, she casts another skin.
I saw her do it as I came in,
Step out of it on younger toes,
Quickly as someone changing clothes;
And brighter than a brand-new pin,
She shone from nape to slender shin,
Naked and shameless as a sin.
That night, there was no mortal caller
To see that woman stand there, taller
Than any man. Well might she stoop
To hoop the silk into a loop
And rummage in her box of treasure
Till she had found an old tape measure;
And as I nodded on a rafter
I heard her quiet, sinful laughter.

EAGLE. Why does she change her old skin?
EAGLETS.   Tell
Us. Why she does it, dearest Crow?
EAGLE. Yes, tell us.
CROW.   I know what I know.
But ask some hermit in his cell
How thought can keep his body warm.
I'll only say that this bad storm
Has come that she may change her form
Once more.
EAGLE.   You have experienced much.
But can you not remember such
A night?
CROW.   Eagle, I never knew
So bad a night since I first flew.
But I grow sleepy.
                    Ask the stag
Of Leiterlone. He saw the hag
When she was young before that.
EAGLETS.   Mother,
Dear mother, ask the stag.
EAGLE.   Don't bother
Us.
      Where is he, Crow?
CROW.   Beneath that jag
Of rock and furzebush.
EAGLETS.   Has he seen

111

So bad a storm?

EAGLE.   Keep quiet!
                                        Stag
Of Leiterlone, beneath my crag
And furzebush, have you ever been
In such a downpour?

STAG.   'Twas I who warned
Diarmuid and Grainne, night and morning.
I knew the larger winds that roar
At daybreak, saw them butting shoreward,
Shadowing Shannon, clapping horns
Of ice, but I was never concerned:
For when they came before the winter
They blew my scent away through mint
And garlic. Over pebble and tussock,
Deer leaped along the summer rock,
But in bad weather, wandered freely
Feeding beneath the forest trees,
Before the Fianna could fire
The cooking pits they hid in briar
And ash. I led my herd of does
To quiet glens beneath the snows.
But men were ever on our track;
And when the thawing pools were blacker,
One time, I ran their mighty dogs
A fortnight through the rainy bogland,
Never snapped a fallen branch
Or struck the brown leaf with my antler
As I went past it. Caoilte swore
To pull me down when I had worn out
The heart of Bran, seethe me for supper
And fling my humbles to his pups,
But I got wind of him. At dawn, once,
The woman who became a fawn
Fled with me to the grassy lairs
And heather tops. Though I was wary
And in my prime, it was her son
Who wounded me with woman's cunning.
Where are the proud that never brandished
A head like mine? And where is Flann
Or Bran? Many a time they started
The chase and yet I broke their hearts.

112

Believe me I have seen the Christians
When they were ambushed in a mist
At Tara change into a herd
Of deer – and yet they have not spared me.
By night and day, I am pursued
With pain and terror in the wood.

EAGLE. But, Runner, have you ever heard
So loud a deluge?

STAG.   Ask the Blackbird
Of Derrycairn for it is perched
Upon my antler.

CROW.   Live and learn!

EAGLE (*imperiously*). A song! –
                Blackbird of Derrycairn!

BLACKBIRD. Stop, stop and listen for the bough top
Is whistling and the sun is brighter
Than God's own shadow in the cup now!
Forget the hour-bell. Mournful matins
Will sound, Patric, as well at nightfall.

Faintly through mist of broken water
Fionn heard my melody in Norway.
He found the forest track, he brought back
This beak to gild the branch and tell, there,
Why men must welcome in the daylight.

He loved the breeze that warns the black grouse,
The shouts of gillies in the morning
When packs are counted and the swans cloud
Loch Erne, but more than all those voices
My throat rejoicing from the hawthorn.

In little cells behind a cashel,
Patric, no handbell gives a glad sound.
But knowledge is found among the branches.
Listen! The song that shakes my feathers
Will thong the leather of your satchels.

EAGLE. But have you ever known a night
As bad, Blackbird, in all your life?

BLACKBIRD. Stop, stop and listen for the bough top
Is whistling and the sun is whiter
Than God's own shoulder in the cup now!

113

Forget the hour-bell . . .

CROW.   O that bird
Will drive me foolish. Late and soon
More grace notes but the self-same tune!

EAGLE.   We *must* find out.

CROW.   I am disturbed
But let me think . . . Hm! Hm!

                                    There is another
Yes . . . he will know.

EAGLETS.   Then ask him, mother,
This very minute.

                   Go and visit

CROW.   His home.

EAGLE.   Where is it?

EAGLETS.   O where is it?

CROW.   Under the falls of Assaroe.
The ancient salmon there will know
The answer rightly if you call him
For he is wiser than us all.

EAGLE.   How can I go on such a night?
And leave my children?

EAGLETS.   Race the lightning,
Dear Mother.

CROW (*eagerly*).   Do. Now I am warm
I'll tuck them in despite the storm

EAGLETS.   And be our grannie.

CROW.   Yes, dears.

EAGLETS.   Hurry,
Now, mother, hurry. No need to worry.

EAGLE.   The north is dangerous and darker.

EAGLETS.   You will be back before the lark-cry
Has made us hungry.

EAGLE (*doubtfully*).   Can I peer
Into the foam of the salmon-weir?

CROW.   Fly down, fly down, but do not look.
His name is stronger than the hook
Men use.
(*Chuckling.*)
                  It broils him like an ember.
Call Fintan?

EAGLE.   Fintan.

CROW.   Yes.

(*Calling after* EAGLE.)

                                Remember

The name is . . .

EAGLE (*faintly far away in storm*). Fintan.

SCENE FOUR

Inside the cave.

AENGUS (*softly*). Father, are you awake?

VIRGILIUS. Yes, Aengus, I am still awake like you.
        Only the young and old are troubled at night.
        God has been merciful to Manus. He
        Is fast asleep.

AENGUS.   But were they really there?
        The voices, Father, that we seemed to hear
        Despite the storm.

VIRGILIUS.   I am inclined to think
        They were delusions of the senses,
        Secular follies of the mind.

AENGUS.   If so,
        What is their meaning?

VIRGILIUS.   They were sent to try
        Our faith to-night.

AENGUS (*in fear*).   But that name, Father, that name.

VIRGILIUS. Come close. Why do you tremble at a name,
        My son?

AENGUS.   I heard that name before.

VIRGILIUS (*alarmed*).   But where?

AENGUS.   In class . . . Our teacher quickly turned the page.
        Father . . .
        (*Slowly.*)
             Is Fintan still alive?

VIRGILIUS.   Of course not.
        He went to Limbo.
        (*Gravely.*)
             Knowledge *is* old, my son,
        Older than us and there are thoughts men suffer
        Which are not fit for books. But try to go
        Asleep now.

AENGUS.   Father, I will try to.
        (*Silence.*)
        (*Softly.*) Archangels, pray for me to-night that I

May sleep like Manus on this pillow of rock.
Let me not dream of evils that afflict
The young, and by your intercession, save me
From the dreadful voice beneath the waters.
(*The storm rages more shrilly through space now.
Gradually it deepens again and far below is heard the
thunder of a waterfall.*)

SCENE FIVE

The Falls of Assaroe.

EAGLE (*above*). Fintan . . .
                    Fintan . . .
                            Fintan . . .
SALMON (*below*). I am here.
EAGLE.   Where?
                      Where?
SALMON.   Beneath the Falls.
Who is it calling from the sky?
What spirit cries my name?
EAGLE.   Eagle I
Of Knock.
             Through leagues I fought, I dared
Unearthly waters flooding the air,
To find your home beneath the foam-pit.
SALMON. Why have you come?
EAGLE.   To ask a question.
SALMON. What is it?
EAGLE.   Tell me of a tempest
At any time, as sudden, dreadful
As this?
SALMON.   I knew the muddy beds
Beneath the Bann, the Suck, the Barrow,
Leaped up the narrows where Shannon topples
In miles of thunder, by torch-lit caves
Of Cong, half choking in the sunlight
And bellied by the Atlantic waves
Plunged down . . .
              down . . .
                    sank into the deeps
Of darkness to a primal sleep.
I dreamed of horrors that had shrieked
Before creation. There the sightless
And deafened creatures grope to life
With deathly gulp: the giant claw

118

Searching the forest of the fronds.
In pulps of sperm, the shapeless maw
Swam slowly past me and mute monsters
Uncoupled one another's armour
Though they were blind.

EAGLE.   I kill at sight,
For I am fearless.

SALMON.   How can you guess,
Poor bird, dressing your carrion meat
With highflown feet, that every creature
We know is eaten by disease
Or violent blow! We are unseasoned,
Unsensed, unearthed, riddle-diddled
By what is hidden from the reason.
How can the forethought of defilement
Be reconciled with any faith
That teaches mortals to be mild?
A thousand years, I waited, prayed
And all my fears were only answered
By agony of ignorance.
How must reality be named
If carnal being is so shamed?
From this humiliating body
And brutal brain, these loathsome scales
Itching with lice that no salt water
Can purify, I cry to God
To pity my madness.

EAGLE.   What are you?
(*Pause.*)

                                    Answer,
Great Salmon.

SALMON.   I am a man.

EAGLE.   A man?

SALMON. A man ...
(*Kindly*)

               your enemy, poor bird.
The selfsame instinct that has stirred
Your wing is stronger than our will.
Innocent infants trying to kill
A bot or housefly know as much
As their own father.

EAGLE (*from storm*).   Icicles clutch

My pins. Shout, shout, for I am hurled
Down gaps of hail,

SALMON.   I saw a deluge
Destroy in rage the ancient world
And millions perish in the surge
Hugeing above each mountain refuge,
I could not keep by subterfuge
My mortal shape. Yet I escaped
Into another consciousness
That did not know me. I lived on.
Men called me blessed. In the west
I prophesied to Partholan,
Divined the arts but knew no rest.
The very plague-pit in my breast
Widened my time. How can I find
In all the ages I have known
The dreadful thought that slowly brought
My consciousness beneath these waters
Where memory unrolls the mind
In chronicles of war, greed, slaughter –
Unchanging misery of mankind!

EAGLE (*joyfully*). The night of the Great Flood! I know
The answer now.

SALMON.   Before you go
One word.
               How did you bait the hook
That I must bite, if pious monk
Pumice my name from lessonbook?

EAGLE.   A scaldcrow told me.

SALMON.   Was she shrunk
And old?

EAGLE.   Yes.

SALMON.   Baldy as the egg
You lay?

EAGLE.   Yes, yes.

SALMON.   And did she beg
For shelter?

EAGLE.   True.

SALMON.   That was the Crow
Of Achill and well I know her ways.
Mummified fingers of the plaything
She gave her children with the great ring

120

Carbuncled by the jewellers
Of Egypt—that was the hand of Nuadha.
Aye, at Moytura, she despoiled
Many a hero. In his boyhood
Cuchullin was her friend. She croaked
Three times upon the pillarstone
Before he died. She was alone
With him in his last moment. Mist
Of blood had hid her from his fist.
She ripped the lashes from each lid
And blinded him.
              Homeless with age,
Her food has changed but not her guile.
On stormy nights when she has crept
Upon her belly like a reptile
Into a nest and the frightened chicks
Cry out that some thing cold and wicked
Is sticking to their mother's wing,
(EAGLE *cries out.*)
She tells her story, makes excuses
(If they are very small and juicy)
To send their parent far away,
That she may overlay and kill them.
(*The* EAGLE *cries out again.*)
What is it, Eagle?

EAGLE (*far away in storm*).   O my children,
    My little children!

SCENE SIX

Early morning: the monks are rowing up the Shannon. They pause to rest and look round them.

VIRGILIUS. Who would have thought there was a storm last evening.
The gravels run so softly.

MANUS. When we are safe
At Clonmacnoise, I will be more myself.
This wilderness is not for journeyman
Or scholar.

VIRGILIUS. How can we convert you, Manus?
Look at that wild-thorn on your left. I hear
An early blackbird in it praising Heaven
Above.
(*As if despite himself.*)
Stop, stop and listen for the bough top
Is whistling . . .

MANUS (*alarmed*). Father.

VIRGILIUS. What did I say just now?
Illusions of the night are still upon us.
(*Half to himself.*)
But why should they conspire against the east?
Well might the ancients warn the fortunate:
'Cave cavernam!'

AENGUS (*excitedly*). No, Father, you were right.

VIRGILIUS. What do you mean?

AENGUS. Look . . . Look . . . that speck within
The sky.

VIRGILIUS. Where?

AENGUS. Coming swiftly from the north.

VIRGILIUS. I cannot see it.

AENGUS. Now a cloud
Has hidden it.
There, there it is again.
It is the eagle.

MANUS. Aengus is right. It is

122

            An eagle. Never have I seen so fast
            A goer.

VIRGILIUS.   I can see her now above
            Us.

MANUS.   She is turning.
                  She is striking from
            The air.

AENGUS.   No, she is swooping to the cliff
            Above the cave-mouth.

VIRGILIUS (*uneasily*).   This is very strange.
            But why is she hovering so heavily?
            Why does she dash her wings against the rock
            Like that?

MANUS.   She must be wounded in the breast.

AENGUS.   I know. I know.

VIRGILIUS.   What are you saying, Aengus?

AENGUS.   I've known it all the time.
                  She is too late.
            Her little ones are dead.

VIRGILIUS.   What do you mean,
            My son? Why is your habit shivering?
            Why are you frightened?

AENGUS.   Father, Father, I know
            The ancient thought that men endure at night.
            What wall or cave can hide us from that
               knowledge? . . .
            (*The voices are fading in the distance.*)

THE END

The Viscount of Blarney

A PLAY FOR RADIO OR STAGE
IN ONE ACT

CHARACTERS

CAUTH
WOMAN
HUSBAND
OLD MAN
POOKA
FOSTERMOTHER
JACK O'LANTERN
GALLANT

THE VISCOUNT OF BLARNEY

*The action starts on a lonely road near the Blackstairs Mountains,
after nightfall, seventy years ago.*

*As the curtain rises, the stage is entirely dark except for a spot,
down, centre. There are two small stools, one on each side of
proscenium. Angry voices of men and an elderly woman are heard
from one of the entrances of the auditorium. ('Put her out,' 'the
lazy get,' 'bad cess to her impudence,' 'chase her out of sight.')
CAUTH MORRISSEY, a young girl, runs through the auditorium to
the stage, centre, down. She has a small fringed shawl around her
shoulder and carries a bundle wrapped in a coloured handkerchief.
She wears shoes but no stockings.*

CAUTH (*to audience*). The moment that I got my toes
       Inside that house, pots came to blows,
       The ash-hole dog began to bark,
       The turf fell out, bog-flame and spark
       Smoked up the flue and red stars of smut
       Shot down. I knew it was a witch
       Had done it, but they called me – slut.
       That woman was beside herself
       Chasing my elbows round the delf,
       Through rings of old potato peels.
       Her sons came at me from the door
       But I showed a cleaner pair of heels
       Than they had ever seen before.
       I thought they wouldn't leave a stitch
       Upon me as I sprang the ditch,
       Except the fancyings of my shawl!
       (*Sagely.*)
       They say when people use bad language
       The devil scribbles on their wall,
       Empties his sack of sins, kicks back
       A dozen hoofs in every stall!
       (*Yawning.*)
       I'm half asleep . . . Will no one help
       A poor young orphan going out

On service, give a little shelter
Until the day peep. Is there no house,
No house in all this neighbourhood
Will take her in without a line
Of reference?
(*Starting back.*)

                                  What's in the wood there?
A wicked tramp . . . must find a rock
And hide from him.
(*Crouches down.*)
(*A woman comes out, down, right, and sits on stool,
before red glow of fire.*)

CAUTH (*looking right*).   A lamp is shining
Behind that window pane. I'll knock.
(*She makes a gesture of knocking. The sound of the
knocking is heard, off.*)

WOMAN.   Who's there?

CAUTH.   It's me, ma'am.

WOMAN.   Who?

CAUTH.   Cauth Morrissey.
An orphan going out on service. I'm lost
Entirely.

WOMAN.   Lift the latch and walk right in.

CAUTH.   O thank you, ma'am.

WOMAN (*rising*).   God bless me, you're exhausted.
Sit here before the fire and rest a minute.
What can have happened you?

CAUTH.   Such a to-do, ma'am
I looked into a shanty near the roadside
And saw a pothook coming down the flue.
It jumped at me and changed into a cartload
Of sooty sparks. The place was smothering.
With smoke and stink of ash and boiling mash,
And seven fellows bawling for their mother.

WOMAN.   Good gracious!

CAUTH.   Big galoots in hobnailed boots!
Tried to play tig with me around the pighouse,
Over a drain and through a patch of furze!
And ma'am, the cursing!

WOMAN.   Must have been the Quigleys,
Fighting and running to solicitors
With every shillingsworth they cut or dig.

You're safe now, Cauth. Is that you're name?

CAUTH. Yes, ma'am.

And . . . could I stay the night?

WOMAN (*hesitating, then making up her mind*). I'll do my best
For you. Himself's a bit cantankerous.
(*Leads her, anxiously, right, down.*)
In here and don't disturb the childer.

CAUTH. Thank
You, ma'am. May God reward your kindness.

WOMAN. Hurry.
The bed is in the corner. He may be back
At any moment now. The crack in the door
Will give you light and when I hear him snoring,
I'll bring you a drop of new milk.
(*Pushes Cauth off, right. Michael, her husband,
comes, down, from the dark stage, lifts latch.*)

HUSBAND (*in a surly tone*). What's your worry?

WOMAN. Nothing.
(*A noise off.*)

HUSBAND. Who's that?

WOMAN. Tim had a little pain
Just now. I'll take him into bed with us.
(*A louder noise.*)

HUSBAND (*grimly, going right.*) He's learned to walk.

WOMAN. Stop, Michael, I'll explain,
You can't go in. She may have nothing on.

HUSBAND. Who?

WOMAN. It's an orphan girl . . . she lost her way.

HUSBAND. She can't sleep here.

WOMAN. Michael, Michael.

HUSBAND. I say
She can't sleep here.

WOMAN. You'll have remorse of conscience
For this.

HUSBAND. I'll have no hop-the-hedge or stray-
By-night inside this house.

WOMAN. But listen, Michael.
(*A crash, off, and howls of children.*)
Merciful Heavens!
(*Following him off.*)
Stop, stop! Don't strike the girl.
Don't strike the girl.

HUSBAND (*off*). I'll cook her goose!
(CAUTH *runs in with clothes disordered, catching her shawl as it is flung after her.*)
CAUTH (*to audience*). I'm back again!
Am I to blame
Because the knobs and screws were loose?
I hardly sat upon the bed
Before the mattress, spring and frame
Fell down.
(*As she fastens her clothes.*)
No thought stays in my head.
I toil and moil. It's all the same.
Foot-water tries to come to the boil
And scald the basin. Sticks want breaking.
The turf is damp. Paraffin oil
Upsets the lamp. The dough won't rise,
The currants come out in the baking;
And onion choppings skin my eyesight,
Although I drop them in the bucket.
(*Sagely.*)
They say the third time must be lucky.
(*An* OLD MAN *comes out, left, spot light, sits down on stool with a book.*)
CAUTH (*looking round*). An old man reading at a doorway.
He wipes his spectacles . . . schoolmaster . . .
Respectable. I'll ask once more.
(*Approaching.*)
God save you, sir.
OLD MAN. God save you kindly, child.
What is your name? . . . don't know your little face.
CAUTH. Cauth Morrissey, Sir.
OLD MAN. The people here are wild
And dread to see a stranger round the place.
Where are you from?
CAUTH. Sir, if it does not vex you,
I'm only an orphan going out on service,
Walking the road all day from County Wexford
And now I'm lost.
OLD MAN (*smiling*). A most deserving case
For supper, bed and breakfast.
(*Sternly.*)
But you must earn

130

Them, Cauth.

CAUTH. Yes, sir, I darn and mend.

OLD MAN. My wife
Does that. You'll have to earn them with a story.

CAUTH. I've no book learning, Sir.

OLD MAN. But you have life
And all of us are on our way to glory –
(*Half to himself.*)
Although the old must riddle their own ashes
To find what's hidden in them, ... senseless work ...
The lashes of the Turk. But awake, my Cauth, or
Asleep, a story stirs the porridge in
The pot. Now listen to this ancient author:
(*Reading from book.*)
'The mind's of such a noble origin,
Man is condemned to see his own blood flow;
Obey that dreadful state or dare to ask –
Impatient in the courtyard, far below,
The executioner puts on his mask.'
You understand the sentence?

CAUTH. No, sir.

OLD MAN. Just
As well, poor child.
(*Rising.*)
And now to earn your crust.
Here is a lantern.
(*Gets it off stage.*)
Go into the barn –
It's part of an old castle – and bring me back
Five sods of dry turf and a story.

CAUTH. Yes, sir.

OLD MAN. But don't go near the corner where the sack is.
Upon your life, Cauth, don't go near it.

CAUTH. No, sir.
(OLD MAN *goes off, left.* CAUTH *comes centre, down,
shading lantern with her shawl, looking up and
around.*)

CAUTH. I never saw so big a barn
Before. What's shining there? A harness
And there's the sacking. Daren't look
Into that corner. Five ... five sods

131

Of turf, he said . . . a story . . . a book.
(*Finding a tool-box, left centre.*)
I must sit down, my head is nodding.
I think I'm half asleep already.
(*Yawns.*)
Or is the lantern wick unsteady?
(*Her eyes close. Gradually the cyclorama brightens
until, at back, centre, through a wide and lofty doorway,
can be seen a starlit sky of Spring. The barn remains in
shadow. Sacking in corner over a box or crate, heap of
turf left. Far away are heard light hoof-beats and a faint
tinkling sound. As the sound comes nearer,* CAUTH
*opens her eyes. During this scene, the words of the
unseen* POOKA *can be followed in the childlike intensity
and eager, changing expressions of the girl's face.*)

CAUTH (*in delight*). The Pooka! The Pooka! I must be asleep now.
The fishermen know by the bubbles and frothing
When he snorts in his shadowy water-hole, deep
Under Shannon. But why is he stopping?

VOICE OF POOKA (*right, outside, cautiously*). Cauth . . . Cauth . . .
Is there anyone there with you?

CAUTH (*rising*).   No, not a soul,
Dearest Pooka.

POOKA.   Then come to the doorway.

CAUTH (*to audience*).   I must
Have a peep at him.
(*She runs to doorway, leaves lantern just outside it,
left, her face gleaming in starlight.*)
                              Nothing . . . nothing but dust
And gray docken.

POOKA.   You're wrong. I am here on my shoes.
(*Importantly.*)
They have thousands of sparks that can hop in the
          dark
Whenever I choose.

CAUTH.   But where can I find you?

POOKA.   In the silver of sight. Now shut both your eyes,
Cauth.
What can you see?

CAUTH (*slowly*). Something that's bright . . .
Moving . . . and mooning along the ground.
(*Turning, as if impelled, until she is facing audience*

again; puzzled.)
I must be looking at a lake
And yet the water makes no sound.
(*Alarmed, opening her eyes.*)
It's at my feet.
(*Catching up her skirt and turning.*)
         It's all around
Me.
(*Facing around again.*)
   Water, deep water.
(*Screaming.*)
           I'll be drowned.

POOKA. Quick, close your eyes again.

CAUTH.   The lake
Is gone!

POOKA.   I know. Why are you shaking?

CAUTH. I saw it twice when I was smaller,
Rising from mud floor, sill and wall.
What was it, Pooka?

POOKA.   Noah's flood,
That's sent to castigate the young
At night. They huddle half asleep
Because their minds have grown too big
For them and keep on falling, falling
Into the pit their terror digs.
Then, wide awake, all of a sudden,
They see that flood-gleam, hide their heads
Beneath the bedclothes, see that flood-gleam
And are so much afraid of it,
They cannot scream until the fit
Is over.
(*Farther away.*)
       Open your eyes.

CAUTH (*turning*).   I see
The moon shining on rock and tree,
Gray docken . . .
(*A faint tinkle.*)

POOKA (*nearer*).   What else?

CAUTH.   A tiny horse,
It must be you, dear Pooka!

POOKA.   Of course,
It is.

CAUTH (*in admiration*). All silvery and speckled.
POOKA (*coaxing*). Come, put your arms about my neck,
        Cauth. Pet me, pat me for a while.
        I see you smiling.
        (*Pleading.*)
                Cauth, be kind.
CAUTH.   Poor Pooka, why are you so sad?
POOKA (*indignantly*). I'm treated badly, north and south,
        Especially on Sunday nights
        At closing time. Carousing crowds
        In public houses struggle and roar
        Around the door-bolt while the barmen
        Put back the bottles on the shelves.
        The married men are much the worst
        And women who take a drop themselves,
        Singing till twelve o'clock and cursing
        And using filthy language.
CAUTH.   I know
        Too well, for when I lived with grand-dad,
        They used to wake me, stumbling home,
        Swearing like mad.
POOKA.   Just think of it!
        When I have found a drunkard sitting
        Upon the ground beneath a shutter
        I have to scare his living wits –
        As if I were a common nightmare;
        And lie beside him in the gutter,
        Then trundle like a whiskey keg
        Between his bow legs, carry him
        For miles and be his boon companion
        Until the shouting moon is dim.
CAUTH.   Poor little Pooka.
POOKA.   Hug me, tug
        My curly mane, Cauth. Let us snuggle
        Together closely, rubbing noses,
        Your little one and mine. No leather
        Or saddle girth has ever pressed me
        And when you've fondled and caressed me,
        Away we'll go.
CAUTH (*doubtfully*).   You will not bite,
        If I come near.
POOKA.   I won't.

CAUTH.   You might.
So promise me.
POOKA.   I promise, Cauth.
(*She puts her hand past doorway, starts back with a cry.*)
What is it?
CAUTH.   Your mane is wet and cold.
It makes me shiver.
POOKA.   Only froth,
My dear.
(*In a sinister voice.*)
          The river Shannon rolled
A dreadful wave above my head
And drove me from its ancient bed,
To-night.
(*Pleasantly.*)
          You must be brave and dare
To come with me.
CAUTH (*recovering*).   I'll try. I'll try.
POOKA.   We'll gallop off, but do be careful
For when I mount into the sky
You'll have to lie along my back
And grip me tightly with your knees.
The hollowing of air is black
At first, a wind comes from the tree-tops
But when the mountains stop their nodding,
We'll see a croppy moon in water
And then look down on field and townland.
CAUTH.   Counting the miles –
POOKA.   Laughing and talking –
CAUTH.   Above the heads of everybody –
POOKA.   In Ireland.
CAUTH.   Wait, dear Pooka, wait.
I'll leave the lantern just inside
The doorway for old baldy pate.
(*Coming back.*)
Now tell me, will we see all Ireland?
POOKA.   Why not?
              Mount Leinster is on fire
Since dusk. I saw upon Slieve Bloom
A jig and reel of yellow sparks –
The gorse was not more gay at noon.

Friends of the dark, the loop of wire
Stretching across the rabbit-run,
The night-line twitching in the pool –
All still.

CAUTH.   But are there cunning witches?

POOKA.   Of course. They gather up the smoke,
Hide in the stable, chain the spoke,

CAUTH.   Creep to the cowshed –

POOKA.   Dry the udder,
And hurry to sour the milking can.

CAUTH.   They have big humps?

POOKA.   They'll make you shudder.
They've nothing on those hairy lumps
And bumps but smouldering red flannel,
And when they turn in cartridge wheels –

CAUTH.   I'll make you gallop all the quicker,
By drubbing gently with my heels –

POOKA.   Disturb the birds in every thicket –

CAUTH.   And never hear the wicked words
Of witches –

POOKA.   leap the iron gates
And hurry up the avenues
Of big estates where nothing stirs
At night but grass, waken the mews
And kennel yard –

CAUTH.   But trespassers
Are prosecuted –

POOKA.   landlords thinking
Evicted men have come to shoot them;
And when we leave these mansions, number
As many little lakes as they
Have windows. All will quickly link
Their arms and light us on our way
To see that place where finch is caught
At last. There, there upon Mount Nephin
All lovers can be safe in thought,
And cap in hand is head in air!

CAUTH.   Let's hurry!

POOKA.   If I go too slowly
Spur, spur me with your little toenails.

CAUTH.   Must I take off my shoes?

POOKA.   Yes, dear.

Then stoop and whisper in my ear.

CAUTH. And when my breath is tickling in it?

POOKA. I'll gallop at a mile a minute.

(*She runs off right.*)

(*The* FOSTERMOTHER *appears in barn from left, back. She wears a short cape and jet bonnet, and carries a small black bag.*)

FOSTERMOTHER. Cauth Morrissey, come here.

CAUTH (*coming to doorway, picking up lantern*). Who's calling?

FOSTERMOTHER. You wicked girl, I'm just in time . . .

I jumped the cemetery wall
At Cleggan, straddled a tombstone, climbed
The quarry until that lantern shone
Outside the door.

CAUTH. Yes, ma'am.

(*Tinkle, sound of hoofs.*)

He's gone . . .

FOSTERMOTHER (*coming between* CAUTH *and doorway*). Aye, gone. I've saved you from the Devil.

CAUTH (*desperate*). No. No. It was the Pooka.

FOSTERMOTHER. Be civil
And please remember who I am,
Cauth Morrissey.

CAUTH. But, ma'am . . .

FOSTERMOTHER. Now hold
That lantern up. Do what you're told.
No . . . higher . . . higher than that.

Dear me!

You've grown much faster than your pimples.
Keep still . . . respectable appearance . . .
Firm chest . . . the arms a little skimpy.
Cauth Morrissey, you'll come to harm.

CAUTH. Let . . . let me go. I do not know you.

FOSTERMOTHER. You know what brought me here so quickly.

CAUTH. No. No.

FOSTERMOTHER. Your wicked thoughts. Don't dare
To contradict. Too fine a comb
Will break its teeth in that wild hair!
When you were small I took you home
And dirty bottle was your mother.
I tried to send you back to heaven
And save the angels all this bother

137

Before you reached the age of seven.
But you grew faster than the lie
That hid your birth, with every cry
Struggled for foolish life on earth.
(*Complainingly, leading girl to tool-box.*)
Nurse children all forget my kindness.
(*Sitting down with horrible affection.*)
Who turned you up when you were bold,
Gave you a scolding for your supper?
And when you fell, have you forgotten
Who kissed the spot and made it well?

CAUTH (*in terror*). Your eyes are staring through the shadows.

FOSTERMOTHER (*fiercely*). Because I've seen young girls, half
    maddened
    By grief and terror do queer thing –

CAUTH.   You squeeze me tightly –

FOSTERMOTHER.   wizen the string
    Of life, sentence themselves to prison.

CAUTH.   What have I done?

FOSTERMOTHER (*half to herself*). My lap is weary
    With all the labour of the years.
    Let the unhappy fill with sighs
    The charitable institutions,
    Wash, wash and scrub without a wage,
    For melting crystal purifies,
    Yet hear in mockery the hiss
    Of scalding pipe: their clock – the steam-gauge,
    Their refuge – a laundry.

CAUTH (*stopping her ears*).   I will not listen.
    No. No. I dare not.

FOSTERMOTHER (*whispering*).   Premature age . . .
    Paralysis . . . Think of the lost
    Raving at night in hospital
    From lock to lock, until their screams
    Are certified . . .
                  What's that? Sssh! Hide.
    The lantern flame.
    (*To herself.*)
                  The plot's the same,
    Misery of fields and little farms.
    Look, tell me who is passing by.
    (*A girl and woman pass outside.*)

CAUTH.   A girl with something in her arms.
          I cannot see it but she is crying.
          (*Puzzled.*)
          Maybe the fairies stole her child,
          And put a changeling in its place.
FOSTERMOTHER. Who follows her?
CAUTH.   A woman.
FOSTERMOTHER.   Wild?
          Purse-lipped?
CAUTH.   I cannot see her face.
          What is it makes me so afraid?
          Tell me, tell me.
FOSTERMOTHER.   A tiny soul
          Has gone to Limbo.
CAUTH.   Limbo?
FOSTERMOTHER.   Yes.
          It's dark there, darker than a hole
          Dug in the ground. No prayer or blessing
          Can reach that place where nothing sighs,
          Wakes, sleeps, for ever.
CAUTH (*kneeling and tearfully*).   I've learned my lesson
          I will be good, never tell lies
          Again, if you will only save me.
FOSTERMOTHER (*raising her up, cheerfully*). Of course I will.
          We'll cut the cards
          And cheat the Joker, call on knave
          And queen to play their ancient part,
          Shuffle with hearts, laugh at all danger
          And catch the dark or fair-haired stranger
          Before his tricks begin. We'll fix
          The future in the present, glue
          The dirty Devil, hoof and horn.
CAUTH.   O thank you, ma'am.
FOSTERMOTHER.   The pack of cards
          Under the sacking in that corner,
          Quick, get it now.
          (CAUTH *goes with lantern, then hesitates.*)
CAUTH.   I beg your pardon,
          Ma'am.
FOSTERMOTHER.   What is it?
CAUTH.   I quite forgot . . .
          The man . . . he warned me of that spot.

139

FOSTERMOTHER. What man?

CAUTH.   The man that read the book
And gave me the light. I daren't look.

FOSTERMOTHER. You're dreaming.

CAUTH.   Maybe a black hound
Or something cold that makes no sound
Is waiting to pounce. Or a corpse might raise
A coffin lid and slowly gaze
At me.

FOSTERMOTHER.   Nonsense. Do what you're bid,
Cauth Morrissey.
(*As Cauth goes to corner, Fostermother points at her,
winks grotesquely at audience, then steals out, left. A
small figure with horns and demi-mask peeps in and
whistles softly, then withdraws. Cauth turns but sees
no one. Figure re-appears at doorway and whistles.
He is dressed in Tudor green and terracotta, with a
buckle belt.*)

STRANGER. She's gone.

CAUTH (*alarmed*).   Who are you?

STRANGER.   Don't you know
Me, Cauth?

CAUTH.   No.

STRANGER.   I'm the Pooka. Yes,
Your little Pooka. Didn't you guess?

CAUTH.   You're not the Pooka. You are old
And hairy with crooked horns. Please, Sir,
Please go away.

STRANGER (*with a few dance steps*). I'm hot and cold.
I'm drizzly and dry, a born teaser.
For when I show my fiery spot
To straying eyes at night, beware
The sudden splash of bog-pool. Mist
And darkness are my doubtful lair
For I am quicker than the kiss
That needy bachelors try to snatch,
As tricky as their coaxing hand,
But stinking as a sulphur match.
(*Darting out a finger at her.*)
What is my name?

CAUTH (*recoiling*)   You're Jack o' Lantern.

JACK O'LANTERN. That's right. No, now give me back my flame.

140

I want to know what's happening
To-night outside the fairy ring.
Two women, who had hid a spade there,
Put something small into a hole
And it was waxen as a candle.
Foul Jack must learn their secret.
(He *grasps at lantern.*)

CAUTH.   Stop.
        The man that gave it to me . . .

JACK O'LANTERN.   Stole
        My property. Let go that handle.
        Let go!

CAUTH.   Help! Help!
        (*A* GALLANT *in eighteenth-century riding costume appears at doorway.*)

GALLANT (*melodramatically*). Villain, you dare
        To molest a young lady!
                      Take that now.
        (*Cuffs and chases him out.*)
                        A pair,
        A pair of smoked glasses to strengthen my sight!
        (*Bowing.*)
        Say! Are you Aurora, that early riser?
        Her cousin, Flora, who fears the hailstones?
        Venus herself – surpassing thought?
        Or the fairest daughter of Granuaile?

CAUTH.   Oh, no, Sir, I'm only an orphan from Wexford.

GALLANT.   The light of her sex, then! I cannot be wrong –
        That grace, that modesty, noted in song,
        Must surely belong to – Miss Morrissey.

CAUTH.   Your honour is joking me.

GALLANT.   Do I make bold?
        You cannot deny your own name. It is known
        Far and wide, both to poor folk and wealthy.

CAUTH.   But how can my name . . .

GALLANT (*smiling*).   You are back in the past
        Where all boxes are crammed when the future is
            doubtful.
        (*With a sweeping gesture.*)
        And I swear by this barn that only last week
        The Viscount of Blarney was speaking about you
        And drinking your health in his castle.

141

CAUTH. The Viscount of Blarney!

GALLANT. Guests were assembled,
The chandeliers burning – I remember distinctly –
The pledge they were drinking was flavoured with lemon,
Demerara and nutmeg. The fair were concealing
Each blush with a fan for the gentlemen showed them
A dashing fine leg as the dancing began,
But every proud lady that kirtled her petticoat
And led up the set was soon brought to heel
For the tune that was played was – *Miss Morrissey's Reel.*
(*Music of a reel is heard.*)

CAUTH. I can hear it, so softly.

GALLANT (*to audience*). The young find a riddle –
Existence! The old give it up.

CAUTH (*to herself*). . . . so softly . . .

GALLANT (*to audience*). And the answer is?
(*To orchestra.*)
Fiddlesticks! Play with more feeling.
(*Italian music.*)
(*To* CAUTH.)
Cupids that cluster on a lovely ceiling
With tiny darts gilded above each lustre,
The cloud-born Goddess revealing her body
Awakens mere sighs. True modesty flying
To closet or screen still fears to be seen,
Because the first lesson in joy must be tearful.
(*Music fades out.*)

CAUTH. O what do you mean?

GALLANT. I'll tell you my secret.
For fear of offending you, dreading refusal,
His Lordship has sent me ahead of his carriage,
To post without stop, with spurring of topboot,
To beg and implore your consent – as I live –
To give him your fair hand in marriage.
As token
Of deepest respect, this heirloom –
(*Presenting a tiara, confidentially.*)
Worth more than
A thousand in guineas.

CAUTH (*rapt*). All shiny.

142

GALLANT.   Accept it –
A trifle of rubies and diamonds.
CAUTH.   I daren't.
GALLANT.   Put it on for a moment.
(*As she does so, he conjures a satin cloak from behind
the tool-box and slips it round here.*)
                          The night air is cold.
CAUTH.   A cloak!
GALLANT.   And a ring.
CAUTH.   Two hearts made of gold!
GALLANT.   It comes from the Claddagh.
                          Your finger . . .
                              Not the second . . .
Third.
        Thank you . . . fits perfectly!
CAUTH.   But how can I wed him
With nothing, no nothing at all, for a dowry?
GALLANT.   Such silking of panel and spreading of gown
On sofa and bed, the latest from town,
And milliners feathering hats by the dozen.
I swear, as first cousin, he loves you.
CAUTH (*dreamily*).   He loves me!
(*He nods.*)
And he's tall?
(*He nods.*)
         And handsome?
(*He nods.*)
                  And darkhaired?
(*He nods.*)
                            Truly?
(*He nods.*)
(*Suspiciously*). But is he . . . a Protestant?
GALLANT (*shakes his head vigorously – then confidentially*).
          Convert . . . newly
Received!
CAUTH (*clasping her hands and looking upwards*). And his eyes?
GALLANT.   Their colour?
(*She nods.*)
           He'll tell you
Himself if you dare him. And now a surprise.
Can you guess it?
CAUTH.   I cannot.

GALLANT. Impatient to welcome
The Bride, he is waiting outside in his carriage.
Black horses, scarce seen in the fleering of tallow,
A pair neck to neck . . . runaway marriage –
Mad kisses through Carlow, breakfast in Mallow!
Sssh!

CAUTH. What is it?

GALLANT. People are stirring outside.
Not a sound. Not a spark –
(*He takes lantern and as he leads her to left corner, up stage, lowers the light.*)
We'll grope here and hide
Until they are gone.
(*Extinguishes the lantern.*)

CAUTH (*alarmed*). You've put out the light.

GALLANT. Of course. Elopements are always kept dark.
(*The crying girl and the woman pass slowly outside on their homeward journey.*)

CAUTH. The pale girl again. She trembles . . . She stumbles . . .
The woman is helping her on.
Where are you?
Where are you? I'm frightened.
(*CAUTH is seen running across the stage, past doorway, without the cloak and jewels.*)

GALLANT (*outside*). The Viscount is coming!

A DEEPER VOICE (*announcing*). The Viscount of Blarney!
(*Bass music, multo agitato, as the cyclorama begins to change to a red glow. A figure appears, tall and handsome, in travelling cloak with tricornered hat. As the newcomer raises his face, he holds a small gold devil-mask and looks at her through it with a quizzical smile. The red glow deepens until it is like the background of an ancestral painting.*)

CAUTH. The Devil Himself!
(*As she screams, there is a black-out. Shuffling steps are heard, left, downstage, and the OLD MAN comes in with a candle calling her. She runs to him for protection.*)

CAUTH. Where am I?

OLD MAN. You're save now. The lantern went out.
You were gone but a tick when herself heard you calling.

I caught up the candle-stick, came out to look.
Don't cry, child. Don't cry. Sure it's nothing at all.

CAUTH (*dazed*). I remember . . . the Pooka . . . the Pooka.

OLD MAN. You saw him?

CAUTH. Yes, truly.

OLD MAN. You looked in that corner –
(*Pointing finger in playful reproach.*)

CAUTH (*protesting*). I didn't

OLD MAN. Good girl. Herself has a clutch in the straw there
And the brown hen is on it.
Some turf for the fire.
(*Giving her sods.*)

CAUTH (*in terror*). That woman . . .

OLD MAN (*excited*). Respectable? Wearing a bonnet?
I know her . . . the night-hag. She fills the next world
With sorrow. Her bag – ssh! – the secret of Ireland.

CAUTH (*almost letting turf fall, feeling her brow*). The jewels are
gone!

OLD MAN. And the heir to the Earldom
Of Hell!
Quick, bring in the turf,
I'm in glory,
For that is a story I heard as a boy.
Not a word now to spoil it.
(*Calling.*)
Wife, put on the kettle
And take out the china.
(*Leading* CAUTH *off, left, down stage.*)
We'll draw up the settle,
When I wind the repeater. But mind you don't utter
A word, keep it all in your head, like a play,
Until you have eaten six slices of bread
With plenty of butter – and saucered your tay!

CURTAIN

145

The Second Kiss

A LIGHT COMEDY IN ONE ACT

CHARACTERS

PIERROT
PIERRETTE
HARLEQUIN
COLUMBINE

Scene: AN OPEN SPACE NEAR TEMPLEOGUE, OR ANY OTHER
ENGLISH-SPEAKING DISTRICT OUTSIDE DUBLIN

THE SECOND KISS

The stage is set with black curtains. On left, front, the garden gate of a villa, bearing the name, 'Cosy Nook'; on right, front, a painted cut-out of a small tree. Right, near centre, a grassy bank. The kiss, with which the play commences, should exceed by three seconds the emotional duration allowed by the Film Censor, for there is no Irish stage censorship yet. As the curtain rises, all is in complete darkness, so that PIERROT *and* PIERRETTE *cannot be seen but their voices are heard in a loud stage whisper.*

PIERROT. Darling . . .
PIERRETTE. Darling . . .
　　　　(*Spotlight gradually rises, showing them clasped in a long kiss.*)
PIERROT (*turning*). Look! the moon at last.
PIERRETTE. Our clock was right.
PIERROT (*smiling*). Only our hearts were fast.
PIERRETTE. Let us go home now, Pierrot, forget the moon.
PIERROT. Why do you want to go to bed so soon?
　　　　(*Rapt.*)
　　　　All maps are silver now. Go where thought will,
　　　　Midsummer fills a million miles of space.
PIERRETTE (*peeved by his reverie*). Pierrot, the moon is rude. It makes your face –
PIERROT (*waking up*). Too pale?
PIERRETTE. No, blue.
PIERROT (*rubbing his chin*). Did I forget to shave?
PIERRETTE. You're laughing at me.
PIERROT. True.
　　　　(*Catching her around waist.*)
　　　　Let's misbehave!
　　　　Do something shocking!
PIERRETTE (*withdrawing*). Quite impossible!
　　　　We're married now.
　　　　(*Suppressing a little yawn.*)
　　　　Come home to bed.
PIERROT (*teasingly*). Who fell

Asleep at nine last night?

PIERRETTE (*playfully*).   I did.

PIERROT.   Then stay

Up late to-night . . .
(*Striking an attitude.*)
          and we'll perform a play.

PIERRETTE (*surprised*). A play?

PIERROT (*nods and points to moon*). Our spotlight.

PIERRETTE.   But we left the door

Wide open, dear.

PIERROT.   What matter to the four

Of us?

PIERRETTE.   The four?

               What do you mean?

PIERROT.   Look round.

PIERRETTE. There's nobody.

PIERROT.   Our shadows on the ground!

PIERRETTE (*happily as they both mime*). I know. We'll chase them
    to the garden wall,
Pierrot, and make them very big –

PIERROT.   and small.

PIERRETTE. For comedy can prove by night –

PIERROT.   that black –

PIERRETTE. Is white.

PIERROT (*hopping*). Poor Pantaloon, who finds a tack
In every carpet slipper.

PIERRETTE.   Columbine?

PIERROT.   The dance that hides the clothes peg on the line!

PIERRETTE (*considering*). No, all that jumping round would weary
    us.

We must walk on like this – be serious.

PIERROT.   Gesticulate?

PIERRETTE.   – like actors that we know.

PIERROT.   I'll be an elongated Romeo –

PIERRETTE (*tenderly*). Stooping to kiss me, dear –

PIERROT.   in silhouette!

PIERRETTE (*leaning on his shoulder*). What shall I look like as
    your Juliet?

PIERROT (*caricaturing in air*). Victorian virtue –

           catching up her clothes

To run –

      all bustle –

bandy whatnots –
nose
More pointed than my own –
and such a chin.

PIERRETTE (*bursting into tears*). I hate your nasty play. I'm going in.
(*Runs left.*)

PIERROT (*following her*). But listen, darling, Don't you understand!
(*She dabs her eyes with a tiny handkerchief. He goes on one knee and catches her other hand.*)

PIERRETTE. You do not love your wife. Let go my hand.

PIERROT (*rising, pleadingly*). Pierrette!

PIERRETTE (*at gate*). Last night you said that you adored
My shadow in pyjamas –
(*Turning as she closes gate.*)
now you're bored.

PIERROT (*centre alone, to audience*). I meant no harm. I hate domestic dramas.
(*Moving left, looking.*)
The windows flash –
two –
three –
six startled eyes
Across the trellises and lawn. She flies
Upstairs and down again to every switch in
The drawingroom, hall, the bathroom, pantry, kitchen,
As if the house in one gigantic huff
Had hidden lipstick, cold cream, powder puff.
(*In anguish.*)
The fuse has blown and all is darkness now.
No . . .
– shaken by her rage a frightened bough
Has fallen down and snapped the electric cable.
I'm wrong . . .
She's found them on her dressing-table –
For in our bedroom, beaming with content,
I see one bulb.
(*Holding out arms.*)
O Darling, do relent.
(*Hesitatingly approaching.*)
She's at our window now. She must have beckoned . . .
But if I am mistaken . . .

151

(*Indicating his heart.*)
                                Wait a second!
I'm right. I knew my darling would be kind.
(*Starting back.*)
Dear me!
                    What's that?
                                She's banging down the blind.
(*Considering.*)
I must be cautious, stay awhile, then creep
Along the banisters, when she's asleep.
(*With sudden resolve.*)
No, I'll endure the dawn, with tragic gloom,
Hugging the sofa in the breakfast room.
My heart is . . .
(*Trying to remember line.*)
                    dated . . .
                                no . . . weighted . . .
                                            deflated . . .
(*Edging right, in a stage whisper.*)
                                                Cue.
(*Edging nearer.*)
Quick, quick, the cue, please.
VOICE OF HARLEQUIN (*right, sepulchral*). Pierrot!
PIERROT (*jumping back, alarmed*).   Who are you?
(*To audience.*)
A ghost as prompt!
VOICE OF HARLEQUIN (*in normal tone*).   Think, Pierrot!
PIERROT (*in terror*).   Harlequin!
What do you want with me?
VOICE OF HARLEQUIN.   I've come to win –
PIERROT (*realising*). To win –
VOICE OF HARLEQUIN.   your wife.
PIERROT (*wildly*).   You can't. She's too demure.
And we are newly wedded.
VOICE OF HARLEQUIN.   Are you sure?
PIERROT (*shrilly*). Yes, yes.
VOICE OF HARLEQUIN.   Your tones are most heart-rending.
PIERROT (*hysterically*). Go back . . . this play must have a happy
                ending . . .
                Back . . . peer through fanlight, dart around street
                    corner,
                Leap corridors. I'll call my wife, I'll warn her,

Tell how you toyed with my confidence the last time
We met, until I prattled for your pastime;
The friend who made my difficulties clearer,
But when they came – the self same disappearer!
The friend, who, when I spoke of all my hope meant,
Was fondly thinking of a new elopement:
The friend who knew the slow words not the fast stick.
My patience stretches, paler than elastic
At breaking point. Back, silent masquerader,
My heart is free of you. I'm not afraid or
Dejected now. I know what devils feel.
I've seen at last –

VOICE OF HARLEQUIN.   the wing upon my heel?

PIERROT.   Hint as you like. I'm strong. I can resist.

VOICE OF HARLEQUIN. You can't decide.

PIERROT.   Who then

      (*Cutely, as a sudden thought strikes him.*)

                         – the dramatist?

VOICE OF HARLEQUIN (*with assumed blandness*). Of course.

PIERROT (*triumphantly producing typed play from pocket*). I have
           you, Harlequin. You tripped

      Into my trap –

      (*Coming nearer but still at a safe distance.*)

              a copy of the script.

The carbon and the ribbon were not nearer
In thought than you and I were, once.

                     Back, sneerer,

For I can prove by every tap and page,
You cannot come to-night upon this stage.

      (*Waits, listening, then investigates cautiously.*)

He's gone.

           I'm really getting very clever.

(*Shaking himself.*)

But what is running down my back?

                      – a shiver!

I dare not risk another prompt.

(*Fingering his forehead.*)

                    What's next?

(*To audience.*)

If you will pardon me, I'll read the text.

(*Reading slowly.*)

'Pierrot becoming sad and rather pensive' –

(*Indignantly.*)
I'm not. I'm feeling very apprehensive.
There's some mistake . . .
(*Turning pages feverishly.*)
         This cannot be the play.
The lines are different. My head's astray.
(*Coming front, reading title page.*)
'A Comedy' . . . this light is much too dim . . .
'By Austin Clarke' . . . I never heard of him.
(*Confidently to audience.*)
I'll read the stage directions, scan the plot.
(*He reads slowly, instinctively obeying each direction.*)
'First, Pierrot moves up, centre –

            to the spot.'
(*The spot lights up.*)
'Back curtains open' –
(*As he waves his hand, reading, they do so.*)
         'Cyclorame – pale blue,'
(*He looks up, nods approvingly.*)
'Sits down on grassy bank' –
(*He does so.*)

        'Music on cue –
He falls asleep . . . and daintily tip-toeing,
A Columbine – from right.'
(*Jumping up and putting script in pocket.*)
        I must be going.
I'm married now.
(*Blowing a kiss.*)
        So, Columbine . . . goodbye.
(*Pausing.*)
I wonder what she's like.
        No harm to try . . .
Precaution: just pretend to be asleep.
(*Sternly.*)
Now promise, Pierrot, nothing but a peep.
(*Sits down, closes eyes and smiles. Smile fades. Opens eyes.*)
No Columbine! I'm much too ill-at-ease.
Ah! something I forgot –
(*Runs to footlights, to orchestra.*)
        the music please!
(*Runs back and sits down as soft music starts, closes*

eyes, then with a happy sigh makes himself more comfortable and falls asleep. The music fades away and there is silence for a few seconds. COLUMBINE *enters, right, upstage, hesitant, and as if in fear. She is dressed exactly in the same costume as* PIERRETTE *but wears a mask. She moves gracefully and yet sadly to left, discovers* PIERROT *and crosses to right. The audience at this time has considerable advantage over the dreaming* PIERROT *and realises that* COLUMBINE *is being played by the same actress who has already appeared as* PIERRETTE. *Slow action.*)

COLUMBINE (*gently*). Pierrot!
                              Pierrot!
PIERROT (*slowly rising, rapt*).   Columbine!
COLUMBINE (*running to him*).   They kept
          Me, darling, in the darkness, though I wept.
PIERROT (*as if to himself*). Imaginative darkness none can share.
COLUMBINE (*in alarmed anguish, as he starts back*). What is it
          Pierrot?
PIERROT (*urgently*). That mask. Why do you wear
          That mask again? Why do you wear it? Tell
          Me, tell me, Columbine.
COLUMBINE (*in gentle reproach*).   You know too well.
PIERROT. Yes, yes, I know too well. Poor eyelids red
          With weeping. Shadow of tears that must be shed.
          (*Trying to be cheerful, with a quick gesture towards her eyes.*)
          To make those pupils dance, my Columbine,
          The poison drops of joy!
                              See how they shine!
COLUMBINE. Only because my lashes still are wet.
PIERROT (*still trying to be cheerful*). We must examine them.
          (*He moves to unfasten mask. She stops him.*)
COLUMBINE.   I dare not yet.
PIERROT. Dark domino, a thought can separate us!
          (*Going centre, right.*)
          What have we done that mind should always hate us,
          The old conundrum need a new solution
          For every turn of brain? Is evolution
          No more – and faith the fashion for bare knees?
          Shall we unscrutinise, uphold, appease –
          With flattery, continual applause –

155

Last exercise of hands and feet and jaws?
Can we be saved, perhaps, by mathematics?
Too hard!
　　　　　Let's be profound.
(*Runs to her pretending to have a stethoscope, leaps
back, pointing triumphantly to her heart.*)
　　　　　Why, even *that* ticks
And proves the universe still goes by clockwork!

COLUMBINE (*sadly, coming to him*). We found the dreadful door.

PIERROT. 　　　　　　　　　　　　But will the lock work
Or bend the hairpin that you gave me, dear,
For key?

COLUMBINE (*softly*). So long ago.

PIERROT. 　　　　　　　　　We reappear
With consciousness and find, for all we think,
The copybook has run off with the ink.

COLUMBINE. Poor Pierrot!

PIERROT (*puzzled*). 　　　　Columbine.

COLUMBINE (*obediently*). 　　　　　　Yes, dear.

PIERROT. 　　　　　　　　　　　What happened
The last time? Did some unexpected clap end
The comedy?

COLUMBINE (*as they sit down*). Think, dear.

PIERROT (*trying to remember*). 　　　　　A countryside
Between the towns –

COLUMBINE. 　　　　　　　where birds had gone to hide
In little woods –

PIERROT. 　　　　　　　No higher than your shoulder –

COLUMBINE. So many birds, the eggshell made them bolder,
Outpecked by song.

PIERROT (*shuddering*). 　　　　But, Columbine, those cries on
The branches after dark and that horizon –
The sun, a burning mine among the trees,
Still there at night, pitfall of armouries,
Fire-washers, huge pig-iron smelting works.

COLUMBINE. Pierrot, we knew the suddenness that lurks
In air to strip the plaster from each room
And foolishly we fled into the doom
Of city after city.

PIERROT. 　　　　Terrible sound
Came faster than sight, killing its own rebound –

COLUMBINE. Obeyed the needle nodding round the dial –

PIERROT.   The rapid calculation –
                           last espial

COLUMBINE. Of expert earth.

PIERROT.   Could skies be starrier?
Expanding sparks and all they carry, err
In dropping cemeteries blown to pieces?
Can passing finger know what it releases?

COLUMBINE. Flyaway bodies lighter than cubes of air
They suck as sweets; young men went up to dare
The sunny prism, gay with tab and facing,
Though future childhood died; specks that were
    chasing
A glory, frail as the uniform they donned,
Chasing it through the vacuum beyond
Our globe.
(*Light begins to dim.*)

PIERROT.   How could poor citizens escape
When solids took again their ancient shape
Of unsubstantiality?

COLUMBINE.   We fled
As ghosts when all belief in them is dead,
A glimmer of white clothes –

PIERROT.   mere phosphorus –

COLUMBINE. For comedy had seen the last of us.
(*They are in darkness.*)

PIERROT (*rising*). Where are you, Columbine? I cannot find
You anywhere.

COLUMBINE.   Here, darling, close as mind.
(*Light rises again, gradually grows gay, with rose and amber hues.*)
Look, Pierrot, a skylight! Laugh and learn your part
Again.

PIERROT (*searching*). My script?

COLUMBINE.   I know our lines by heart:
(*They sit down.*)

COLUMBINE. The trivial circumstances that tormented
Our waking hours, the authors who invented
Excuses when we tried to run away
Together – lest we spoil another play.

PIERROT.   And all the wicked gossiping and fuss
That seemed to make our love ridiculous.
Dark gallery and pit, those hidden faces.

COLUMBINE. Appointments kept –
PIERROT.   but always in wrong places.
          (*Unhappily.*)
          That park bench in the rain, the dredge of leaves,
          I sat there wrapped in miserable sleeves,
          All winter. Then I heard a great clock strike
          The dark; and climbed the railings –
COLUMBINE.   and the spike
          That tore your jacket –
PIERROT.   bruised my arm –
COLUMBINE (*tenderly*).   I bound it –
PIERROT.   And left an iron kiss.
COLUMBINE (*softly*).   That night, I found it
          Above your heart – another violet.
PIERROT.   But we were always happy when we met.
          The picnic rolls –
COLUMBINE.   enough for two –
          (*He sits at her feet.*)
PIERROT.   ... that day
          Among the mountains over Fiesole!
          The bread we carried –
COLUMBINE.   bigger than a baton.
PIERROT.   The wine-fall in the flask at noon.
COLUMBINE.   We sat on
          The ground among rock-roses in a pine wood.
PIERROT.   The paper napkin that you wore – how mine would
          Keep falling down.
COLUMBINE.   That sausage –
PIERROT.   peppered!
COLUMBINE.   pink!
PIERROT.   A clown might envy it –
COLUMBINE.   each bite –
PIERROT.   a drink.
COLUMBINE. The world went wrong –
PIERROT.   yet right –
COLUMBINE.   because the moon
          Came out to see the sun –
PIERROT.   an hour too soon.
COLUMBINE. At dark we heard a serenade below,
          The double parts that kept together –
PIERROT (*holding her hand*).   slow
          Upon guitar –

COLUMBINE. and fast on mandolin.
PIERROT. Those voices answering through thick and thin,
Such melody – we stopped to listen –
COLUMBINE. kissed
More often than we meant to, dear,
PIERROT. – and missed
The tram.
(*As a tremendous idea occurs to him, getting up.*)
Wait, Columbine.
COLUMBINE (*obediently*). Yes dear.
PIERROT. I wonder
Was all that misery, each stupid blunder
Our share, because we weren't always good.
COLUMBINE. Rock-roses do not grow in every wood,
Pierrot.
PIERROT. Suppose . . . how can I put it . . . Well
In order to become respectable,
Suppose that we . . .
you promise not to frown . . .
COLUMBINE. I promise, dear.
PIERROT. . . . get married, settle down.
COLUMBINE (*laughing*). The first time either of us thought of
asking!
PIERROT. You will?
COLUMBINE (*rising*). Of course.
Now I can dare unmasking!
Pierrot, don't look till you have counted three.
(*He covers his face partly with his hands and counts
slowly with lip mime. She turns, throws away mask
and turns round again, hiding her face now with her
hands as if in playful parody of him.*)
PIERROT (*turning*). Why do you smile yet keep your eyes from me?
Your very hands reflect them as they shine –
COLUMBINE. And hide the blushes –
(*She turns away so that her face is still hidden as she
lowers her hands.*)
of your Columbine!
(*She runs off right, followed by* PIERROT.)
COLUMBINE (*far away*). Pierrot!
Pierrot!
PIERROT (*off*). Columbine.
Where are

You, dear?

(*Nearer again.*)

        Where are you?

(*He appears at back against cyclorame, from right.*)

              Have I gone too far?

(*Bewildered, he runs off, right, again.*)

I cannot hear you calling.

(*The cyclorame gradually becomes a darker blue and a low ominous drumming is heard.* PIERROT *is seen backing in from right, in terror, towards the stage. Drumming becomes louder, stops, as* HARLEQUIN *leaps in from right. Through the eye-slits of his demi-mask appear goggles. He carries a little rod or wand.*)

PIERROT.   Harlequin!

HARLEQUIN. All darkens, Pierrot. Top begins to spin
And hum: the final giddiness of globe. Isle,
River and rock – geography is mobile.
Mankind arrived too late to learn the truth,
But roars each time it cuts another tooth,
Fighting to gain possession of those toys
Which end in silence, but begin with noise.
If hotheads play at giants, hit too hard,
What matter if the building blocks are charred?
I am the spirit of all new inventions
Known for their speed and excellent intentions.
My pantomime was once the sweating stoker,
A funny fellow with a red-hot poker.
I found a smaller act to save that toil
And on a billion tons of heat and oil,
I fed my new performing flea, the spark
That tickles happy travellers through the dark:
And while you fall in love, each time, more frantic,
I talk in air, I leap the great Atlantic;
So prove my right, Pierrot, to take the stage,
The spirit of the quick in every age.

PIERROT (*wildly*). Back, back! Your balanced couplets are a trick
To catch my Columbine.

HARLEQUIN (*deprecating*).   The hemistich
Is far too wooden.

PIERROT (*more wildly*).   And you substituted
That play for mine –

HARLEQUIN.   and so electrocuted

                        Your missing heart!
PIERROT.   You loathe me.
HARLEQUIN.   Yes.
                                                    But true
                        To friendship, put the other point of view.
PIERROT.   Back, Harlequin, I know your roof at last,
                God's messenger – a midge upon the blast,
                The devil striving to be orthodox –
                The coffin-lid of hope . . . Jack-in-the-box,
                Black in the face with rage that cannot hurt,
                A tiny upstart waggling in a shirt
                And jumping to a wire-pull, halfway in
                And halfway out, the toyman, Harlequin.
                All history shows the harmless and the meek win,
                When gone are spangle, diamond and sequin.
                (*The cyclorame has become bright again.*)
HARLEQUIN. Pierrot, I think you've lost your sense of humour.
                No brush above the chimney ever drew more
                Than bags of soot. Fire likes a little smoke!
                I meant it all, believe me, as a joke,
                (*Indicating.*)
                A painted lath, a borrowed pair of goggles
                At which your pained imagination boggles.
PIERROT.   Another trick!
HARLEQUIN.   No. No. Your love endures.
                And Columbine? She is already yours.
                And just to prove no wife could be so fond,
                Pierrot, I will pretend to have a wand.
                (*Low drumming is heard.*)
PIERRETTE (*off, left, downstage*). Pierrot!
                (HARLEQUIN *smiles, vanishes in black-out, during
                which back curtains are drawn.* PIERRETTE *appears
                at a garden gate, in white silk pyjamas, carrying a
                Chinese lantern. She has an embroidered wrap and
                pretty mules.*)
PIERRETTE (*running to him*). Pierrot!
PIERROT (*still dazed*).   Pierrette!
PIERRETTE.   Can you forgive
                Your naughty little wife?
PIERROT (*by rote*).   How can I live
                Without you, dear?
PIERRETTE.   And yet I left you, all

                                161

Alone!

(*Anxiously.*)

      Your sleeve is dusty.

                        Did you fall?

PIERROT (*nervously*). No. No.

PIERRETTE (*as she brushes his coat*). We must not quarrel any
        more.

BOTH.   We promise truly.

PIERRETTE.   And you do adore
My shadow?

PIERROT.   Even now when it has fled –

     (*Sighing.*)

Wish for the moon!

PIERRETTE (*giving him lantern*). I brought this one instead.

PIERROT.   You think of everything!

     (*She looks up, alarmed.*)

PIERROT.   But you are frightened?

PIERRETTE. The clouds are strange, Pierrot,

                 Suppose it lightened!

PIERROT (*soothing her playfully with a triplet*). Only a summer
        storm among the hills.

Down comes the rain, chases the silly rills
Into the great new reservoir and fills –
A milli-millimetre!

              You remember.

The day we saw it all, the mile-long camber
Of concrete –

PIERRETTE (*softly*). Dear, the week of our engagement –

PIERROT.   The travelling crane – you asked me what the cage
        meant –

The chain, the steam that grovelled in mud and
        marling.

PIERRETTE. Now let the clouds come down in buckets.

BOTH.   Darling!

     (*While they are clasped in a long kiss, the curtain
     begins to descend.*)

PIERROT (*to stage hands*). One moment, please.

     (*The kiss is renewed.*)

     (*At last PIERROT picks up lantern and they turn
     towards the garden gate.*)

PIERRETTE.   I left the curtains undrawn.
Look, flowering trellises and half the lawn.

PIERROT. No light in any villa now but ours.
PIERRETTE (*rapt*). Rock-roses in the garden –
PIERROT (*smiling*).   keep late hours.
     (PIERROT *closes the gate and the curtain falls.*)

CURTAIN

Liberty Lane

A BALLAD PLAY OF DUBLIN
IN TWO ACTS WITH A PROLOGUE

Author's Note

The late F. R. Higgins was the first to write a verse drama about Dublin's 'low-life'. *A Deuce of Jacks* was based on an anecdote about Michael Moran, better known as Zozimus, a ballad-maker, in the early part of the last century, which tells how some practical jokers held a mock wake for him. This one-act play, written in a vigorous, irregular measure, was produced at the Abbey Theatre and might have been a success but for the unsatisfactory ending. Later, it was printed in *The Dublin Magazine*.

During many years, I thought over the play and when I had learned more about dramatic technique, I ventured to make some changes in the last scene, in the hope that these would render it effective. The Lyric Theatre Company, founded in order to maintain the new movement in verse drama, offered to hire the Abbey Theatre and give several Sunday performances of the amended play, but failed to obtain permission from the Literary Executor.

Eventually, I could not resist adding to the new ending my own version of the traditional story.

Austin Clarke

NOTES ON THE TEXT
Ballads of Zozimus: *Ballad of Donnybrook Fair*. Attributed by the late D. J. O'Donoghue to a journalist of the time. An interesting example of the wheel-and-bob stanza.
Swift: from *Epilogue to a Play for the Benefit of the Weavers in Ireland*, 1721.
O'Rourke's Feast. This translation appeared in a volume of mine entitled *Flight to Africa*.

CHARACTERS

THE PROLOGUE

MR EDWARD CARSON
CAPTAIN TERENCE O'NEILL
MARTIN MCGUCKIN
MR TITMARSH THACKERAY
MR CHARLES LEVER
A WAITER

THE PLAY

PATRICK DELANEY
MARTIN MCGUCKIN 'ZOZIMUS'
ZOZIMUS
MR WILLIAM BROWNE
MR DENIS CLARKE
FATHER SULPICIUS
KEARNEY, *a ballad singer*
O'LEARY, *a ballad singer*
MAGRANE, *a ballad singer*
HUMPY SODLUM
GORT WHELAN
COLLEEN OGE
BILLY BOLAND
MRS LISA BOLAND
MRS NELL FLAHERTY

MRS HANNIGAN
THE TOUCHER MAGUIRE
NOBS FAHY
PHELIM BRADY
FRED FURY
MIKE MYLER
BRIAN O'LYNN
BIG JIM PLANT
MOLLIE MALONE
MRS MULLIGAN
DAN KENNY
DANNY BOY NED FLYNN
DANIEL O'ROURKE
DERBY DOYLE

Actors and Others

PROLOGUE

A private lounge in the Shelbourne Hotel, Dublin. Left, small screen, Mr Titmarsh writing at a desk. Two long windows at back. Voice of a fishwife: 'Dublin Bay Herrings! Dublin Bay Herrings!'

MR CARSON. What will you have, Captain O'Neill?

CAPT O'NEILL.   The old
          Reliable.

MR CARSON. I'll pull the bell-rope.

                                        As I
          Was saying, I opened *The Freeman's Journal* at the
              second
          Page, column three, this morning. What do you think
              I read?

                              A new subscription for a statue
          Of Father Matthew, to be executed as soon as
          He shines above.

CAPT O'NEILL.   Too many flies on that ceiling!
          (WAITER *enters.*)

MR CARSON. Good morning, John.

WAITER.   Fine morning, Sir.

MR CARSON.   Two balls
          O' malt, please.
          (WAITER *leaves.*)

                              Think of it. Monster meetings
          In field or market town, from Skibbereen to,
          Say, Smithfield. Populace taking the pledge, hands up
          To Heaven. And the result – the public-houses
          Empty.

CAPT O'NEILL. Cart-horses pulling up and looking
          Surprised when they get a 'Go wan ow a' that!' from
              their driver
          And a flick of unwilling whip.
          (WAITER *returns.*)

MR CARSON. Thanks, John.
          (WAITER *ready with water-jug.*)
                              The same as usual.

(WAITER *leaves.*)

          The banks
  Foreclose and twenty thousand people –
CAPT O'NEILL.   That's
  So.
MR CARSON. Emigrate to Liverpool, fare paid, with
  Their kith and kin.
CAPT O'NEILL.   Steam-packets, stokers, busy.
MR CARSON (*raising glass*). And now the emancipated are
    cheering themselves
  Like us.
CAPT O'NEILL. Pledging to take the pledge again
  Next Lent.
MR CARSON.   The country is going to the bad.
  The very potatoes are rotting.
          And now young Davis –
  I knew his father when he lived in Baggot Street –
  Wants Catholic, Protestant, to unite. It's worse than
  Repeal.
CAPT O'NEILL. Well, I'm a Presbyterian, as
    You know. My father carried a long pike
    In '98 and wore the Green in Antrim
    Town.
MR CARSON (*admiring*). Yes, but his son has a British uniform –
CAPT O'NEILL (*smiling*). Not hidden in a hayloft!
MR CARSON (*lowering his voice*). Are you a Mason?
    (*The other shakes his head.*)
    I'll nominate you.
CAPT O'NEILL (*laughing*). Did you ride the buck-goat?
    At midnight in Molesworth Street, Mr Carsoni –
    Sorry, I meant . . . er . . . Mr Carson.
MR CARSON (*offended*).   Sir.
CAPT O'NEILL. Only a joke.
    (*Gets up, looks out of window.*)
       – and talking of jokes, there's
  Martin McGuckin, hurrying to the Hotel.
MR CARSON.   The actor?
CAPT O'NEILL. And party impersonator, last of the rakes,
    Relative of Sir Joshua Barrington.
    Drink up your whiskey, Mr Carson, or he'll sword-
    stick
    You for a sovereign from your fob. He's playing

A practical joke for a bet, to-night in the Coombe –
A dangerous spot – and the odds are against his
    keeping
A dirty shirt on his back or his cranium
Uncracked. Last Monday, he challenged me at the
    Club
And in a trice my pocket had been *touché*.
(*They hurry out.* MR MARTIN MCGUCKIN *enters.*
Followed by WAITER *with tray.*)

WAITER. Your ball o' malt, Mr McG.

MR McGUCKIN.   Good! Don't drown
'The poor craytur', Johnnie.
                        Leave a few shamrocks floating
On it.
(WAITER *leaves.* MCGUCKIN *comes forward, recites*
in flat Dublin accent.)
At the dirty end of Dirty Lane
Lived a dirty Cobbler, Dick McClane;
His wife was, in the old King's reign,
A stout brave orange-woman.
(*Glances at broadsheet.*)
On Essex Bridge she strained her throat
And six-a-penny was her note.
But Dickey . . .
(*Hears a cough, turns, sees* MR TITMARSH *at door.*)
Excuse me, Sir, I didn't see you at all.
A stranger to this country?

MR TITMARSH.   Yes, English. On
A visit. My name is Titmarsh.

MR McGUCKIN.   Mine's McGuckin.
Pleasure to meet you, Sir.

MR TITMARSH.   I couldn't help hearing
Your ballad.

MR McGUCKIN.   Not mine, Sir. It's by Zozimus,
Our Dublin street-bard, our blind Homer come
To his last city.

MR TITMARSH.   What a strange name he has!
It's not quite Irish!

MR McGUCKIN.   He earned it, penny by penny,
With a hymn he composed about a forgotten Pope
Called Zozimus, who lived in the fourth century
And converted –

171

(*Lowering voice.*)
                    a fallen woman.

MR TITMARSH.   Curiously
           Enough, I've been writing a ballad, too, entitled . . .
           Er . . . *Mr Maloney's Account of the Ball.* I'm trying
           A bit o' the brogue.
           (MCGUCKIN *shows alarm.*)
MR TITMARSH (*smiling*). It's not finished yet.
MR McGUCKIN (*hastily*). Goodbye, Sir.
                                        Bianconi will wrap you in his
           New waterproofs, the cadgers and 'childer' beat
           His chargers to the canal-boat.
                                        And don't forget
           To visit Blarney Castle.
           (*Looking in again.*)
                                        I come from there.
           (MR TITMARSH *comes forward with paper and tries
           to recite in a thick brogue.*)
MR TITMARSH. Begor this fête all balls does bate
                At which I've won a pump and I
           Must here relate the splendour great
                Of the Oriental Emperor.

           There was Baroness Brunser that looked like Juno,
                And Baroness Rehausen there,
           And Countess Rouiller who looked peculiar,
                Well, in her robes of gauze in there.

           There was Lord Crowhurst (I knew him first
                When only Mr Pips he was)
           And Mick O'Toole, the great big fool
                That after supper tipsy was.

           There was Lord Fingall with his ladies all
                And Lord Kileen and Dufferin
           And Paddy Fife with his fat wife:
                I wonder . . .
                            gruffer . . . rougher . . . puff-her, in . . .
           I wonder how . . .
           (CHARLES LEVER, *who has entered quietly, supplies
           the rhyme.*)
MR LEVER.   I wonder how he could stuff her in.
MR TITMARSH. Lever, begad.

(*They shake hands.*)
                    You're welcome as the Muse in
Her peplos.
              Thanks, I'll dedicate my new
Book, *Irish Travel Sketches,* to you.

MR LEVER.   I'll be
Much honoured, Thackeray.
                         I just called in
To invite you for dinner at my place in Templeogue
This evening: carriage outside the Shelbourne here
At six –
        and bring Maloney with you, of course.

THACKERAY. Delighted!

MR LEVER (*smiling*). Has Mr Titmarsh found much by the Liffey-
              side
For pen and crayon?

THACKERAY.   Rags and robes.
                         I saw the
Right Honourable Lord Mayor, Mr O'Connell
Among his Councillors in a black-oak Parlour
At a dingy green-baize table, in crimson robes
With sable collar, white satin bows, cocked hat –
Black as a lunar eclipse in a pale sky!

MR LEVER.   She's back again.

THACKERAY.   Who?

MR LEVER.   The Comic Muse.

THACKERAY.   Then, the Abbey
Street Theatre, last evening, stage-Irish farce,
No . . . 'pathriotic draama.'
                    And you?

MR LEVER.   Toppin'
The marnin', brothing the bhoys!
                   Charles O'Malley,
Rechristened Tom Bourke, still gallivanting,
    drinking,
Quadrilling, tasting a kiss behind a fan that
Stops feathering – and pure as the celibates
In their new Government-granted College at
Maynooth.

THACKERAY.   Think, my dear Lever, of our own
    licentious
Old Masters.

MR LEVER. Sterne.
THACKERAY. Fielding.
MR LEVER. Smollet.
THACKERAY. And poor Dickens
Now, keeping the tester curtains drawn.
(WAITER *enters.*)
Forgive
Me. What will you have?
No, I insist.
MR LEVER. A drop
O' whiskey.
THACKERAY. Waiter!
WAITER. Yes, Sir.
THACKERAY. Two balls o' malt,
Please.
(CHARLES LEVER *and* WAITER *both look
surprised.*)

CURTAIN

ACT I

A disused marine stores in Liberty Lane. Table with bottles on right, small casks. In left recess, a rigged bed, stools. Entrance right, up a few steps. Exit, left.

PAT DELANEY. Please hurry now, Mr McGuckin, it's a quarter
                Past eight and you must have gargled
                Six chasers of seven-year-old to a quart
                O' plain. So be on your guard
                To-night.
                (*Church bells.* McGUCKIN *looks puzzled.*)
                        That's the carry-on at St Patrick's.
                Soon the boys will be here for a stiffener
                An' if they get wind of your play-acting tricks,
                There'll be another stiff
                On the slab to-morrow.
McGUCKIN (*with broken bit of mirror*). Just one more touch
                Of grease-paint.
                            'Me gob' is too red.
                More flour.
                (DELANEY *hands it to him.*)
                      Thanks, Pat.
                                I must look touching.
                For the wake . . .
                (*Claps on wig.*)
                        And now I'm ready.
DELANEY. Bejases, you're the living dead spit o'
                  The corpse of Zozimus
                Some day in Mercer Street Hospital,
                  Penny-eyed, completely unsozzled.

                You worked like a Trojan at his whiskers.
                  (*Bitterly*) Poet, my foot! I'll give him more digs
                In the ribs for he cheated me, guzzled my whiskey
                  An' got me thrun out of my digs.

                There's a jar on the shelf near the bolster.
McGUCKIN. Not yet. I need a rehearsal

175

To sober myself. Are the doors bolted?

DELANEY. They are. All's dark as a hearse-cloth
In St Augustine's. I stopped the key-holes
   With rags.
(*Chuckling.*)
              When you codded the crowd
That day, play-acting on Essex Quay, Sir,
   An' the tin whistles an' crowders

Were jeered in the gutter by butties an' gutties
   An' not a make in their mugs,
I nearly jacksed my wipe-gut
   With laughing to see long mugs

Outside in the rain at the public-houses
   With divil a hope of naggin
Or pint, their droopy moustaches an' cat-licks,
   As they cutaway'd home to be nagged.

McGUCKIN. You have another laugh coming, Delaney.
   It's part of my bet, but mum's
The word. It will liven up Liberty Lane.

DELANEY. Is it strawmen, Sir?

McGUCKIN.   No.
           Mummers.
(*He picks up blackthorn stick. Lights dim as he comes
forward, groping, into spotlight. Vague figures gather
in background.*)

'ZOZIMUS'. Gather round me, Boys, for well you know
   St Patrick was born in Bull Alley.
Some say your man was Taffy, the so-an'-so,
   But that, Boys, is up my Ball Alley.

Am I standin' in wet or a paviour's puddle?

VOICES. On dry land, Zozimus.

'ZOZIMUS'. I'm not, ye desaivers, I'm swimming the Poddle.
   If I go down a manhole, I'll moslem
The lot of youz, string up your black-an'-white
      puddings
   An' sausages.

VOICES.   Don't squeeze your lemon.
   But give us sweet word of St Mary,
They called the whoor of Jerusalem,
   How she varted,

                              An' sold her mare's tail
              For a luvely pot of balsam.
'ZOZIMUS'.   Will you wait
              Till I scratch myself under the oxter?
              Do you think I'm a Pro-Cathedral waite,
              The blessed donkey or the ox?
VOICES.   Sing *Pharaoh's Daughter*
                              Prodigal
              Son
              Strike up, Zozimus.
'ZOZIMUS'.   Go long to Hell with all Protestants.
              An' may we never simmer.

              I'll tell you now of Dirty Dick
                  An' swipe them orange fellas
              With their Antient Concert Rooms, their dickies
                  An' college ducks an' umbrellas.
              (*Tin whistle as he recites.*)
              At the dirty end of Dirty Lane
              Liv'd a dirty cobbler, Dick Maclane;
              His wife was, in the old King's reign,
                  A stout brave orange-woman.

              On Essex Bridge she strained her throat,
              And six-a-penny was her note.
              But Dickey wore a bran' new coat,
                  He got among the yeomen.

              He was a bigot, like his clan
              And in the streets he wildly sang
              O Roly, toly, toly, raid, with his old jade.
              (*Enter the real Zozimus.*)
VOICE (*truculent*). I'm a Proddy.
VOICES.   Then be St Balize's disease
                  An' his holy flannel, I'll poke out
              Your swollen tonsils.
                              I'll chapel-o'-blaze you
                  An' expose your hoky-poky.
'ZOZIMUS'.   Be cripes, you won't, you straw-foots, you big
                  Galoots. He's a Dublin man
              Like myself.
                          Shake hands, Sir.
                              Them bigots

Were never emancipated.

'ZOZIMUS'. Men and women, who's that imposterer?

VOICE. Zozimus, himself, Sir.

'ZOZIMUS'. Are you seein' my double?

                                 Sure, he's taken my posture
    An' stolen my songs an' hymns.

Come, Boys, grasp his posteriors,
    The scruff of his neck, an' pitch him
Into the Liffey or I'll bate the posthumous
    Out of him on my pitch here.

Don't you know he's really Beelzebub,
    That fly-god, an' he's got you
By it, an' your daughters by the tub
    For his name is the Unbegotten?

'ZOZIMUS'. Don't mind that foul-mouthed blackguard, Boys.
    He stinks like Anna Liffey
An' his language is all blague –
    But I'll blacken his analectas!

Come on, you unsunned Cimmerian,
    Though you're not dimensional,
I'll take you on with your Mary Anne,
    Her tail an' what I won't mention.

('ZOZIMUS' *and his rival contend silently with sticks.
The effect is uncanny. Lights dim, leaving them in the
spotlight.*)

DELANEY (*to* McGUCKIN). By all the holy Mysteries,
    They're not Dublin men
At all. So we'd better be scooting, Mister.
    Them's ghosts an' we're seein' double.
('ZOZIMUS' *and crowd fade out. Lights up. Loud
knocking.* McGUCKIN *lowers a drink.*)
The doss, quick.

                     Those droners'll need a stiff one
    An' if they get wind of your play-acting
They'll want a real wake and yourself as the Stiff
    For nothing less will please them.
(*He opens door and the Ballad Singers enter. He
moves candle to end of side-shelf, leaving* 'ZOZIMUS',
now in bed, in the shadow.)

KEARNEY. Is he bad?
DELANEY.   He couldn't be worse, man.
    His toes are turning up,
    His head rolling round like a mangol-wurzel
    An' he's newly at the turnpike.
KEARNEY (*at bedside*). Cheer up, my aul' Geranium;
    No better clay's in pot.
    Your bud will redden an' bloom in the rain
    Though you're paler than poteen now.
'ZOZIMUS' (*cheerfully*). You're right. I'll chew my quid o' baccy,
    Pinch snuff an' quit my moaning.
    Your hand, Kearney, and may Bacchus, not
    Vartumnus, possess Pomona.
O'LEARY. Cheer up, like us, you'll be well-lit
    To-night, my aul' Gasoleer, an'
    Your recitations won't be littered
    For a long time yet.
'ZOZIMUS'.   That's O'Leary.
O'LEARY. Cheer up, my aul' Segochia. You're good
    For many another Lent.
    An' no descendants will scatter your goods
    Till you get back all you lent
    To those bummers down in Clanbrassil Street.
'ZOZIMUS'. That's so.
MAGRANE.   An' I've come here to recite
    Those ballads bright as the brassy knobs
    Of your double-bed – a sight

    You've never seen – when I'm well-oiled,
    And your songs like Sesame,
    Lovely an' yellow as its oil
    'An' gayer than foxglove,' sez Sammy

    My friend –
'ZOZIMUS'.   Magrane.
MAGRANE.   You'll warm the bed-sheets
    Till your flowers o' speech are cut down
    By time, declare bold words from your broad-sheets
    Like Emmet in the wood-cut.
'ZOZIMUS'. Start up the wake for my living corpse
    An' vigilate the Nation
    Before the white-an'-red corpuscles
    Are cold and my last carnations

Shed, for I'll stay, my fingers, in the pink
    An' tell of untarnished
Wreath of amaranth, pansy, pink,
    Till I come to my tarnation.
    (*Crowd of men and women with bottles enter. Some women go respectfully to the bed.*)

DELANEY.   Come all ye, men an' women, fill up
    Your cans with a rozimer
An' give our Zozimus a fillip
    Before he goes.
                   The rosin's for
The fiddlers till they've done their accompaniments
    An' if annie interrupts
Their Bs an' Fs, the Boys will encumber
    The back-lane with rupture-belts.

HUMPY SODLUM. An' after the ballads, we'll dowse the dips,
    Play *Hunkering*

GORT WHELAN.   An' *Cutchee-coo*

COLLEEN OGE. An' *Croppies Lie Down* when you're feeling dippy.

HUMPY SODLUM. Yes, Girls, an' *Fan-me-Cool.*

BILLY BOLAND. With *Wind up the Tick-tock*

GORT WHELAN.   An' *Hic Haec Hoc*

MRS LISA BOLAND. An' *How's your Cockalorum.*

HUMPY SODLUM. Girls, knock your cups back till you hiccupped
    An' beware o' the Marrion Cocklers.
    (*More guests arrive.*)

MRS FLAHERTY. Mrs Hannigan, did you ever see the like
    Of that in a Christianised land,
    Those dressed-up hussies, them ikey wans?

MRS HANNIGAN. I've seen a lot from the landing
    Winda: young wans an' fellas hugging
    An' mugging, but to escort
    Them lassies here – ask Mrs Huggins –
    Is terrible. I'd scorch
    Their fal-de-lals.

MRS FLAHERTY.   To think of street-walkers
    In this respectable place.
They should be working in Walkingstown
    At the mill, not taking the place
Of their betters.

MRS HANNIGAN.   The wonder-working Franciscan,
    Who preaches Hell-fire to the say-gulls

An' all of them other Cispontines
    Should be told. He'd have a say
In the matter.
MRS FLAHERTY.   Aye, Father Sulpicius
    Would deal with their sins of occasion
An' frighten them like the pis-skators
    Who pull out their big eels on the Quay.
MRS HANNIGAN. You're right, ma'am, all brazen-faced wall-
        pushers
    From the red-hot Kipps of Mabbot Street,
Short-timers in doorways at Ussher Island.
    There's Blanketty May and Peony Mab.
An' –
THE TOUCHER MAGUIRE. Did youz never hear tell o' Saint Mary,
    The Whoor of Jerusalem,
With her luvely buzzom, the night-mare
    Of christianers.
MRS FLAHERTY (*to the* TOUCHER). Lemmy
    Go!
THE TOUCHER MAGUIRE. Jewmen, the infidel Moor,
    Sure when they had clapped an
Eye on her handy behind, Mrs Moore,
    She poxed them, she soft-sored, she clapped them.

But, Zozimus, the Bishop, convarted
    The Whoor o' the East, baptised
And wet her all over in gallons of Vartry
    Till his holy volume capsised her.
CHORUS.   Till his holy volume capsised her.
THE TOUCHER MAGUIRE. She gave the crabs to the nuns in her
        convent
    And they sent her out to buy blackwash,
For they found them very inconvanient,
    But she stopped to pray with a black-man

An' left the Sisters of Mercy to scratch
    Themselves an' when she returned the
Next week, she kept them up to the scratch
    An' they had to turn her out

In tears with her fare to Constantinople.
    So she gave them her boils, but
Before she could get to the Consulate there,

The Turcos redipped an' boiled her.

CHORUS. The Turcos redipped an' boiled her.

NOBS FAHY. An' she wasn't the worst. The King o' the Beggars,
Bold Dan O'Connell, sure he fathered
The half of us all from Kilbeggan
An' Birr to Puck Fair.

PHELIM BRADY (*menacing*). Whisht, Fahy!

NOBS FAHY. Sure, he's famous for his hortations
An' nobody can deny it.
An' he'd bate Kind David when he was hoary
Yet always nigh it in his pavilion.

PHELIM BRADY. By the blessed mumps
Of St Blaise, I'll make you a tenor.

NOBS FAHY. Get back, you cut-purse.
I'll mummify
Your lights at Tenebrae.

FRED FURY (*in corner*). Sure they say he's infatuated
With a lassie who won't be converted.

NOBS FAHY. That's true.

PHELIM BRADY. Ah dip it in fat, chew, ate it!

NOBS FAHY. He's a hard chaw, Dan O'Connell.

THE TOUCHER MAGUIRE. Don't mind them, Mrs Hannigan.
They're
Trying to badger you, an'
Get up your dander. But I'll hand it to
You, if you're feeling that bad
By the Back o' the Pipes at eleven
To-night with due respects,
If you'd like a bit of levitation.
But you'd better put on your specs!

MRS HANNIGAN. Get along, you smutty Corkonian,
You want all the works for nowt.
I'll pepper-pot your polonio.

MIKE MYLER. Eh, ma'am, I'll lend you my knout.

MRS HANNIGAN. You Cossack.

BRIAN O'LYNN. Ah, leave the woman to her sheeny
And mind the rip in your pants or
Some Colleen Oge will dish your drisheens
When you've warmed up the cooking-pan.

So, back to Coal Quay, my shandy-gaffer.

THE TOUCHER MAGUIRE. I'll not. I've paid my corkage.

(*Peal of bells.*)

BRIAN O'LYNN. The window-breaking Bells of Shandon
      Have just come up from Cork.
     (*Delaney intervenes.*)

DELANEY. Now for Come-all-yes, Entertainments,
      So go steady with the booze
   My Boys. Don't guinness your containers
      For we don't want any boos.

BIG JIM PLANT. Pat has a half-nelson up his sleeve
      To give us all a start,
   I've seen him peel his biceps, the sleeveen.
      We're waiting, Pat, so start.
   (*Two of my great-grandfathers come in.*)

DELANEY. Will you look who's here!
                Mr William Browne
   Who owns the tannery in Watling Street.
   (*Chuckling.*)
                 He does them brown
   With ballads, bitter as tannin –

   Those victuallers and vintners, flour-an'-salt merchants
      Of Thomas Street and the Cornmarket,
   Not to speak of haberdasherers, robbing mercers,
      With his scorching words and remarks.

   All know he's the friend of ballad-makers
      An' slips each a silver crown
   To sing him songs at their shop-doors for make
      An' wing from the nudgy crowds.

   I came in to greet you for I heard a great sound
      As I passed by with Denis Clarke
   So good evening to you, all and sundry.
      He's my confidential clerk.

CLARKE. One of the Clarkes from Black Ditches, Blessington.

MR BROWNE (*lowering his voice*). I'm told the bard's on his sick-
      bed
   Since Monday. We'd like to have his blessing –

CLARKE. Though we hear no sweep o' the sickle.
   (*They go over to bed.*)

DELANEY. An' now we're having some grand new ballads
      For our visitors.
           Kearney:

VOICE. Spifflicated.

DELANEY. O'Leary, my lad!

VOICE. Paralytic.

DELANEY. The Meathman:

VOICE. Canned.

VOICE. They're all of them langers.

VOICE. Yewerinated.

DELANEY. Ah! potes will be potes.
So Mr William Browne, you're in.
That liquor was too potent,
Now one of your ballads.

MR BROWNE. Here's a broad-sheet
I picked up at Skinners Row.
The language in it? Well, rather broad.
(CLARKE *whispers to him.*)
Sorry, I found it near Roe's
Distillery – so don't tell the Missus.

CROWD. We'll swear on a sack of Bibles, Sir,
Or take the pledge from the missioner
Although we are fond of imbibing.
(*Tin whistle. He recites in the traditional manner.*)

MR BROWNE. As I went up their Nelson's Pillar
The steps went round and round,
An' who should come down them but Lady Sackville!
An' her drawers were coming down, too, My Boys.

CHORUS. Her drawers were coming down, too.

MR BROWNE. 'The string of me whatnots is broken entirely'
Sez she, an' her luk was a sly wan.
'Would you like to see a fine pair o' legs,
Young man?' But I turned the blind eye, My Boys.

CHORUS. An' he winked with the seeing wan.

MR BROWNE. She pulled up her skirt to fasten the doings,
'It's a very large size,'
Sez she, when I gave her a helping hand,
'An' you tuk me by surprise, My Boy.'

CHORUS. He tuk her by surprise.

MR BROWNE. As we came down from Nelson's Pillar
She thanked me for my trouble.
'We'll meet again,' sez she, 'in the Lar
Above the streets of Dublin, My Boy.'

CHORUS. Above the streets of Dublin.
(*Applause. He goes aside with* DELANEY.)

MR BROWNE. How do you like the bran' new wig
    I bought last week for Ascot?
DELANEY.   It's black as a bag of coal from Wigan!
    That's best for nuts. Though if you ask

    Me, Bill, I like the pepper-an'-salt one
      An' the other, a natty nasturtium,
    You sported that time you won
      A packet at the Gran' National.
MR BROWNE. If my wife buys a new Dolly Varden,
    I wear a lighter toupée
    For there's nothing like variety
    Whenever there's debts to pay.

    I've one for every day in the week
      And each of them makes me cheerful.
    Sure, the wigmaker knows my little weakness
      So here's to your very good cheer!
    (*They drink. He slips a few sovereigns to him.*)
    A special contribution.
DELANEY.   Two golyons!
    (*Goes to bed.*)
    Zozimus, feel an' bite them,
    My angeshoir.
'ZOZIMUS' (*to* MR BROWNE). By your goloshes,
    My gallstones an' the last bite
    O' bread, Mr Browne, I can digest
      In my latter solitude,
    My thanks.
              We'll spend then on fun and jest
    Before the clergy call my tune.
    (*My two great-grandfathers leave.*)
DELANEY.   We're slipping out for more of the hard tack.
    So don't wake the invalid.
    His gizzard has had a dire attack.
    We'll send for a leading physician.
    (*He leaves with some others. General merriment,
    fiddlers start to play.* BRIAN O'LYNN *and* MOLLIE
    MALONE *dance a jig.*)
BIG JIM PLANT. Whack, fol-the-diddle O, the diddle O!
MRS MULLIGAN. Arrah, fol-de-rol, the titty O!
BIG JIM PLANT. Sure, they say, my dear Mrs Mulligan,
    It's the Pride of the Coombe;

And that's the spot where we all began
    Our first wee sup with a coo, my Boys.
(*They whirl with the other couple into a four-handed
reel.*)

CURTAIN

ACT II

Wild merriment. DELANEY *and others enter with more drink. He claps for silence. Fiddles and tin whistles start.* BRIAN O'LYNN *and* MOLLIE MALONE *mime as* DELANEY *recites a ballad of the time.*

DELANEY. Oh! 'Twas Dermot O'Nolan McFigg
That could properly handle a twig.
   He went to the Fair
   And kicked up a dust there,
In dancing the Donnybrook Jig
   With his twig.
Oh! My blessing to Dermot McFigg!

The souls they came crowding in fast,
To dance while the leather would last,
   For the Thomas Street brogue,
   Was there much in vogue,
And off with a brogue the joke passes,
   Quite fast,
While the cash and the whiskey did last.

But Dermot, his mind on love bent,
In search of his sweetheart he went,
   Peeped in here and there
   As he walked thro' the Fair,
And took a small taste in each tent,
   As he went.
Och! on whiskey and Love he was bent

And who should he spy in a jig,
With a Meal-man so tall and so big,
   But his own darling Kate
   So gay and so neat;
Faith, her partner he hit him a dig
   The pig,
He beat the meal out of his wig!

Then Dermot, with conquest elate,

Came up to his beautiful Kate;
  'Arrah! Katty,' says he,
  'My own cushlamacree
Sure the world for Beauty you beat,
  complete,
So we'll just take a dance while we wait.'

The Piper, to keep him in tune,
Struck up a gay lilt very soon,
   Until an arch wag
   Cut a hole in his bag,
And at once put an end to the tune
   Too soon.
Oh! the music flew up to the moon.

To the Fiddler says Dermot McFigg,
'If you'll please to play "Sheela na gig",
   We'll shake a loose toe
   While you humour the bow.
To be sure you must warm the wig
   Of McFigg,
While he's dancing a neat Irish Jig!'

(DELANEY *addresses the crowd.*)

DELANEY.   This is the first centenary
    Of that great patriot
Dean Swift, who died in eighteen-hundred
  An' forty-five. Pay-roll

An' bribe was scorned by our noble Drapier.
  He dipped an' raised his pen.
All England shook; for he tumbled the drays
  An' cartloads of Wood's pence.

The Quality have forgotten his toil
  But the Coombe Boys still remember,
While ladies grimace at toilet table,
  They bless him on Ember Day.

He wrote a pome for Webster, tailor,
  Who abided in Weaver Square,
When times were bad in the retail trade.

FRED FURY.   He was always on the square.

It's a pageant of famous charácters

(*Cheers.*) An' regardless of great cost
We present the march-by of our actors
    Arranged in Liberty Costumes.

Come all ye, industrious Huguenots
    With your wonderful frieze
That has never snapped a threadknot
    Although you eat fries on a Friday.

DAN KENNY. Some say the pathriotic Dane
    Enjoyed two mutton chops
Of fast-days, though he was clean-shaven
    An' had no mutton chops!
('ZOZIMUS' *sits up, blankets around him and recites
in clear English.*)

'ZOZIMUS'. *An epilogue by Dean Swift*
Who dares affirm this is no pious Age,
When Charity begins to tread the Stage?
When Actors, who at best, are hardly savers,
Will give a Night of Benefit to weavers?
Stay – let me see, how finely will it sound!
Imprimis, from his Grace an Hundred Pound,
Peers, Clergy, Gentry, all are Benefactors;
And then comes in the *Item* of the Actors.
Item, the Actors freely gave a day –
The Poet had no more, who made the Play:
(*The Actors line up in costume and come forward in
turn.*)
But whence this wondrous Charity in Players?
They learned it not at Sermons, or at Prayer:
Under the Rose, since here are none but Friends,
(To own the Truth) we have some Private Ends.
Since Waiting-Women, like exacting Jades,
Hold up the Prices of their old Brocades;
Well-dressed in Manufactures here at Home,
Equip our Kings and Generals at the Coombe.
We'll rig in Meath Street Aegypt's haughty Queen
And Anthony shall court her in Rateen,
In blue shalloon shall Hannibal be clad,
And Scipio trail an Irish plaid.
In drugget drest, of Thirteen Pence a Yard.
See Philip's Son amidst his Persian Guard.
And Proud Roxana fired with jealous Rage,

With fifty Yards of Crape shall sweep the Stage.
(*She whirls, unrolling the crape, then stops, half clad and dashes off.*)
In short, our Kings and Princesses within,
Are all resolved the Project to begin;
And you, our Subjects, when you have resort,
Must imitate the Fashion of the Court.
(*The Actors parade, march off. Conversation.*)

DELANEY. We now present *O'Rourke's Great Feast*
    With all the props an' effects.
    The wash of its drink would have choked the gratings
    If they'd any.

DANNY BOY.   Sure, Dane Swift fecked
    That song from the Irish.

DERBY DOYLE.   Two hussies came
    From England, dressed in their best
    To nobble him but he soon hustled
      An' bustled that pair o' besters.

NED FLYNN. But what did these shinannikers want from
    The Dane?

DERBY DOYLE (*lowering voice*). A touch o' the relic.

NED FLYNN. Why didn't he marry the wealthier wan
    An' leave his relict?
    The rhino?

DANIEL O'ROURKE. Them black Prodistants say
    Our relics are only divarsions.

DERBY DOYLE. Will some-wan give that bostoon a prod?

DELANEY (*impatient*). This is a longer version.
    (*He brings a drink to* 'ZOZIMUS', *general amusement. Fiddle and tin whistle, actors enter, speak and mime in spotlight. Crowds in dark, down stage.*)

'ZOZIMUS' (*narrating*). Let O'Rourke's great feast be remembered
    by those
    Who were at it, are gone, or not yet begotten.
    A hundred and forty hogs, heifers and ewes
    Were basting each plentiful day and gallons of pot-still
    Poured folderols into mugs. Unmarried
    And married were gathering early for pleasure and
    sport.

ACTORS (*speaking and miming*). 'Your clay pipe is broken.'
                    'My pocket picked.'
                    'Your hat

Has been stolen.'
                    'My breeches lost.'
                                    'Look at my skirt torn.'
'And where are those fellows who went half under
    my mantle
And burst my two garters?'
                         'Sure, no one's the wiser.'
'Strike up the strings again.'
                      'Play us a planxty.'
'My snuff-box, Annie, and now a double-sizer.'

'ZOZIMUS'. Men, women, unmugged upon the feather-beds,
Snored until they heard the round clap, the step-dance
Again, jumped up, forgot to bless their foreheads
And jigging, cross-reeling from partner to
                        partner, they trampled
With nail in brogue that cut the floor to shavings.
'A health, long life to you, Loughlin O'Hennigan.'
'Come, by my hand, I'll sing it in your favour,
You're dancing well, Marcella Gridigan.'
(*A spotlight shows floor with a couple going to bed.*)

ACTORS. 'A bowl, Mother, and drink it to the last drop'
Then came a big hole in the day.
                              Light failed.
'Shake rushes for Annie and me, a blanket on top
And let us have a slap-and-nap of decent ale.'
Merciful Heaven, whoever saw such a big crowd
So drunk, the men with belt-knives of slashing,
    stabbing,
The women screaming, trying to hold up trousers
And others upon the table, twirling an oak-plant!
(*More actors take part.*)
The Sons of O'Rourke came rolling from the doorway
In somersaults of glory. Bachelor boys
Were boasting, cudgelling more, more, more,
'My father built the monastery at Boyle . . .'
'The Earl of Kildare and Major Bellingham were
'My . . .'
           'Sligo harbour, Galway, Carrick-drum-rusk.'
'And I was fostered . . .'
                    'Pull the alarum bell!'
(*Bell sounds.*)
'A blow for your elbow grease.'

191

'A kick in the bum.'
'Who gave the alarm?' demanded one of the clergy.
And swung his big stick – not as a censor.
Right, left, he plied it soundly to asperge them
In blood-drops, gave a dozen three more senses.
The friars got up with their cowhorn beads to haul him
back, dust his habit.
                    Three Reverences tumbled
Into the ashes; Father Superior bawling
Until that congregation went deaf and dumb!
'While I was studying with His Holiness
And taking Roman orders by the score,
Yiz sat on a settle with an old story-book,
All chawing roast potatoes at Sheemore.'
(*Lights up. General confusion, ructions, then silence
as* 'ZOZIMUS' *enters, striking out with his stick.*)

'ZOZIMUS'. Who's that imposterer ye're wakin';
    With Guinnesses an' doubles,
Instead of me? Am I awake or
    Is my mind seeing double

Since I heard the news in Smock Alley
    A while back?

DELANEY.   It's 'Zozimus'
    That's passing.

'ZOZIMUS'.   It's down your alley alright
    To find my didymus.

Have I no share in my own passing
    Or the dibs for the noddin' plumes
And your collecting from passers-by?
    Don't I live by my holy plume?

I've converted them wans in the tenements,
    An' magdalen'd the lot.
Throw me my half-share o' the tin
    Or I'll uncify you all like Lot an'
His pillar.

'ZOZIMUS' (*sitting up*). He's the imposterer
    An' he wantin' my sacred death-dues.
He's some play-actor who's taken my posture
    An' he'll razzle-dazzle with my jewels
O' song.

'ZOZIMUS'. Boys, don't you know he's Moloch,
The fish-god with only one fin,
Who keeps the cod-banks an' covers his molluscs
An' bosses the old Fin-nations?

'ZOZIMUS'. The name is Dagon, you ignoramus,
An' I'm swimming the booty.

VOICES. Begod, we have two Zozimuses
('ZOZIMUS' *jumps out of bed.*)
And both of them in their boots.

'ZOZIMUS'. He's changing to Vercingetorix.
Where are you? (*Striking out.*)

VOICES. There
Beside you

Where?
Here

'ZOZIMUS'. Here
He's a ventriloquist
And he's turned my senses inside
Out.

God in heaven, have youz no pity
On the blind man who tried to save youz
All from the Everlastin' Pit
An' get the Penny Savings
Bank to protect your wings?

MRS MULLIGAN (*moved*). Hold back the
Poor Jossers. They're long-lost twins.
Their way is dark an' unbeholden
An' their eyes have never twinkled.
(*A man at main door.*)

MAN. Quick, men and women, the back-lane exit
From the Hell-fire Franciscan
Is striding the cobbles to make an example
Of youz all to-night and fire
You tails, so keep them where they belong.
(*Watching from door.*)
He's running now with his skirts up.
He's turning the corner of Long Lane
An' he'll pull up your boards an' skirting.'
(*Crowd rushes for the side-exit. 'ZOZIMUS' gropes for
door followed by 'ZOZIMUS'.*)

'ZOZIMUS'. Wait for the Blind man. Are youz all decamping,

Leaving me to his mercy
An' Flaming Flowers?
                                        Where's my aid-decamp?
Am I to end up in Mercier's

With splints in the Casualty Ward,
    Sitting up in a pose
Of Plaster-o'-Paris? Is this my reward
    For a lifetime of composing?
('ZOZIMUS' *pushes him out.*)

DELANEY (*winking at* 'ZOZIMUS'). Come on. I'll guide you to the
            door
    For it's your only chance.
He's not got your name in his dossier
    An' you'll not be in Chancery
Before your napper has been boxed.
(*To* 'ZOZIMUS'.) There's whiskey to add to your diet
On the shelf.

'ZOZIMUS'.   Give me that cash-box.

DELANEY.   I won't.

'ZOZIMUS'.   I'll make you the diet
Of worms.
    (*Steps. He blows out candle, hurries to door.*)

'ZOZIMUS'.   What's this?
                                        My box of grease-paints.
    I've got you now. I'll careen
Your bottom before I cut the painter
    So tell that to the Marines!
(FR SULPICIUS *appears in moonlight at doorway.*)

FR SULPICIUS. Hide your misconduct, jereboams,
            In darkness, knowing your sins
Have sent me. Hear my Placebo
    And kneel down, married, single.

It is against the Bishops' ruling
    To hold a wake, put beads
Aside. School-children know strap, cane, ruler,
    When Brothers lay bare obedience,
Yet *Sacrilegia super defunctus*
    Is committed, to-night, by parents.

DELANEY.   Father, we took no soup. Them Funkers
        Fled to their top-back pair
    O' rooms.

FR SULPICIUS. You came for a filthy purpose,
Neglected religious duties,
Insulted our Faith, my sacred stole,
And never pay your dues:

Indulging in shameful practice
And known abominations
Songs, games, that encourage lewd acts,
Disgrace our Catholic nation.

DELANEY (*coming forward, servile*). 'Twas only a spree for Tom
Malone
To warm his cockles with chat
An' a few pints, poor twilight man
For his teeth are chattering.

An' he couldn't say the Litany
With us, your Reverence.
He felt so bad, we never lit any
Candles for his two aul' grand-aunts
Crying their eyes out.
I'll get the flint.
(*Strikes in vain.*)

FR SULPICIUS. What's wrong?

DELANEY. Be the sufferin' Jases –
Excuse me, Father.
(*Showing tinder.*) That mean aul' skinflint.
It's worn out, an' I've no sulphur
Matches.
I'll lead you to the poor old sod –
I mean – the dying man.

FR SULPICIUS (*at bed*). Now try to tell your sins.

'ZOZIMUS' (*in low voice*). Sodomy,
Three rapes, man-slaughtering,
An' fornication, seduction – when I'm sodden
For I'm Tom-any-Moll.
Notorious from Birr to Blacksod,
See the mots an' animals run!
(*Half sitting.*)
Incest and other carnalities,
Likewise necrophilism,
An' divers deeds of bestiality
An' I've not had my fill, for
To-night, I'm going to commit murder –

195

Martin McGuckin will freeze.
And they'll report this murky crime in
   Tomorrow's *Freeman's Journal.*

Delaney, you've had two jokes, but this time
   Zozimus holds the Joker.
(*Getting up.*)

DELANEY.   Holy St Francis, he's mad.

                       Mind out, Father!

'ZOZIMUS'.   He'd better.

           This is the last joke.
(*He tumbles out of bed, swinging stick, stumbling after them as they rush out. Pause. Stage dims as he comes forward into brightening spot.*)
Come all ye, listen to my song.
   It's about a fair young maid –
Moryah – an' won't detain you long,
   For her bill was soon marked 'paid'.

In Egypt's land contagious to the Nile,
King Pharoah's daughter went to bathe in style.
She tuk her dip, then walked unto the land,
To dry her royal pelt she ran along the strand.

A bulrush tripped her, whereupon she saw
A smiling babby in a wad o' straw.
She tuk it up and said with accents mild
'Tare-an-ager', girls, which of yiz owns the chee-ild?

'Tare-an-agers' . . .
(*Silence.*)

         So, that's it.

              The very ghosts
Are absent.

         The Shakesperian O
Is surrounded by darkness.

               It's time for me to go.
       The comedy is over.
(*Dazed.*)
But pray, who am I?

          Zozimus
Drunk?

     Or Martin, his man?
And who the Hell – for I must know –

Is the Stage Manager?

(*Slow steps.*)

The ghost of Zozimus!

DELANEY (*returning*).   He's gone.

'ZOZIMUS'.   That's not the right queue.

DELANEY.   Well, then, he bottled his way through that scrum
           All roaring for a curer,
     Ghost-pale. He slipped on a cabbage
           Stalk in the gutter outside.

     A mot picked him up and the Boys are cabbing
           Him to the Meath. A side-car
     Is rattling more paralytics on.

McGUCKIN (*taking off wig*). Delaney,
           You devil, you'll get your money
     And another fiver for the delay.
           My backers will settle on Monday.

DELANEY.   We'd better skidaddle, Mr Martin
           McGuckin.
     (*Putting down stick.*)
     (*Meaningly.*) His stick.
                    I'll close
The place up. Go by the Bird Market
     Or your jokes will soon be clovered.

I'll hide to-night from the Liberty Boys
     In the ruins of St Kevin's Abbey
Nearby. Those fellows will be boisterous
     An' rougher than the Abbots of
Missrule, you told me about, rampaging
     Before the High Altar, an' gargoyles
Grinning outside at Sins on the ramparts.
     But first I'll have a gargle.
(*Goes to table, tries bottles, mugs.*)
Piss.
      Mother's ruin.
                What's here?
                            A ball
O' malt?
                  No, not one dram.
(*Leaving.*)   A
Notable conclusion to your balderdash!
(McGUCKIN *puts on wig, then slumps to the floor.*)

197

DELANEY (*at door calling*). There's more to poetic drama.
　　　(*Moonlight shines on prostrate figure. Spot dims.*)

SLOW CURTAIN

St Patrick's Purgatory

FREELY ADAPTED FROM
THE DRAMA OF CALDERON

CHARACTERS

EGERIUS, King of Ireland
PATRICK, a slave
LUIS ENIUS, an adventurer
A CAPTAIN
PHILIP
LAEGARIUS
POLONIA, daughter of Egerius
LESBIA, younger daughter of Egerius
PAUL, a peasant
LUCY, his wife
TWO CANONS
ATTENDANTS AND OTHERS

ACT ONE

Scene I

Upon the Irish cliffs.

	(*rushing in.*)
EGERIUS.	That slave . . .
CAPTAIN.	Stop, stop, my lord.
LAEGARIUS.	Halt, great Egerius.

LAEGARIUS. Where Ireland ends, air is insidious:
Danger inclines.

LESBIA. Come back, dear Father,
Come back. You know the hill-path
Is shuddersome –

POLONIA. The cliffs
Of basalt, abrupt and slippery.
Look down at the cave-whirl of the sea,
The combers that climb above themselves.

LESBIA. The skiffs
Are hurrying, unnetted, from the tumble of bay.
What foot-ring can you find in the fall of
billow?

EGERIUS. Just now, brighter than the edge of daylight
Raggled by storm, as I lay on my pillow,
I had a fearful vision for I thought
I heard the rise of that measureless water
Below and the great serpent which enwinds
The fourth heavenly sphere,
Illumining the atmosphere
With seven coils was gliding
From the ocean bed.

LESBIA. Dear Father, it
Was only a dream.

EGERIUS. Rather
An omen of violence to come.
I stood alone, it seemed, in the palace hall
And from the prism of morning sun, a young man

Stepped in. His gold hair was a-flame,
Flame tipped his curls but did not fall
And from his mouth and nostrils came
Another flame as though his lungs
Were burning but without the smoke
Of crickle-wood. Quickly I tried
To lift the broad-sword at the bed-side.
The metal melted. My dagger was broken
In three. Confounded, I dropped it,
Before the reach of hands could stop him,
He darted, an incendiary, to the cots
Where you, my daughters, small again,
Still mothered, were lying asleep
Beneath the fold of linen, warmth of sheepskin.
He stooped above you with a mock gentleness,
Blew lightly – and your innocence was blotted
Out. Funerary cinders glowed, blackened, leaped
Beyond the doorway. Tiny dress
And golden toy lay on a settle. That slave –
For the tunic he wore was short and scant –
Turned with a vacant smile . . . was gone.
The footsteps of the infanticide
Were left across the floor and still they shone
And I could hear them running outside.
Then, I woke up.

LESBIA.   Chimeras
Afflict us all. They come from eras
Long past; serpent, Pan-head
Peer from the fluted column, cave-bed.
But listen, I hear a trumpet sounding
At sea.

CAPTAIN.   A ship is in our fishing grounds.

POLONIA.   Father, you know that I have always doted
Upon the upward, double note
Of the trumpet, great breath that blows
Our fighting-men together, the clash of blows
Upon the edge of battle. Give me leave
To hurry to the shore and watch the leaving of
Row-boats, rope-turn, dropping of canvas:
Perhaps our Philip's galleon is stranding.
(*Exit.*)

LAEGARIUS.   Come, my lord, to the brink that wrecks;

                       Green waves that break on a yellow shore.
                       See the galleon with castled decks –

CAPTAIN.   High lanterned poop –

LAEGARIUS.   And oyster-coloured sails

EGERIUS.   No, no. My mind is dim with forboding:
                       Sea-monsters, giant clams in their abode.

LESBIA.   Look, Father how the stately vessel
                       Glides, figure-heading the wave crests,
                       Blue bannerets flying at the truck, the yards
                       Outspread. Bay with Venetian glass
                       Is dot-dashing messages that pass
                       Uncoded

EGERIUS.   What is it, child?
                       (*Storm.*)
                                 The heavens collide,
                       Ocean becomes a waste: Neptune
                       Emerges in his car; the trident,
                       Held high, commands the roll o' the tide
                       And now his sea-green horses out-step
                       The storm: his shell is at his lip:
                       The storm drives past. I cannot see the ship now.

POLONIA (*returning*). Father, we are too late.

EGERIUS.   What is it,
           Polonia?

POLONIA.   Nereids let down
                       Their sky-blue tresses for they have spirited
                       The ship below. Each wave is a down,
                       A hollow. Look how Erato, Galatea,
                       Thetis, Glauca, Amphitrite,
                       Are pearling the foam; they lash their fishtails
                       And billows go higher than the sails did.
                       Can you not hear Aeolus cheeking
                       The wind that rushes out of his cave
                       Obediently? There are the cheek-straps
                       Of the horses rolling with Neptune's car
                       Wheeling in the clamour of the breakers.

LESBIA.   The Nereids are porpoising the waves:
                       They plunge, roll backward, pap and navel.

POLONIA.   I heard a trumpet from the starboard:
                       A cannon ball leaped from its smoky den.
                       Philip was drowned with all his men.
                       I ran to the shore, calling; my teardrops

Were saltier than the spray. My fears
Were right. Our Philip has been drowned
And on the shore is nothing but sound.

EGARIUS. My dream is out. Am I an Atlas
To bear this weight? The sea-torn altar
Draws men to death or misery
And our misfortunes are foreseen.

PATRICK (*faintly below*). A moi!

LAEGARIUS. I hear a cry.

EGERIUS. What can you see?

CAPTAIN. A man is near the shore.
He's gone.
No, there's his head, like a black pea.
He's trying to help another, his companion,
Half-sinking.

LESBIA. Unhappy mortal creatures,
Do not despair. Strike out with hands and feet
Beyond the Nereids that tangle white limb with
Blue tress. The shallows are near, swim, swim.
(*Enter* PATRICK *and* LUIS ENIUS.)

EGERIUS. That is the slave
I saw just now in the palace hall.
I marvelled for his gold head was a-flame,
Flame tipped his curls but did not fall
And from his mouth and nostrils came
Another flame.

PATRICK. That conflaguration,
Monarch, was once a burning brake
Upon Mount Horeb, symbol of our faith.
These virgins in robe and veil soon
Will leave the world, together partake
Of holy bread and wine in the name
Of the truth that we commemorate
By simple service at a table.
Almighty God has saved us.

LUIS. The Devil
Saved *me*.

LESBIA. I pity the distress
Of these two shipmen.

POLONIA. Rather be pitiless.

PATRICK. Show mercy to strangers cast upon your shore,
Half-naked under the jaws of a foreland.

204

We beg for shelter in the name of God.

LUIS.

I don't.
                    Fling of mackerel, cod,
May cut the net. I take whatever comes.

EGERIUS.

Who are you, thrown on our coast, fireball
Above you, down-burst of cloud, rumble
Of sky-bolt, your ship untimbered, unhulled?
What are your names? What is the rank these
    coloured
Rags at your hips have hidden? Tell me.
My daughters call on the gods. But I
Have no belief. We're born, we die,
And that is all. None prize our ashes.

PATRICK.
                                        Great
Egerius, I bow to you.
My father was born in Ireland, his chaste
And faithful wife a Frankish lady,
I was given the Latin name
Patricius at the font and made
A little Christian, learned to pray
Before I was unswaddled, uncradled,
Or yet could toddle a step. Daily
My parents taught me the glorious names
Of those who led the battling angels
Who fought together in the Great War
Of Heaven and cast into the flame-pit
Below the armies of the unslayable
Rebels for ever.
                    I knew the pains
Of parting when I reached the age
Of four. My parents separated.
Convent and cloister hid their faces
From me for life. A pious matron,
My foster-mother, loved, educated
Their child. Five days from holy day
To day, the sun had wheeled and blazed
Upon its axle. Five times, displayed,
The Signs of the Zodiac were raying
The Heavens when the Almighty gave me
A sudden knowledge of his favour.
Gormas, a wealthy blindman, came
To me and begged my blessing. I raised

My hand above his head, making
The sign of the Cross. A sudden blaze
Of sunshine filled his sockets. Dazed,
He blinked, then, overjoyed, was gazing
At the world again. He threw his oak stave
Upon the ground. He knelt and praised
That wonder sent by God. One day.
A snow-storm swept over the braes
And dales. A mighty thaw invaded
Our lowlands, carried cattle, hayricks
Down, rivering streets and byeways.
The water rose within the basements
Of houses, shops, with box and case.
Strange fish goggled at window panes.
Children on rafts were racing by.
My elders called on me to stay
The flood. Humbly, I made
Another Sign of the Cross. Our Saviour
Was merciful. The mud came back
Again. One morning in early April
I walked with some in meditation
Along a shelly round of the bay.
We saw a three-decked galleon sailing
Shoreward: a long boat with twenty raiders
Put out with flash of lifted oar-blades.
They captured, manacled, bore us away.
Their captain, Philip de Roqui, braving
The will of heaven, kept me in chains,
For I was healthy, fit for sale,
Until that storm had come to break
My foot-ring, cast me here to crave
Your royal protection.

EGERIUS.   Insolent slave,
I have no time for a debate
Upon your miracles. They break
The laws which we discover in Nature.
Better for us the humble state
Of ignorance.

PATRICK.   In future ages,
This unblessed land in which you reign
Will be renowned as the Isle of Saints
And Scholars, so many of the faithful

Will take their final vows, proclaim
The mysteries of our salvation
Throughout all Europe.

LESBIA.   Dear Father, pity
The stranger. See how his forehead is lit
With augury.

POLONIA.   Must he forgo
The lash and the toil of slavery, go
Unmanacled? Is he a Joseph
Trailing a many-coloured coat
Among the wise Egyptians, boasting
Of dream, prognostigation, omen?
Far sooner would I die, be shown
The shades, then resurrected, bone
By bone, than be a Christian.

PATRICK.   Lady
Your sister and you will be ours, arm-laden
With the white flowers of piety.

LESBIA.   Father,
I pity Patrick, slave of fire,

POLONIA.   Not I. This man is more exciting.

LUIS.   Then listen, lady, to my confession
Of gallantry, sins of the flesh,
With sidelong glance. Egerius,
Great King, whose very word is plenty,
I am a Christian, but different
From Patrick, the slave of fire. I've spent
My days in duels, violence,
My nights, with music and caresses.
I, too, am an Irishman, from head
To heel; my name – Luis Enius.
My father was banished when I was weaned,
And fled to Perpignan, settled
There, traded in kegs of brandy. The Seven
Planets have shed their influences
Upon my nature. The fickleness
Of the horned moon, the wit, drop-silver
Of hermes, pride of Jupiter,
The darker rings of Saturn, cruelty,
Courage of Mars. Sol taught me to spend
My substance, take all easily,
But most I owe to Madam Venus.

Who can resist that naked one?
I've worshipped the whorl of the shell
That whirled her to Cytherea,
Foam-delicate, led by Zephyr,
Who brings the flowers and frost on his breath;
Yet did not dare to come too near.
While yet a youth of seventeen
Or less, my hand was on her cestus,
Faint with the loveliness that Greece
Yielded to Rome. How can I tell you
Of the gay ladies who seduced me,
The later duels I fought, the rapiers
I broke in Spain, the husbands deceived
On midnight cushions? Yes, rape, even,
Was counted among my crimes. From presses,
Half stifled by pot-pourri of dresses
Or chambering under double beds,
I leaped, kiss-blown, from balconies,
While torches lighted from door-way, street,
Down alleys, leaving the coverlet
In boudoirs, oval, tapestried
With naked gods and goddesses,
While a young wife pulled down her night-dress
And, pale with all our joy, scarce whispered
My name, as though I were Cupidon,
The wingleted. Was I contented?
No, not until I shared the secret
Of incest. Cloaked, with my close friend,
A silken ladder, I scaled the keep-house
Of a nunnery near Toledo
Where a step-sister of mine was kneeling
One night, counting her ivory beads.
Her body lay in my arms, all weak,
As I carried its light weight to my pommel.
Quickly, I rode to a secret place
And, shameless, impatient at her pleas
For pity, I uncoifed, unguimped
My handsome sister as she wept
And kicked. But suddenly a sweetness
Filled Sister Gonzaga and she yielded,
Surprised by the heaven of the senses,
Before I could remove her flat-heeled boots,

Our bout of bedding was renewed.
So I debauched for the seven weeks
Of Lent, a Bride of Christ. Wearied
At last by sin, my savings spent,
I tried to pimp my sister, bordel
Her boldness to others. She fled to a convent,
Too amorous for true repentance.
Soon after, by ill-luck, I was held
A prisoner by Philip de Roqui,
Battened, kept prisoner under deck
Until the frolicksome Nereids threw me
Gaily, with Patrick, at your feet,
Imperitent adventurer.

EGERIUS. Though I detest your foreign creed,
I like your gaiety, impudence,
Elegant leg, so, if you will serve me,
As general, come to the palace, undress
In my Roman thermae. Towel, compress,
Attendants, wait: and you are welcome,
Luis Enius.
(*To* CAPTAIN, *pointing to* PATRICK.)
   Guard him well.
(*To* LUIS.)
       Come
(*They leave. Two soldiers lead* PATRICK *away.*)

Scene II

Open country. Cottage on left, off stage. LUCY *and* PHILIP *come out.*

LUCY.   Sir, I hope that the featherbed
               Was comfortable; our simple meals,
               Bacon and cabbage, milk, oaten bread,
               To your liking.
PHILIP.   Lucy, at this moment
               You cannot tell what I am feeling.
               (*Coming nearer.*)
LUCY (*with a smile*). I think I can.
PHILIP.   At night in your home,
               When you had turned your back to your husband,
               Thoughts of love kept me awake, banding
               My forehead with heated iron. I
               Resisted the temptation, tried
               To pray to Heaven. How could I rest
               When lidded eye-glance was immodest
               And I could hear you siding in sleep:
               A man, one inch of lath, between us?
LUCY.   I, too, was lying awake, Philip,
               Sharing your empty arms. Come, take me
               Quickly into them now, lip
               To lip. Come closer, hip
               To hip. Before you say farewell
               At noon, this tight embrace will kindle
               The tinder in the box we know so well
               When the spark is jumping out of its skin.
PAUL (*entering. To audience*). Great Heavens above my head,
                    what's this?
               My wife and our new lodger kissing.
               My bumps are bigger. I scratch my poll.
               Am I the poor hard-working Paul?
               Five times, my wife has cuckolded me,
               She cannot learn to keep her worsted
               Stockings from falling down in rings. The worst
               Comes out in married women. She's bursting

210

For every codpiece that goes by.

LUCY.   Gilded shadows play fast and loose
With one another where your Lucy
Has thanked the tempest on the sea
That cast all heaven in her arms
And took away her common sense.

PHILIP.   Come, we will turn the sky-blue day
To darkness again and every sense
Shall be in our delighted touching
Of this-and-that, of such-and-such,
No lovers name.

PAUL.   Damn their embraces.
I'll beat her badness out with my braces,
When he has left the house.

LUCY.   What is it,
Philip?

PHILIP.   Your husband.

LUCY (*to audience*).   I could spit
On him!

PHILIP.   I must get ready to go.
(*To audience*) What would Polonia think of me?
Better to be snapped down at sea.
(*Exit.*)

PAUL.   I've caught my lady in the act
Of cuckoldry.
               Up with your skirt,
Out with your . . .

LUCY.   Do not talk so coarsely.
You have mistaken a simple action.
You only saw your Lucy flirting.

PAUL.   This time you'll get a hundred strokes
Behind the hedge.

LUCY.   I'll bargain for fifty.
And fifty pinches to-night.

PAUL.   Then swear
That you will give them.

LUCY.   Without my shift on.
But wait a tick. When bottom's bare,
Husbands take pleasure in the stick.
So give me only twenty-six
And make them harder when I yell.

PAUL (*to audience*). This rhyming match is much too quick

      For my dull noddle. How can I tell
      What's next? She may enjoy a skelping,
      Want more. So, why should I oblige her?
      (PHILIP *re-enters.*)

PHILIP.   Farewell, Lucy.

LUCY (*sadly*).   Farewell.

PHILIP (*to* PAUL).   Farewell.

PAUL.   Before you leave our humble dwelling,
      Sir, may I thank you for the kinder
      Favours you have bestowed on us,
      By sharing the pleasures of my bedroom,
      Quite satisfactory – as I trust.
      Moreover, I am honoured that you like
      My wife and hurried to her at a glance
      Whenever I had turned my back.
      I pray you've not abused your health.

PHILIP.   Stop. Lucy is a paragon
      Of goodness.

PAUL.   This shovel wants to strike you.
      Take up your bedsores and be gone, Sir.
      (LAEGARIUS *enters.*)

LAEGARIUS.   Philip, my Lord, the Court is mourning
      A month for you. We saw your galleon
      Driven between the jaws of the foreland,
      Spars, tackle, poophead, flung upon
      The coast.

PAUL.   He is a lord!

LUCY.   Yes, Paul,
      Now is the time to bare my back
      For all the kisses I gave him.

PAUL.   I'll fall
      Upon my knees before him.

PHILIP.   I swam
      To a cave, dripped through the brambles,
      Beyond a sandhill, came to this cottage
      Where our good fellow and his wife
      Lifted the latch, oatmealed the pot
      Upon the hook.

LAEGARIUS.   You should have come
      To Court.

PHILIP.   I was afraid the King
      Might be angry when the hold

Filled and my men were too frightened to pump
 ship.
For how could timber and bulkhead hold
Our bullion? Fireball, thunder, fork-lightning
Uncaptained the wheelhouse.

LAEGARIUS.   Come with me now,
Surprise the downcast Court and dry
The tears of your Polonia
Until she gives you 'oh' for 'ah'.
(*Exeunt.*)

LUCY (*to audience*). My Paul will find the Frenchified kisses
Of that court lady on my mouth
When he exchanges his 'that' for 'this'.
Tinder is glowing in the box,
Although the steel has never struck
The spark for it. Better a cuckold
Than nobody. I'll coax my husband
To give me those five-and-twenty wallops.
A merry shepherd shares his wallet,
Big water-gourd.
      (*To* PAUL) Come, Husband, tuck
   up
My skirt and turn my cheeks to the wall.
(*They enter cottage.*)
(*Enter* OLD MAN *and* PATRICK. *Sound of slaps
within. He knocks. Pause. He knocks again and
waits.* PAUL *and* LUCY *come from cottage.*)

OLD MAN.   Good-day to ye, Paul and Lucy. I bring
This youth to tend your flock on the hillside
And keep the paw from your pen. Take care
Of him. Put out his daily swill
For he's the property of the king.

PATRICK.   Good sir, I am a slave, ready
To do whatever you may need
If it is virtuous. Beat me too,
(*Bows to* LUCY.)
With knotted thongs or brand me deep
If I am tardy, disobedient.

PAUL.   He shows respect.

OLD MAN.   He's learnt his lesson
Abroad, they say.

LUCY (*to audience*).   Has Heaven sent

This wonder down? Or Phoebus left
His team to drive the sun astray,
Replanet the night? What hand has bent
The ivory bow? The innocence
Of this young man is dangerous.
It darts around me, all in flame
Until my limbs are resinous.
I'll teach him the sweetness of the senses
That blossoms the hedges, lilies the byre.

PAUL.   A golden head upon your platter
Again. If you're so ready to unlace
Your petticoat, you'll grow too fat.

LUCY.   I'm young and healthy. Is it wrong
Of me to love the human race?

OLD MAN.   Farewell, I must be getting along.
(*He goes.*)

PAUL (*pointing to sky*). Run off, young man, before that skylark
Takes to the open. I must save
Myself from another pair of horns.
My wife before the turn of morning
Would twiddle your kiss-curls and every sense,
Rose-hip, unlily, your innocence.
Fetters are gone. There is the world.
Quickly follow the little goat-track
Along the hill, climb over the stile
Into the field of gorse. A mile off
Near fox-grass, fescue, timothy,
There is a holy well that curses
Gravel and stone. You'll come on black
Basalt, columning to the sea.

PATRICK.   God keep you, Sir, and you may trust me.
I am no fugitive from justice
And I obey for the first and last time
The word of a generous master.
High King of Heaven, I would pray
In such a spot as this, among
The celandines and meditate
At dawn before the lark had sung
Alleluia at Your gateway,
Hidden by showers, tending the sheep
Along the slopes as they went cropping
Through daisies no whiter than their fleece.

214

PATRICK.   Is it Your will I should not stop here
Preparing my soul for Paradise?

PAUL.   Who's there? Who are you looking up at?

PATRICK.   Almighty God who made the world
In seven days, the blueness above
Your head, the ocean and the land,
The fish, bird, beast and lastly man,
His wonders are written in the Book
Of Genesis.

PAUL.   Why did He do it?

PATRICK.   Before Time and the Beginning,
There was joy in Heaven. The Prince of . . .
(*A golden glow on right.*)

VOICE OF VICTOR. Patrick.

                    Patrick.

PATRICK.   Who are you?

VOICE.   One
Of the Seraphim.

PATRICK.   I see the sunlight
Become prismatic.

PAUL (*to audience*).   He must be dotty.
I'd better be going now. This spot
Is full of snake-bites.
(*Exit.*)

PATRICK.   Too great a wonder
Darkens the mind of mortal before
Its brilliance, ivory, rose –
And yet I seem to see four wings
Whose delicate poisings veil a face
Too glorious for earth. The robes
Of star-shine are diaphanous
Wreathed with jasmine, arbutus: the vans
Are silver.

VOICE.   Patrick, have no fear,
For I, Victor the Archangel,
Am sent from Heaven to protect
And give you this important letter:
(*To* PATRICK.)

PATRICK.   Am I not a slave,
Poor, unworthy, born for fetter
And brand?

VOICE.   Unroll and read.

PATRICK.   'Patrick,
          Apostle of Ireland, hurry to save us
          From mortal ignorance and woe'.
          What is its meaning?
VOICE.   Do you not know
          The voice that calls you over wave?
          I dim myself. Look in this mirror.
          What can you see?
PATRICK.   A multitude
          Of men, shawled women, little children
          Who beckon me, a darksome wave
          Behind them and a mountain filled
          With the huge coilage of demons.
VOICE.   You see
          The Irish people who await
          Your coming. Go to the gallic Church
          Where Sanctus Germanus, pious bishop
          Stays for your ordination. Clad
          In brown habit; thence to Rome
          There to receive the pallium
          From Celestine, the present Pope.
          Obey in confidence the wishes
          Of Heaven: then, three years of study
          At Tours, in the household of St. Martin.
PATRICK. How can I find the way?
VOICE.   No trouble
          To heaven-goers. We'll fly
          Above the weather to Gaul. My speed
          Is seven hundred miles an hour,
          But when the sky is free of cloud
          And icicles, I can exceed it.
          (PATRICK *rises into the air.*)
          (LUCY *enters, half in tears.* PAUL *following.*)
LUCY.   Paul, Paul, I knew that it was Phoebus.
          I might have clasped a real god.
          Seen my arms shine around his body
          And known his ardour though I am feeble.
          It's all your fault.
PAUL (*pleased*).   Look up at the sky.
          My rival's no bigger than a fly now.

216

ACT TWO

Scene I

In the Palace. LUIS *and* POLONIA.

LUIS.   Polonia, I have won and lost
        Love, mantled myself at a shrine-corner,
        Waited, with stars, until the morning
        For a mask, false smile, or tossed
        Away the risks of an elopement
        By torchlight, coach; attack of brigands
        Bouldering a track; a brig
        At anchor: out of a play by Lopez
        De Vega. Now I am overtaken
        By hands of folly. How can I dare
        To ask you humbly if you could care
        For me since Philip wants to make you
        His wife? Why should I boast of a few
        Midnight affairs, merry intrigues
        Got by a galliard on a gigue,
        Quick, stolen comfits in a pew?
        How can I try to seek your love
        When Philip is my rival? He
        Is better born than I am, free,
        And easy at Court in pointed ruff.
        I've spent my life in the service of Mars,
        Fallen like him into the net,
        Struggling with Venus in scented letters
        That scattered our folly, showed us stark
        Naked throughout all Naples. Though I
        Have bivouacked in despair, got up
        To victory before the sun-god
        Was out, I fear to meet your eye.
        Three years, I have waited in the hope
        Of winning your love.

POLONIA.   You have it. Philip
        Means less to me than this playful fillip

(*She flips her fingers.*)
Betray me to your arms. Elope
With me to-night. The prophecy
Of Patrick has disturbed me. Unguimp me.
Unrobe my virgin breast and limbs
And take all, all, there is to see.
Teach me the first sweet moves in the game
Of love. Beat round the bush. The shame-bird
Tumbles to bow of ivory.

LUIS. It's Philip.

(PHILIP *enters.*)

PHILIP. Sir, have you forgotten
You were a ship-slave of mine, manacled
Beneath the deck I walked on, man
For sale to the Moreiscoes? You got
Away on a wave; the Nereids
Your rescuers, when my vessel was cast
On Ireland. Billow, thunder-bolt
Had loosened every staunchion, bolt.
Poseidon ruled. The silver tiddlers
Were winged or swam into the canvas.

POLONIA. Stop, Philip, stop.

PHILIP. Come, draw your sword
And your last breath. Polonia
Is mine. Dance to this tra-la-la.
Egerius has given me his word.

(*They draw their swords.*)

(*Enter* EGERIUS, LAEGARIUS *and* SOLDIERS.)

EGERIUS.   Stop, gentlemen.
Put up your rapiers. Explain
The meaning of these passes. Plainly
Your combs are up

LUIS.   I must defend
My honour –

PHILIP.   And I, Polonia.
This vile adventurer and rake-hell
Would steal my promised wife, forsake –

LUIS. And send her home to her Papa!

(*They leave, fighting.*)

EGERIUS. Call up the palace guard. Send for
The irons. Bugle the walls.
                                        Captain,

218

Follow that dangerous outlaw, capture
And bring him, doffed, into my presence.
Laegarius, I have heard too late
That Patrick has returned to Ireland,
His gold curls visible in fire
And none can stop him. Men relate
Miracle and marvel that are astonishing.
They say a Burgundian king who had him
Waylaid and tied with a magic gad,
Was swallowed in lava when the ground
Opened. The midday sun went spinning
Upon one wheel. Thunders were unbolted.
The rabble fled. The palace bolted
Its doors.
           He turns men into sinners.

Scene II

The CAPTAIN, SOLDIERS, LUIS, *a prisoner, the* KING.

CAPTAIN.   We have the Christian. He killed
            Two of my men before his rage
            Surrendered him, fighting with skill,
            Thrust, cut and parry, excellent sword-play.
KING.   Double security. I'll try him
            To-morrow on the charge of courting
            My elder daughter, killing two gardai
            In the course of their duty.
LUIS.   I
            Refuse to recognize the court!

Scene III

LUIS *in Prison cell.* POLONIA *enters.*

LUIS.	Polonia!
POLONIA.	Luis, I have bribed

The guards. Forgetful of coming lashes,
They wipe the froth from their moustaches,
Share out the money. I've come to guide you
For in a minute from now, the postern
Will be unlocked. Horses are saddled
Outside and when my bags are staddled,
We'll gallop together. Ship is astern.
This jewel will mount us, this diamond
Will chandle, provision, a caravel:
Its Highness lies on purple velvet
And is well named the Demi-monde.
Two oceans will bring us to India,
This ruby jungle us in a howda,
And you will teach me by starlight how
To hunt gazelles. Polonia
Is ready.
(*He is about to speak. She stops him. They leave.*)
(*Enter* CAPTAIN, EGERIUS *and others.*)

CAPTAIN.   My lord, my lord, the prisoner
Is gone. Cell-door is open. The guards
Have sentenced themselves, bolted, barred,
Pot-housed. Not one of them can stir.

PHILIP.   Polonia has run with him.
The wards were turned with a golden key,
That tides an impatient ship at a quay,
All sails.

EGERIUS.   Nothing but brow and hymn
At dawn. These Christians are revolting
To me. Has Patrick overthrown
Our genealogy and throne?
Families divided, the young revolting.
He calls up auguries of fear.
The sub-kings give him expensive gifts

To save their souls when he has lifted
His hands to Heaven. Far and near,
Pastureland, river-isle, great herds
Of cattle, flocks, are given to Abbot
And Bishop. They weary of clay cabin,
And bless the banquets that have heard them
Turn dogma into national gold.
Patrick threatens to come with spell,
And charm to teach me how to spell
And write on sheepskin. If he shows
That flaming head of his in chine
Or fairy wood, I'll send him back
With his forged bull and wealthy backers
Feet foremost to Pope Celestine.
(*All leave.*)

Scene IV

Sound of hoof-beats. At the edge of a wood. Enter POLONIA *and* LUIS.

POLONIA.　　　　　　A holy traveller and sage
　　　　　　　　Came, when I had been pigtailed, a Hindu
　　　　　　　　Who told me what dusky lovers do
　　　　　　　　Before they are fifteen years of age,
　　　　　　　　And taking carbuncle from his turban
　　　　　　　　One day, because, he said, it suited
　　　　　　　　My eyes, explained the Karma Sutra
　　　　　　　　To me, magnificence of the Durbar.
　　　　　　　　We'll glide from the palm-trees, parroting,
　　　　　　　　Into the fiery shades of temples
　　　　　　　　Where all has been exemplified
　　　　　　　　And resinous gum-drop, charcoal, sparkle.
　　　　　　　　We'll see the sculptured walls of love
　　　　　　　　Where men and women in the nude
　　　　　　　　Sinew the seven changes of
　　　　　　　　Position practised by all lovers,
　　　　　　　　Instructed by the sacred books
　　　　　　　　Elbow mistaken for bold ankle
　　　　　　　　Above, bosom for rump or back,
　　　　　　　　Leg-grip for arm. Amorous lookings
　　　　　　　　Play hide-and-seek. Turvy is topsy.
　　　　　　　　Reverent women on twos or fours,
　　　　　　　　Gather the pollen of the blue lotus
　　　　　　　　Until the pale stalk is nodding.
　　　　　　　　Lengthwise, their eager mouths a-suck
　　　　　　　　Couples with supple limbs combine
　　　　　　　　To form the mystic sixty-nine.
　　　　　　　　Sweet nature flows within the huckle.
　　　　　　　　Krishna, he told me, had come to show men
　　　　　　　　And women how to gladden. He wandered
　　　　　　　　From jungle creepers to village pond,
　　　　　　　　Gaping at fairs, snake-tricks of showmen.
　　　　　　　　He met, by the forest track, the herd-girls,
　　　　　　　　Who laugh and never let a man go,

Bathing in pools beneath the mango
Trees, where the splashing is never heard
When they drip out or are floating up,
Their breasts pointed as golden pitchers.
He piped a twin-note, cool in pitch,
That seemed the cry of Kokila.
In princely disguise, he came to court
To watch the ladies palanquined.
Each felt, from muslin curtains, his keen
Glances and longed for him to court her.
So he met Radha, his spiritual
Love. Lightly she fled from him, alarmed.
One night, she jasmined into his arms,
Hip-deep in petals, and he knew her.
Next morning she bent from hand-glass to mirror
Examining each scratch and love-bite
On her back, but the redder were out of sight.
Arrow of flowers had brought no fear
To her. She fingered the box of mascara
And drooped each eyelid, carefully henna'd
Her toe-nails to the gold of a guinea hen
And from the Kunda, saw the faraways:
Snow-line of Siva, forested slopes
Of the Himalayas. Suddenly, Krishna
Was by the marble pool. The goldfish
Leaped in the net. Night-lily opened.

LUIS.　　　　　Dearest, we'll spread that counterpane
From India over us, all starletting
And Milky Way.

POLONIA.　　　　　　　　　　The sun is setting.
See how it makes our bed of flame.
(*They enter the wood.*)

Scene V

A wood. POLONIA *and* LUIS.

LUIS.   All say that beauty is dangerous.
        I walk in fire. The toying
        Of lovers brought destruction to Troy
        And drives the very gods to lust.

POLONIA.   And do you think, strange man, I am
        So beautiful?

LUIS.   Yes.

POLONIA.   And, perhaps,
        Dangerous?
        (*He nods.*)
        Then, what will happen
        Me?

LUIS.   Dearest, eternal damnation.

POLONIA (*alarmed*). What do you mean?

LUIS.   I dare not take you
        Abroad. Pursuit is much too close.
        We cannot strip it off like clothing,
        Last night. The very plants are bladed
        As in the desert. If I leave you,
        A monstrous enmity will wait:
        The day and night increasing its weight
        Of woe, I hear the cry of Eve,
        The mock of time.

POLONIA.   You are a Christian.

LUIS.   A bad, though honest, one. I told you
        My crimes, how many church-bells tolled for
        My victims, how often this supple wrist
        Was turning and how many a sword
        Was joined by mine, of the women
        I have seduced until their timid
        Touches were bolder.

POLONIA.   These are the words
        That demons use. O have mercy –
        Mercy. What have I done except
        To let you enjoy my maidenhead's

                    First pangs, what more have I?
LUIS.   These jewels
                    To unlength the miles, catch wind with tack
                    For France or Spain – whatever betide
                    Me – strike a bargain with merchant jew,
                    Ungum his cobweb.
POLONIA.   Is this a dream
                    From which I must awake? Are these
                    The moon-bewildered shadows of trees
                    Or waxen shapes? Are you a demon?
LUIS.   Yes.
POLONIA.   Spare me, fiend. I am afraid
                    Of the earth, of nothingness, extinction
                    Of mind. To live is but to think.
LUIS.   Then live forever in the flames
                    Of hell, deep in sulphurous lake
                    Or pit, where all non-Catholics
                    Are tortured, pierced by barb and prick
                    Of arrows that eviscerate them
                    Down there, the naked limbs are cindered,
                    Flesh-hooked in cauldrons of boiling pitch:
                    Howling of demons, unhuman scritch.
POLONIA.   O God of Patrick, save a poor sinner!
                    (*She rushes, right, followed by him, brandishing
                    his dagger. A scream. Pause. He returns.*)
LUIS (*hesitating*). She fell in flowers and seemed to smile,
                    Flowers that are crimsoned as she fell.
                    Ideas turn horrible, horrible.
                    O God, am I a necrophile?

Scene VI

Outside PAUL'S *cabin.*

LUCY (*within*). Who is it?
LUIS. A traveller. I lost my way
Among the nettles, then stumbled here.
LUCY. Wake up,
Paul. There's a man at the door.
PAUL. Why should
I leave a warm bed? Tell him to go.
LUCY. You're snoring again. He may need food,
Shelter.
PAUL. Sir, this is no inn.
Man in the Moon's your sign.
LUCY. Stop, Paul,
He's knocking so hard the door may fall in.
On us.
PAUL (*enters*). Don't tear the place to flinders,
Sir. Legs are tumbling into clothes.
Who are you?
LUIS. Never mind. Quick, show me
The way to the coast.
PAUL. Follow the track
Around that hillock, beyond the turf-stack,
The gorse and heather-field. A stile
Is hidden by hawthorn. Less than a mile
Through fox-grass, fescue, timothy,
There is a moon-lit well that cures
Gravel and stone in wealthy and poor.
You'll see beneath the rows of black
Basalt, columning to the sea.
LUIS. Take me as far as that pagan well.
LUCY. Stay
Sir, until the morning. You are welcome.
PAUL. I'll be your guide, sir, before my wife
Has time to show you another way
So near, no man has need of guide.

Scene VII

LESBIA.
        Father, dear Father, let us turn homeward.
Our horses are bitted. Hundreds of soldiers
Have searched sky-hidden forest, the open
Country, beneath dark cloud, the lonelier
Hillsides, river, sand-bar, shore.
No sign of them has shown
Itself. Our poor Polonia
Is gone.

KING.
              Then, earth must have swallowed them
With sudden rift of rock and groan,
Fearing my vengeance that has grown
Too great for human veins. I rode,
Night-long from military post
To post, while messengers were posting
By, pulling myself from the loadstone
Of grief.
(*Enter* PHILIP.)

PHILIP.
             All night, I thorned, I brambled
Through moonlit woods. When rays were bad,
I lost the leaf-track of the badger
Then found the moonlight had kept my shadow.
It ran lightly before or after me
As if to mock the motionless shades.
Dawn scarcely left the clouds, sadness
Had filled the middle air, the lark
Shook raindrops from his flight, thrush tapped
An empty shell.
              I turned, saw track
Of feet on the clay, little and large,
Then, shivering from a lower branch,
A tearful strip of purple rag.
I hurried forward, my sight half mad
As fear and grief. On the stained grass
Polonia lay, stabbed, stir, ravished.
Come but a step beneath this ash-tree.
She fell on flowers, a bloody gash
Beneath her left breast.

228

KING.
         Philip, no more. I
Cannot endure this grief. I have borne
Too much already. What evil drove
The dagger through the frightened robe
That has such loveliness? What colder
Delight has this vile Christian known
Before he fled to the unknown?

LESBIA.
       Words have no mouths. I only feel
The terror, the anguish, that were seen
By his unnatural eyes.

PATRICK (*within*).
           Repent
Ireland, repent. The gates of Heaven
Are closing. Only a stinted ray
Between the eastern vapour reflects
The fading goldness of that beam.
Cornstalk will rot, grass turn to sedge;
Multitudes, pleeted as lepers,
Will spectre the day. Repent, repent.

KING.
     Who can be shouting there?

LAEGARIUS.
           Patrick,
The runaway from farm and hayrick,
He travelled from the Continent
By air, landed without risk
And scatters our holy fire on hilltops,
Blaspheming against our faith, hits off
His voice from rock and quarry pit,
Lifts up the crook of his snake-stick,
Preaching as proudly as the Pontiff.

PATRICK (*enters*). Repent, Ireland. Forget the past.

KING.
     Why do you raise your voice, Patrick
In a stricken place? Beneath those branches,
That tried to save her to the last,
My beloved daughter, Polonia,
Lies dead, slain by a Christian hand.
Men troubled by their fantasies,
At midnight or reasoning in trance
Have faddled the day with unreal dogma.
We live alike, we die, then pass
To our oblivion. Priestcraft
Is vain as abstinence or fasting.
No charcoal smoke can save us. Mankind
Has known its fate since the first dragon

Laid eggs among the rocks. Anguish
And death are here. What passionate
Despair can bring the murdered back
To life?

PATRICK.   Egerius, the will
Of the Almighty. At this moment
The spirit of the girl is hidden
In darkness, waiting His decree.
The unbaptised have been condemned
To everlasting torture, however
Good or evil their lives. Mercy
Alone can save them from such.
There is another state or place of being
That theologians have deduced
By reason, a state or place between
Heaven and Hell, which learned schoolmen
Call Purgatory. Travellers
To Ireland will find a dreadful entry
To it, a lonely island, mist –
Surrounded. Stories of water-serpents
Have shadowed the truth of its existence
Unnamed in Holy scripture. Profit
From pain and terror of descent
Below the earth will soon increase
And visions spread.
                Henry de Saltrey,
The Knight Owen, De Parethos,
Jacobus de Voyagine, the Seigneur
De Beaujeu, Father Ranult Heyden
And Dionysius, the Carthusian,
Giraldus Cambrensis in a learned
Volume, and other foreigners
Will piously record the wonders –
Unknown to the Irish, superstitious,
Valinglorious, as their kings – thought-rending,
Horrible things:

KING.   What will brave men
See, down below?

PATRICK.   From island-bed
To bed, kneeling on penitential
Stone, pilgrims will make the round of penance,
Fasting, turn widdershins with *Pater*,

Ave Maria, go with *Credo*
Barefooted in simple skirt of linen,
Be locked in the Cave, descend the steps
Until there are no more of them.
Above the pit-rim, dizziness
Is waiting; turmoil, fire and stench
Below. Shrieking of naked men
And women, their lacerated bellies
Impaled on iron poles, red-hot
And barbed. Demons in their hundreds
With prong and pitchfork, leathering
Their clawed wings, place the wretched sinners
In vats of burning oil, or on grills
Of fire and in sulphurous
Or icy lakes, that burn or freeze
Their open forks: see fetters
Of flame, inextricable legs
And arms that cannot find a head.
From a thin bridge, twelve miles in length,
Archbishops wearing smoke-braided vestments,
Which they have soiled at altar or in vestry,
Are hurled into the emptiness
Of their false vows. But heretics
Will come, deluded ecclesiastics
Close up the Cave. Yet penitents
Will stay, to fast on bread and water,
Life is stone-hollows. Protestants
Will claim our simple services
Are theirs, and black-clad clergymen
Wive piously because our deacons
And parish priests are married men
Until at last in the twentieth
Century, cars will speed on petrol;
Then, angel-led Sir Shane, a convert,
Will give the Isle of Penitence
To us and cunning architects
Build a basilica, to shelter
The spot where knight-at-arms, crusader,
Went down to Purgatory.

KING.   Better old
Ignorance than this inventory
Of woe. Patrick, how can you tell

So clearly what is yet to happen,
Prove in act the incredible?

PATRICK. By raising your daughter from the dead.

KING. The dead?

PATRICK. Yes, King.

Laegarius, send
For stretcher-bearers.

(*Soldiers enter, they bear in the body of* POLONIA.)

PATRICK. In the name
Of God the Son who shared the daylight
With us rise from the dead!

(*Nothing happens.*)

I claim
Your unwilling soul from Limbo, name
The deceased Polonia.

Obey.

(POLONIA *rises, distraught: all draw back in awe.*)

POLONIA. O save me, save me, I am lost
Among the shadows, the wrath
Of the Almighty has tossed
Me down from rock to rock; the unpathed
Forests with stooping branches close
Around my footsteps. I run from glances
That pierce the sky, strip off gay clothes
Belying my body from navel to wame.
Look on this filthy fornicatrix.

(*She leaves, her voice can still be heard.*)

KING. What oriental trick is this,
Patrick, you offer as miracle?
I have seen women fall into
A swoon that seemed the very pit
Of nothing, men in sudden fit,
Roll up, or bound, in acrobatical
Frenzy, half recover their wits.

POLONIA (*she comes and goes wildly throughout the scene*).
Repent before the Judgment Day, repent
Your lust. Valley and mountain shake with the
wrath now
Of the Almighty. Where have I been pent
In terror, yet nothingness? What zigzag pathway
Can aid the toes that hurry where earth is rent
And from his lair, the hunger-waiting beast

Descends into forest mire, huge horner, unseen,
Where darkness keeps on edge the pointed bill?
The knottings of root and gnarl are many-eyed,
Fungus is spreading slowly from chill to chill
Pallid as limbs of mortals who have died,
And under their twisted branches oaks are piled,
Worm-phosphorescent. How could I believe
The gold-rot lamps of Midas, that deceive
The senses? Echoes, halloa'd me, calling 'come',
And in a vision I saw an island cave,
Above it a boulder of granite that seemed tumbling
Yet never fell, but clung, despairing, to clay
Despite its weight, like the human spirits, numb
And hopeless, to the body. Under that big rock
I heard the cries of the tormented, mocked
By devils, with rage in leathern vans, thin whip-tail.
Among the shore-reeds, half-naked, dripping, I
    rushed,
Soul, snatched out of my body in an instant,
Behind a stake. The ripples had been roughened.
A smoke or cloud rose from the hidden pit.
The lake was stormier. The shore-reeds glistened.
The rain beat on my soul. Body was mist.
Fly, fly, from Lough Derg. The water-serpents mail
And cog their coils, fantastic as the foam
And in the mountain hollows, pagan tales
Are phantoming at night. The world is woeful,
Let no one else uncover this dire cave-mouth
Look down at the agony, the writhings of torsos,
Or hear shrieking of millions in their torment.
Repent before the Judgment Day. Repent!
(*Exit*).

PATRICK (*to the* KING). Come with me, obstinate unbeliever,
Come with me quickly to that treeless
Island within the lake, half seen
As rain in mist. No plover or peewit
Has nested by it. Among the shore-reeds,
A boat is moored beside a heaping
Of flints, so old we shall have need of
Invisible hands to row and keep it
From sinking fast. Under the steeper
Granite, there is a track no feet

Have trodden to a cave, sunbeam
Has never gilded. There you will dree
The horrors of a future decreed
For all who sin, the fiery scree
That brings the stiff-necked to their knees,
Men, women, sodomed to a shriek.
(*All go out.*)

Scene VIII

Left, a red glow. Right, a golden and heliotrope radiance. The voices are above the clouds.

DAGON.　　　　　My Lord and Master has kept in vagueness
　　　　　　　　This island, encircled with its vapours
　　　　　　　　That far-eyed hunter or cattle-raiders
　　　　　　　　Might not suspect the actual flame
　　　　　　　　Beneath the earth. Ancient temptation
　　　　　　　　Returns, for priests and laymen break
　　　　　　　　The second commandment, dare to raise
　　　　　　　　In chapel new graven images
　　　　　　　　Of the unseen. What hand will raze
　　　　　　　　These infamies? Fly through the haze
　　　　　　　　To Heaven, bend your back, Victor.

VICTOR.　　　　What will you do below?

DAGON.　　　　　　　　　　　　　　　Evict
　　　　　　　　Or drown in the tumult of the waves,
　　　　　　　　The saint and his acquaintances.

VICTOR.　　　　Dagon, I knew you when you gazed
　　　　　　　　In Heaven beside me, bright not stained,
　　　　　　　　And saw you headlong in an air-raid,
　　　　　　　　Your wings shot down by the vibrations
　　　　　　　　Of a passing sky-bolt. Your threat is vain.
　　　　　　　　Celestial visions are unsainted.
　　　　　　　　Men swarm the Cities of the Plain,
　　　　　　　　Indulge in old abominations.
　　　　　　　　Their punishment must be made plain
　　　　　　　　To them again, all, all, the details
　　　　　　　　Be manifest. The island-cave
　　　　　　　　Shall be a hazy mirror, framed
　　　　　　　　By Ireland.

DAGON.　　　　Never, vile Archangel!
　　　　　　　　(*Black out. Thunder, lightning, flash.* DAGON *is
　　　　　　　　seen as a mediaeval Demon, with tail, horns, three-
　　　　　　　　pronged fork;* VICTOR *in silver mail, with
　　　　　　　　brandished spear and sword.*)

235

Scene IX

The Island Cave. Red glow. EGERIUS *and his company.*

EGERIUS.	Laegarius, be the first man To go below the earth's crust.
LAEGARIUS.	I daren't Sir, sky is threatening.
EGERIUS.	Captain, Renew old battle scenes. Hot air Is good. Come, take this celibate's story and cut it short
CAPTAIN.	Why do you joke, My lord, when black clouds hide the smokers Blitching below?
EGERIUS.	Philip – the turn of the youngest
PHILIP.	I have no wish to burn, Sir, For twenty years in slake or brimstone.
LESBIA.	The rain clouds are lower. All is dim, Lake-water and island.
LAEGARIUS.	Stand aside, Egerius. This is suicide.
LESBIA.	Father, come back.
EGERIUS.	Must I decide To stay on earth or go inside The cavern? As Euridyce, Polonia vanished from the springtime. I'll prove these torments are pishogues And rid our homes of superstition. We cast the shadows of our own self-fears, Empty reflections of the spear-heads No smoke has rivetted with iron Can dare to assail the King of Ireland. (*He enters the Cave. The fiery glow is intensified and thunder rumbles.*)
LESBIA.	The cave reddens. (*She goes.*)
PHILIP.	The waters whiten.

This is no place for mortals.
(*He goes.*)

CAPTAIN.   My men
Stand to for instant orders.

LAEGARIUS.   The lightning
Is earthed.
(*He goes.*)

PATRICK.   Manifest, O God
Of Israel, your anger. Smite
Your foes. Send down the fire of Sodom
Upon the unbelievers. Princes
Of Median, Reken, Zur and Hur,
Still march Against the faithful. Hurl
Their chariots of war back. Blight quince,
Unwine the pomegranate, strip down
The vine-stock. Let the strata swallow
Brass altars, curses choke the swallow.
Let foreskins of the Gentiles seize up.
Look down upon the circumcised
In spirit. Reward our host of knees.
Increase and hallow their midnight seed.
(*Storm.* PATRICK *prays like Moses, hands uplifted.*)

ACT THREE

Scene I

A street at night. LUIS *and* PAUL *with lantern.*

PAUL.   Here we are back in Ireland, Sir.
Three days are gone yet you do not stir
From bedroom, cellar, or our tavern
Until the night-time, when the street-walkers
Wait at the corner and windy lantern
Lengthens the shadow of leg and skirt
Below.
          Are we in danger once more?
                        How often
Since you belaboured me in foreign
Parts, I have shivered when your rapier
Was up at the dawn. I was your second,
Rattling my fear with every second
Until my waistband burst.

LUIS.   No danger
Is here.

PAUL.   Then why do you pretend
To be a Spaniard, with pointed beard,
Long hair-trim, mighty ruff, peppering
Dishes with Catalonian swear-words,
Mulling your wine with them? I heard
To-day, elbowing about the market
Fruit stalls, that King Egerius,
Our King, never came back from Hell,
And Lesbia, his younger daughter,
Is Queen. There was a strange rumour
Of poor Polonia.

LUIS.   Don't mention
Her. May she rest. No monument
Can hide the sight of her remains.

PAUL.   But there is something I must tell you.
Patrick, who now is haloed in Heaven,
Raised . . .

LUIS.   Do not speak of him or her.

PAUL.   But, Sir, the Cave . . .

LUIS.   What Cave?

PAUL.   The entrance
> To Purgatory. A mile of waters,
> A misty island in Lough Derg,
> Disclosed it, proved to unbelievers
> A truth beyond the argument
> Of scholars and astrologers
> Who tumble the skies about our ears.

LUIS.   Enough of this.
>   An enemy
> Of mine, a wily courtier,
> Lives in this street, his residence
> Around the corner, twenty steps
> From where we stand. Make ready
> With me to kill him as he enters
> His home.

PAUL.   Sir, runaway legs
> Are better than arms.

LUIS.   The first, the second,
> Night that I waited, my attempt
> Was vain for a heavily cloaked stranger
> Came suddenly between us, silent,
> Grave. I followed. He disappeared.
> To-night the past will be avenged.

PAUL (*softly*).   We're not alone, Sir. Your mysterious
> Comrade is here. Before my legs
> Give out and leave me cobbling the kerb,
> I'll hurry off to an appointment.
> (*He goes.*)

LUIS (*to stranger*). Stop, Sir, I pray you, stop.
> (*Follows him off.*)
> (PAUL *returns.*)

PAUL.   Defend
> Me Saint Anthony of the Thebiad,
> Dishes appear in hot rows, banquets
> Float on the air and lovely women
> With little on, are eyeing me; they bend
> Pink-elbowed on their palace beds,
> Eunuchs unrobe and bath the pets.
> (PHILIP *enters.*)

239

PHILIP.   Fellow, who are you?

PAUL.   Another Sancha
Awaiting that famous duellist,
My master-at-arms.

PHILIP.   I was mistaken.
Three nights in turn, I've seen a stranger
In a black mantle, so tall and slender,
I thought, by God, he had no flesh
Upon his bones. He mongrel'd my steps,
Then disappeared as if I had docked him.

PAUL.   I am fat and greasy, Caballero.
My name is Paul, a cowardly fellow
Returned from Spain, the Netherlands,
My wages shot out of my pocket
By musket ball and cannonade.

PHILIP.   Take this. (*Gives money.*)

PAUL (*pleased*).   O, Sir.
(PHILIP *leaves.*)

PAUL.   Saint Anthony deserted me.
I'll melt this bit of gold in pleasure.
No poxy hairshirt of a hermit
Can ease the seven weeks of Lent.
But where's my master? That great big booby
Of mine has tried to say boo, boo
To bogy, bogle or bugaboo.
(*Clash of swords.*)
What's that?
                  The pair of rapiers
Is out.
(*He goes.* STRANGER *enters followed by* LUIS.)

LUIS.   Stand, Sir, before death challenges
Your jest.
                Who are you?
(LUIS *snatches back the cloak and sees a skeleton.*)

STRANGER.   Luis Enius!

LUIS.   Help, help.
(PAUL *runs in.*)
                Who is it in that jerkin
Of bone?

PAUL.   Poor Paul, your humble servant.
Why have you borrowed my pair of tremblers?

LUIS.   I followed that stranger quickly to end

His insolence but as I leaned
And flung his cloak back by the hem,
To find out his identity, Paul,
Beneath it was a skeleton.

PAUL. Come back to the inn. I am appalled.
We need a large one.

LUIS.   Empty sockets
Were glaring at me. Skulls and pelvis
Were whiter than my ghost. I fell
Into a vision of the Cave
You told me of and I was sinking
To nothingness, and then I wakened
From dream to dream upon the brink
Of Purgatory, borne in spirit
Where human beings are broiled on spits,
Skewered from shank and groin to armpit
Upon the sizzling grills. Across
The narrow Bridge of Dread, twelve miles
In length, Bishops and Kings are tossed
Into the brimstone, heavy pride
Unbreeched. There I was shown a woe
Beyond the martyrings of Rome.
Farewell!
(*He goes, left.*)

PAUL (*to audience*). Old Boney has turned his noddle.
I'll see him on Tib's Eve, God help him!
(*Shawled girl on right,* PAUL *turns and sees her.
She goes. He waits. She returns and smiles. He
winks at audience and follows her.*)

241

Scene II

LUIS *and* POLONIA. *Near Lough Derg.*

LUIS.   God save you, Lady –

POLONIA.   and save you, Sir.

LUIS.   Three days I have journeyed from green to grim,
From light to dark, on a pilgrimage.
For I heard tell in towns of a Cave
Where steps lead down to Purgatory.
Now I am lost in mist. Is it a fireside story?
To frighten sinners?

POLONIA (*pointing*).   Beyond this bog
Blackish with rain, there is an island
Across lake-water, less than a mile from
Reeds. The Cave is under a rock
Half tumbled from the clinging clay.
For centuries in anguished grip, it has remained
About to fall, yet never falling
Despite its mighty weight. The soul
Within us bears as great a load
Of sorrow, knowing in vain the scalding
Of tears. There is a sandy cove
Hidden by rushes where you will find a rowing
    boat.

LUIS.   Lady, how can I find that haven?

POLONIA.   I
Will be your guide, for I have lived
Three years alone here in a withied
Hut, helping travellers who cry
At night from quagmire, sudden bog-pool.
Berries and hazel-nuts from the forest are my food.
The wild goats spare me milk. Kind hands
I have not seen, put oaten bread,
Honey beside a holy well.
I pray for those who think me mad
And fear this place. A little chapel
With carven figures of saints and patriarchs, a
    Chapter

242

House, bless the island. Peace within.
Mists hide it with a weeping silence.
The very rocks weep and the tiles.
Two Canons meditate on sin,
Punished by Purgatory in turn
Before the altar. Candles of pure beeswax burn
There all the day and night.

LUIS (*aside*). The Tempter
Whispers that she is from the grave
And yet those lovely ringlets waver
With the light breeze around her temples.
Who was it died on flowers? Could it
Be my Polonia? I want to know her spirit.

POLONIA (*aside*). He recognises me. I shrink from
The dagger, thrusting my agony,
The nothingness.

LUIS. You do not speak.
Take all the adultery I think
Of even now. Let soul be flamed
In Purgatorial depths until I am unmade.

POLONIA. First, twilled in penitential habit,
You will receive humbly at daybreak
The wine, the unleavened bread, and pray,
Bare-kneed upon the painful grit.
The Canons will unbar the iron
Gate, torching the steps, until they are ruddy with
fire.
The mist is greyer. Here is the boat.
Step in and take the oars. I will
Unknot the rope. See how the spindrift
Is hurrying towards us. It is the will
Of God that storm is coming down
With more of blackness. But He will save you
And bring that ancient boat into its safety.

LUIS. Lady, I thank you with a sigh.
You seem like one I knew, the same
Expression, sorrowful now and grave
As mine.

POLONIA. Luis, I recognised you
The instant that we met. I am
Polonia.

LUIS. Her spirit, then?

243

POLONIA.   No, I came back,
For Patrick brought me out of Limbo,
LUIS.   Undo my crime. I kneel and beg.
POLONIA.   You are forgiven, Luis. The dreaded
Grave calls to both our bodies, the limbs
That mingled once will perish.
LUIS.   Ah,
Too late the love that made us one, Polonia!

Scene III

On the Island, cave on the right, off stage.

1ST CANON.   The mountain mists are thickening,
Day after day.
2ND CANON.   They cling or drift
About the fernless rocks.
1ST CANON.   On pillar
And cornices, the shadowy figures
Of Adam and Eve, the Crucifixion,
Limbo, are scarcely visible.
2ND CANON.   The little echoes in crack and crevice
Around us might have perished.
1ST CANON.   No pilgrim
Has come for many weeks.
2ND CANON.   Listen,
I hear the splash of oars, the click
Of the rowlocks.
1ST CANON.   Come.
LUIS *(enters)*.   Father,
I floated for hours in this coffin, black
And ample, the lake so dark with mist,
The world seemed uninhabited.
Then, suddenly, I saw the landing
Post, heard voices above, ran up
The steps to show these guilty hands.
Quick, Fathers, bring me to the Island
Cave. Conscience sears me. I know the brand
Of Cain.
1ST CANON.   My son, be patient. Sinners
Cannot repent so quickly, rid
Themselves of what they have done.
                                                            Beginning
Is less than end. The fast and shrift
Come first.
LUIS.   I have the necessary
Permission.
                        Break the seal and wax

245

A Bishop endorsed.

1ST CANON.

Dear Son, consider
The danger of the Cave, the risk,
For many pilgrims have entered it.
Few have come out.

LUIS.

Reverend Canon,
How can I tell you of the scandals,
The crimes, of one too passionate
In life to live. The very Spaniards
Whose cities I have known, shrank back
From one whose violence was so black with
Adultery, rape, manslaughter.
How often I have been balconied,
Deceiver of dark-eyed women, husbands,
Escaping from the scented arms
That held me, breasts that would have damned
A hermit! How could such fury last?
Incest came next: a tall, handsome
Step-sister of mine. I schemed, I planned,
Then scaled at night the hush on the bastion
Of a great convent, unkeyed, captured,
That prize and clasping her on my saddle,
Rode to her violation in darkness.
Perverted by demons, I tried to pander
Her body, see it in the act.
She fled one night into sanctuary.
Banished from Catalonia,
I wandered through France, the Netherlands,
Came back and saw in vision this island
Cave; shadowy figures writhing in pain
Beckoned and pointed to the flames
Below.

I cannot wait.

1ST CANON.

Then stay awhile
Until this Father and I instruct you.
A sudden pain is ready to trip you
Upon the steps. Endure it. Go quickly
Down to the last step.

2ND CANON.

Vertigo,
The son of ancient Madness, sits there,
Whirlwindily, above the pit,
Trying to catch up with his smithers,

246

<pre>
                         All dots and dotted dashes spinning
                         Around each other, soot-black or lit
                         By sparks.
1ST CANON.   When eyeballs, legs, are giddy,
                         The dream will sweat you out of your skin,
2ND CANON.   The horror and the void begin.
1ST CANON.   Reflect again upon the risk.
LUIS.   I cannot wait.
1ST CANON.   You are determined?
LUIS.   Yes.
1ST CANON.   Then come with us.
               (Sound of bolts. Hollow footsteps.)
LUIS.   Father,
               I am within the Cave.
               (He cries out.)
                              A dagger
               Has pierced beneath my left pap.
               (Faintly.)
                                        I pass
               To nothing.
                         Help, help me.
1ST CANON.   I fear for him.
2ND CANON.   Look how the mist is deepening.
               Demon and saint dissolve from pillars.
1ST CANON.   Adam, Eve, wake. The Crucifixion
               Begins.
2ND CANON.   The forest depth is astir.
1ST CANON.   Short legs pursue:
2ND CANON.   The long ones bolt.
1ST CANON.   Come let us push the bar and bolt.
               (They go, sound of clanging gates.)
</pre>

Scene IV

The two CANONS *cross stage to Cave.* POLONIA, LESBIA, PHILIP, LAEGARIUS, CAPTAIN *enter.*

LESBIA.   Before you have brought us near
                The Cave, tell us why we are led
                From green to grimness of mist, water,
                To see the spot where Father, like Empedocles,
                Was follied to flame.

POLONIA.   Dear Lesbia, soon you will see the will
                Of God, strike down on us in light,
                But while we are waiting, speak to me of your
                    own troubles.

LESBIA.   Polonia, you have lived three years here, light
                Of heart, though chilled under a rough
                Roof-tree by drip of rain, your soul at peace,
                And left with me the crown,
                (*Pointing.*)
                As heavy as that rock which seems to fall down,
                Yet never falls, but clings with centuries
                As we to our mortal clay.
                I need a husband now to help me rule
                This much divided land. My very sleep
                Has gone from me. My daily thought is foolish
                As notes that jig in a sunray.

POLONIA.   Then, marry Philip, he is pure and good,
                Noble by birth.

LESBIA.   If he will take his queen,
                I will.

PHILIP.   Marsh-marigolds are at my feet.
                I walk through flowers.

POLONIA.   God bless you both and bless your children. Now
                The moment comes. A man
                Whom all of you have known, stricken
                By pangs of conscience, eager
                To rid himself at last of wickedness
                Within the island-cave,
                Has fallen, unbridged, into the flaming leagues

         Of purgatory with fellow-sinners whose day
         Is done. Last night I prayed and seemed to share,
         In vision, his fate, one with that tortured one
         Forever.

LAEGARIUS.   The monks are swinging back the gate.

CAPTAIN.   Flung up by demons to keep that pilgrim burning,
         Lava and brimstone try to reach the air.
         (*Sound of gates. Hollow steps are heard.*)

ALL.   Luis Enius!
         (LUIS *enters wildly and leaves, left, his voice still
         heard.* POLONIA *follows him.*)

LUIS.   The Day of Judgment comes.
                       Repent!
         Repent! Valley and mountain shake with wrath
         Of the Almighty. My spirit has been pent
         In terror and despair. What zigzag pathway
         Can aid the flying feet upward to rock
         Or hidden crevice where the hungry beast
         Is laired or carry down the evil body to
         Hideous forest?

ECHOES.   – O rest! . . . rest!

CURTAIN

NOTE: Few of the thousands of our pilgrims who visit Lough Derg every year have heard of Calderon's play, *El Purgatorio de San Patricio* of which this is a free adaptation. The original patterns of rhyme and assonance are kept. Assonance in Spanish verse is peculiar for it is used in lengthy passages in which each line ends with the same vowel sound. 'Perfect rhyme' or *rime riche* is used occasionally in this adaptation as a novelty.

    Black-outs can be used between the scenes; the places may be indicated by simple, conventionalized cut-outs.

The Characters wear Spanish costumes of the 17th Century.

The Frenzy of Sweeny

A LYRICAL PLAY

CHARACTERS

SWEENY, *King of Dalaradia*
EORANN, *his wife*
COLGAN, *his brother-in-law*
ST. RONÁN
THE HAG OF THE MILL
THE SWINEHERD'S WIFE
THE MADMAN OF BRITAIN CARADOC
ST. MOLING
THE SWINEHERD
MAELMORE, *second husband of Eorann*
MONKS and others
HALLUCINATORY FIGURES:
Centurion, Scribe, Sheela-na-Gig, Irish runner,
The Greenman, Decapitated Heads, Conal and Emer

ACT ONE

Scene I

Sound of storm. A bare stage with different levels. SWEENY *is seen in a central spot, heavily bearded, shaggy-haired, ragged. Towards the end of his soliloquy, the other characters in the play appear in the background, dimly lit, watching him.*

SWEENY.   Run, run to the sailmaker –
While I pluck the torn white hedges
Of sea to crown my head –
And tell him to bind hard the canvas
For the waves are horseheaded to-night;
I cracked a thought between my nails
That they will light a candle
When I swim from the loud sea-grass
To the oratory of Moling.

Storm is masted in the oakwood
Now and the fire of the hag
Blown out by the tide: in wet smoke
Mannanaun splashes by with a bagful
Of music to wager for the food
In a hall where the women mull
Ale; workmen dream of their furnace
And the male jewels that are alive:
But I hear the hounds of the black queen race.
As I nest in the drenching ivy.

The rain is drowning in Glenveigh
Where once the vats of brightness poured
Until the wet green branches hid
The long ridge of the boar:
Garlic was good there and the pignut;
Upon the tops of the wells
A tender crop was rooted –
But the wild man in the water
Was feathered like a hawk to the foot.

253

I hurried at evening
From the glen of birches
When longer shadows
Were cropping
Their way: on a sudden,
Darkness was nearer,
Hazels had ripened,
I heard the rain drop.

Far down a hollow
Of sloe-trees, a bird
Ran under the fences
Of rain, for a tall man
Followed, his one eye
Redder than turf
When it is stirred:
Far down the hollow
Sloe-bushes ran.

A drove of boulders
Was crossing the ford:
O to what household
Do you hurry unbidden
Swineherd, Red Swineherd,
That men may carouse?
Breathe on their eye-lids,
And bound to the rafters
May three naked women drip
Blood; in their hearing,
Strange laughter and rapine
Of phantoms that tumble
From nothing, till fear
Empty the bladder,
Swineherd, Red Swineherd,
And shadows madden
The heart like a drum.

I hurried to the paddock
While stablemen were brawling
And under the bellies
Of horses I crawled:
Dark, dark was the harness,
(The wheelwright said I was mad)

But I flung back the lock,
Bolt, loosed forty hoofs to
The storm in the grass.

A juggler cried. Light
Rushed from doors and men singing;
'O she has been wedded
To-night, the true wife of Sweeny,
Of Sweeny the King!'
I saw a pale woman
Half clad for the new bed:
I fought them with talons, I ran
On the oak-wood – O Horsemen,
Dark Horsemen, I tell ye
That Sweeny is dead!

Stark in the rushlight
Of the lake-water,
I heard the heads talking
As they dipped on the stake;
Who runs with the moon
When ravens are asleep?
It is Sweeny, Little Sweeny,
Looking for his mind.
I broke the horns of a goatherd
For I heard them on the water
Call: *Sweeny, Little Sweeny*
Is looking for his mind.
But Robbers, dark Robbers, I tell ye
That Sweeny is dead!

If I sleep now, the hag
Of the haggard will steal
My feathers, though I drowned her
In the pool of Achill
That has no sound.

When tides were baying
The moon, in a glen
Of stone, I fed on
Grey cowdung: a hundred
Men hauling a slab
Upon the great dolmen
Of Sweeny the King, fled

255

From the shovels and barrow.
Nailing, I dug up
The gold cup, the collar,
And hid them in rain.
But how can mind hurry
As reeds without feet,
And why is there pain in
A mind that is dead?

I have heard the little music
Of Midna, I have seen
Tara in flame and a blooded moon
Behind the Ridge of Judgment . . .
But how can they find out my name
Though they are crying like gulls
That search for the sea?
Nine years, I hurried from mankind
And yet, O Christ, if I could sail
To the rock-isle of the Culdees,
I would sleep, sleep awhile,
By the blessing of Saint Moling.
(*Black out. Storm. Voice of* SWEENY *is heard.*)

SWEENY.   That otter
Again. That otter whiskering the water.
Why must I dream of what he carries in
His mouth?
(*Morning light reveals the stage again.* St. Ronán
*with monks measuring the land outside the royal
house, which is off stage left.* Sweeny *rushes in clad
in a nightshirt, followed by his wife in nightdress, but
wrapped in a cloak.*)

RONÁN (*sternly*)   Sweeny,
Sweeny, King of Dalaradia,
Go back to bed.

EORANN.   Come, dearest.
                   (*explaining*) Urether
Will scald him if chill of the grass strike up.
(*Raising her hands.*)
                                  Then,
Blankets and pints of barley water.

SWEENY.   Ronán,
I heard your monks plotting again, shovel

To spade.

RONÁN.   We are here to build a church by the lake-side
And the foundations are already footed.
(*Rapt.*)
A church with roof pent as the Ark, archway
With carven heads of Bishops in a row,
Pillars with intertwined serpents, bead-knot
In semi-circle, champhering. The stone
Will sing to us of Prime, the latch of book-shrine
Conceal the Latin uncials within
Silver reliquaries, the rattle of hand-bells,
Bees will bring wax to candle the altar,
The deer come to our green.

SWEENY.   Ronán, be off
With your illuminations: turn about,
The only gift you'll get from me.

RONÁN.   In a vision,
God sent me to this favoured spot. Three times
The vision stood up with wing-beats as I lay
Asleep at Cluanmacnoise.

SWEENY.   Not vision but pride
Has warmed your truckle. Fasting, hand-bell in fist,
Will never own a sod of mine. Be off.
Obey the secular law at once.

RONÁN.   Sweeny,
Your word will call up darker wing-beats.

SWEENY.   Why
Should King fear any threat?
(*He seizes the saint's psalter.*)

RONÁN.   Stop, hand will burn
For this. Come, give me back that blessed psalter.
(*Sweeny goes right, and hurls it into the lake, off stage. A splash.*)

SWEENY.   Frogman
May dive for it.

MONKS.   Look, Father, look,
A miracle for our pens.

                           See how that otter
Goes down,
           comes up,
                    mouthing it to the shallows,
(*Slower.*)

Then lays it,
    Respectfully,
        among the bullrushes,
As though it were the infant Moses in
His wicker cradle –
      and awaits your blessing.
(*St. Ronán blesses the otter.*) The red,
      the purple ink,
Run off with the lettering.
       The Gospel of
Saint Luke is unvowelled.
        But Saint Matthew in his smock,
Goes dry-shod.

RONÁN.   Sweeny, bad King, I put a curse
On you.

EORANN. Stop, holy Father, my husband repents
That throw. His temper is always short as grit
Before he has topped his breakfast egg.

RONÁN.   Lady,
He will repent in the Devil's own time.
(*To* SWEENY.)
        Run, barefoot,
Wandering, witless, in the big Forest
Of Munster, in rain, ragged, feathered from crown
To foot, sprint on to the springiness of trees,
Your shivers hidden in cleft, on ridge, your palsies
In river pools. Run, run with taggle of screechers
Who hurry to Glen Bolcan. Up into the air,
Next month and be damned to you.

EORANN (*as he leaves with* MONKS). O may the Dove
Unparaclete your tongue.
       Come back to our feather
Bed. Dear. You need a drop of the 'creature'.
(*She wraps her cloak around* SWEENY *as they leave.
Black out. Sound of drumming, battle cries. The voice
of* SWEENY *is heard.*)

SWEENY. Why must I dream of death again?
(*Sounds of battle off, as the stage brightens.* SWEENY
*enters, wearing crown. Shadows of soldiers on
cyclorama.*)

SWEENY.   Am I
That ill-fated King of Dalaradia?

Is this bare plain the battlefield
Of Moyra unrolled by careful scribe or monk
On vellum?
                    Fear plucks, stomachs my kneecaps, men
Come out of their wounds, shapeless as cries,

                                                            Brand
Is weapon that strikes in prongs. Fork is a pitfall,
(*As shadows pass across the cyclorama.*)
Look there, there, in his yellow cloak. Congal
Goes by with Maeldun, Andrach, Brasil, the Bard,
Ardaun, Drostair, the Druid. Their blood stumbles,
From thickets. Blade in hand, come Garrad Gann,
Fergus, Ailill and Aulas of the rock-holed
Ships.
            Deep in a covert, Domnall Breas,
Aed Purple-Mantle, Congal Maen, Art, Rgys
And Howell hide under a battle-bush. Half-gone,
Maddened at heel, I see great Congal Claen
Hover in air. See, balder than a goose-egg,
Cuanna, the Fool, has cast a little dart up
At him.
                    Fear plucks the ravel of silk sleeves
From me.
                    I charge into the chilling arms
Of our religion.
(*As stage darkens, the voice of* ST. RONÁN. *is heard.*)

RONÁN.   Sweeny, Sweeny,
Late King of Dalaradia, run, barefoot
Wandering, witless, into the big Forest
Of Munster, in rain, feathered from crown
To craw, alight on the springiness of trees,
Your shivers hidden in cleft, on ridge, your palsies
In river pools. Run, run, with the struggle of screechers
Who go to Glen Bolcan. Up, up, into
The air.
(SWEENY *casts off his crown, waves his arms up and
down, rises in the air and flies off, right.*)

Scene II

(A forest edge, mountains in distance. Stage has several levels.)

SWEENY.　Cold, cold, the snow-storm, cold the winter
　　　　　That bars and bolts, the months that wince.
　　　　　Half-naked, I clamber to misfortune,
　　　　　Thornbush whistles a dreary tune.

　　　　　Once I was ruler of a kingdom,
　　　　　Now I am homeless, without kin,
　　　　　Without company, without music.
　　　　　My horses stale in their mews.

　　　　　I, who had shirts of fine linen,
　　　　　Must wander by snowing brake and linn.
　　　　　They say that I unpaged the Psalter
　　　　　Of Ronán. No bread or piece of salt

　　　　　Is mine. I hop from treetop to mountain-
　　　　　Top, preen on an icy precipice, mount
　　　　　The wind that blows me to the pinewood.
　　　　　On sorrel, on half-dried roots, I pine.

　　　　　Gallant my entries for the cup-race.
　　　　　Mangers are empty. Days erase
　　　　　My memory. All has a limit,
　　　　　All but the aching in my limbs.

　　　　　See how my wife undoes her girdle
　　　　　For a new husband. She girds at
　　　　　Me, thinks that I am dead. Distressing
　　　　　Story; she walks out in a gay dress.

　　　　　Far, far, from illumination, reading,
　　　　　I splash wearily to a reed-bed.
　　　　　Once I was flattered by the bardic
　　　　　Benchers. Now the high door is barred.

　　　　　Cold, cold, the snow-storm, hard the winter

260

That bars and bolts, the months that wince.
Half-naked, I clamber to misfortune,
Fall half-asleep in a faery fort.

How can I find a lasting foothold
On cliff or in gully? Inch is a foot.
Once I was seated at the banquet,
Now sit alone on a river bank.

I pluck and crack my store of filberts,
Soft is in hard. I eat my fill.
A saint drove me into rainstorm.
The winter sun has a watery ray.

When the new ale is topping the flagon,
What shelter is in the withered flag?
My wife has bared her lovely haunch
To another husband. I groan and munch

A stalk. I offended the man with the halo
And now I am scarecrowed by sleet and hail. O
I chucked away his heavenly budget.
He stands his ground. He will not budge.

(*A hooded figure is seen near him.*)

Pool is a lake. River is breaking
In a brown flood over bush, brake,
Now. Torrents are whiter around the inches.
A man secretes, though stomach pinch.

(COLGAN, *the miller, disguised as a monk, comes
forward.*)

SWEENY (*aside*). A trick of air.
COLGAN.   Sweeny, Sweeny
Five winters have kept your rags unseen.
Half-light of reason is in your eyes now.
Pot fills. Your kindred wait: surprise
At every door.
                              Come
                                        To my dwelling, rest
In comfort. I have searched in many a forest,
On the islands of Lough Ree, enquired
At monastic doors from acolytes, choir-men,
Bannered your name.

SWEENY   I will not parley
With you. I am no servant of my past.
I shelter in Glen Bolcan, dine
On cress and brooklime, far from the sign
Of cross.
                      But on a rainy Tuesday
I'll kneel outside a chapel: shoeless,
Confess my wicked sleep. I know you
By the little eye peeping from drugget cloak,
My wily Colgan.
                        Men will spring
From bush, women with barndoor fingers
Wait to singe my feathers.
(*Light dims. The figure retires, unhoods, revealing
Sweeny's wife.*)

SWEENY.   Eorann,
My wife, here. Everyday I random
On mountain ledge or in the forest.
I lie on dampness, scarcely rest.

You frolic at night with a new husband,
While I am under saintly ban.
I lose my strength in sleep: torment,
Affliction of unmarried men.

You have forgotten your old friend, your warmth
Thighing with his in bed. Great wars
Were fought for women. Our pastime
Was double and dear in the past.

Joyful at night the secret sharing
Of one flesh. Now, in the rain, I seek
An ivy tod: sleet coming down.
You stretch a yawn on the pure down.

EORANN.   Sweeny, dear friend, I want to stay here
With you and be your night-warmth, your stay,
Under the misting trees, comfort
To you when hunger, hardship, come.

Remember how often after my flowers,
I sweetened myself with elder flowers
For you. I sigh for the sowing I shared in:
I was the furrow, you, the share.

SWEENY.   Am I a seedsman?

EORANN.   I was told
You died.

SWEENY.   Although no bell was tolled?
Who said it?

EORANN.   Ronán, the wicked saint.
He had a vision.

SWEENY.   Another trick
To clip my feathers.
                    You are a phantom.
Can shadow get by shadow, bear, in fact?

EORANN.   Come, lie with me, I'll prove it.
                              Touch
Is go, although your words are touching.
(*He touches her arms and steps back.*)

SWEENY.   Woman, I fear an ambush. (*Pointing.*)
Men could be birds in that bush.

EORANN.   Wait, wait.

SWEENY.   Eorann, you are too fair
For sleep beneath a cromlech.
                              I fare
Alone.

EORANN.   I hear the red stag belling
His mate.

SWEENY.   I am summoned to Moy Mell.
(*He leaves. Black out. Voice of* SWEENY.)

SWEENY.   Where am I?
(*Turning, as faint light comes up.* CENTURION *above.*)

CENTURION.   Hi, there! What century
Is this?

SWEENY.   The wrong one?
                              (*To himself.*) Try
Again.
          Look, look, from gulling rain,
There in a sprint of sunlight,
That comes to earth, makes light
Of every step, runners
Are racing into shelter,
But no word comes. What ails them?
Is there slumber in new ale?

But see, the Queen of the red-heads

263

Has guessed at their tidings.
Before a mouth is ready,
She drops a needle-stitch,
Says all that is needful.
There is nothing on the tide,
Not even a sail or hull in
The harbour. What woe betides?
She stands by a blue-green web,
Calls out, 'Cuchullin!'

Clang of the armourers
As they scour the weapons.
Iron in strength of arm
And shoulder-blade has slept
Too long. They exercise
Stab, uppercut, thrust.
Shadows, double their size,
Mock from the wall as they must.
Tame falcons, in alarm,
Stoop to the doors, are gone.

Hooded by rainstorm,
Miling from Connaught,
By cloud, hill-water
They fly up
The air, gold-rust
On wings. That rustle
By cairn is a hawk,
Supper in claw.

I know that taboo
Of the hero.
                    Cuchullin
Dare not behold
Bare women. That is
The fit, the death-hold.
(*Listening, right.*)
Ah! hullaballoo
As Maeve commands
Girls, women, to strip of clothes
And shame. No man is
Left, only whiteness.

At the open door-ways,

A row of whiteness,
Cheeks pale, for fear
Cannot blush.
Inside the cheer of clothes:
They have stopped the onrush
Of the Ulstermen.
Cuchullin, eyes closed,
Fiery-faced, stern,
Lifting his shield,
Flies; Ulster before
Him. Charioteers
Are gone as the tears
Of women and girls half
Turn to laughter.
(*Left, a scribe is seen at his desk by candlelight.*)
Mochua, the scribe,
Looks up at his candle,
That hurries each page
For the ink is alive.
To-night he is penning
The best of all stories,
But what is its name?
(*Steals left, looks over shoulder of scribe.*)
The Intoxication, I know it,
Of the Ulstermen.

Ignoring the Border,
The pickets, they drove
Far south. Valley, rock
And hill are disorderly
With rumble of echoes
As the horses gallop
On, short neck to neck,
Unable to stop.

I'll call on my bard
To warn them.
(*Goes right.*)
(*Loudly.*) That house is
Constructed of iron.
Emergency exits
Are bolted and barred,
Beneath is a pit

Of faggoted fire.

Barrelled, kegged, tunned,
The Ulstermen snore.
But Cuchullin is rousing
The dormitory,
He jumps to his feet
Now. Is he too late
To perform a new feat? . . .

Now come the druids,
Raising a wall
Of darkness with cry
And cauterwaul.
Nem, Dak and Druithen,
The doorkeepers, bolt in
The northerners
Who try to bolt out.

Jewels in that darkness,
Open and glisten,
Emerald, garnet,
Amethyst.
Conall, then, Briecriu,
Grab for a fistful.
All blink, blow out,
Change into hissing
Pots that boil over.

Blackness is fire,
Scratch is a scald,
Nails come from claws.
Heroes are bawling
As jewels leap up
Leggily, meet
Every yell with hiss,
Miaow, or growl.
The warriors cower
From druidic mist.

I leap from the cattery
Of Cruachan, spells,
Enchantment, around me,
Swim down the centuries,

Drip from Shannon,
To the heaven-sent
Monks, with their spelling-
Books under the Round Tower
Of Inish Scattery.
(*A red light glows around him. He staggers forward.*
The scribe disappears.)
Always the same story.
I am lost in the flame of
Saint Patrick's Purgatory.
(*Black out.*)

ACT TWO

Scene I

The Forest. COLGAN *enters.* SWEENY *looks down from a tree,*
behind the proscenium.

COLGAN.   Sweeny, I am your foster-brother
Come before the hard frost.
Sad the tidings that are spreading.
Your father, mother, are dead.

SWEENY.   Sad, indeed, is that heavy news,
Worse than ever I knew.
A mourner, stripped by the pitiless,
I stare into a pit.

COLGAN.   Another and more grievous tiding
That came with the ebb-tide:
Your gentle wife is dead from grieving.
Why do you shake the leaves?

SWEENY.   Household without a gentle housewife,
That is to die without housel.
O Colgan, this is the heart's needle,
That cold that none can feel.

COLGAN.   Fearful and loud what I relate now,
Sorrow that comes too late.
Your loving sister is dead, no respite
In a world of spite.

More sorrows come in a great number,
A woe that makes me numb:
Your winsome daughter went in autumn,
A child who was never naughty.

More, more, poor King, your little son
Has gone from play and sunlight.
Never on hill or in holding,
Will a mother coax or hold him.

268

SWEENY.   Here is the sink of misery
             Deeper than Lough Ree,
             The babe that prattled, 'Dadda, Dadda',
             Memory, memory, will dandle.
             (SWEENY *comes down from his tree.*)

COLGAN (*smiling*). This is our green road. Come with me,
                  eastward.
             Happiness, happiness, feast.
             All are alive in Ulster, and happy,
             All, are waiting without mishap.

             Though you have roamed by the Twelve Pins
             Of Connaught, far from tirl-pin,
             Too long, my Sweeny, you have pondered
             By holly tree, hill, pond,

             Climbed the heights of Glen Bolcan. Here,
             Come to the mill-house by the weir.
             Barber will lather, shave you, wash, trim
             Locks, and make your person trim.

             (*He leads away the dazed* SWEENY. *Black out. In the mill-house, suggested by drapes,* HAG, *in hooded cloak, on stool by turf fire.* SWEENY *plucks invisible strings. A few harp notes.*)

SWEENY.   Stag on the westward ridge, melodious
             One, clamourer with your high nodes
             Of point and time. Below, the roe-bucks
             Are grazing in a dappled row.

             Oak, mighty one, my shelterer,
             I lie beneath you, acorn in shell.
             Crush of your bark will cure a mastoid,
             Swine root among the years of mast.

             The water-willow is never hostile.
             I pull down wetness, cross green stile.
             Frail blossom of the catkin. Baskets
             Are woven, supple as your sap.

             The wicked blackthorn, claws sharp as Pangur
             Baun's. Each prickle is a pang.

Appetite has been well sustained by
Those berries, juicy, darksome, stainful.

The yew-tree, gloomer in churchyard. Coffins
Go under it, funeral cough.
The yewy yew thickens: a sturdy
One. Winds blow strong. It is unstirred.

Aspen, the trembler, leaves a-racing
Fast as competitions in Thrace.
I hear within it the sound of fray.
That whispering makes me afraid.

Hateful the ash, a nub for chariot.
Let every branch above be charred.
Avoid the ash that brings contention.
Quarrel on chessboard, blows in tent.

Apple tree shaken by many hands,
Wider spreader out of pink bloom, handsome
One. Bark for tanning, wealth in garden.
Sweet crop that every man must guard.

Elder that women strain, boil twice.
The bark will dry the pus in boil.
Out of the flowers will come a greenness.
Dyers make the dark and the pale be seen.

Holly, cold light in woods, silver
As winter moon, icedrip from sill.
The leaves are fierce and disagreeable
Although they glitter like filagree.

Pleasant the whiteness of the May,
I smell and pluck it while I may,
Go by it in the twilight, listen
To music coming from rath and liss.

Pleasant, also, the lofty beech
That comes down to the river beach.
Under the shady shade, I drag
My weariness, sore-footed, bedraggled.

Briar, deceitful friend, you hold me

With tiny fingers, unholy one,
Drawing a drop from small or big vein.
I jump away. Your tricks are vain.

Birch, the smooth, the blessed, sent down
From Heaven, with summer grace and scent,
Delicate one: breezes are leaving
Half of your sweetness with other leaves.

Dear hazel, bring an end to my story,
Pantry of plenty, my winter store.
Sweet, sweet, is the brown-covered kernel:
Good bite for galloglass and kern.

Stag of the topmost ridge, melodious
One, clamourer with your high nodes
Of point and time. Below, the roe-bucks
Are grazing in a dappled row.
(*The* HAG *wakes up and does a few jig steps. He
whistles a tune and capers with her.*)

HAG. Come on and sport your rags, Sweeny
The Mad, compete with shank and shin
Until your ears are dinning.
We'll take the Twenty-seven Leaps
Through Ireland. Up, man, follow your leader
From Kilmacduagh to Inish Celtra,
Tubber-na-Molt to Tulach Minn
And Tulach Mulaga, thick by thin,
Over the causey to Loch Erne
Mock holy figures by the doorway.
See in a somersault the Round Tower
On Inish Scattery turn, then bounce
Across Lough Derg to Ossory,
By the cross at Ferns, newly embossed,
To Killimure, with folderol,
By stick and stone. You lead, I'll follow.
We'll swim to the Skelligs. In a skelter
Of holiness, we'll randy it, outswive
The heavenly conjunction.

SWEENY. (*She jigs.*) I won't ride
An old gee-gee. Men would deride
That mount.

271

With every leap, your twattle
Is noisier. Ugly your twuzz, your twat.
I will not tweak or tweedle it
Because you're in your jumping fit.
No diddied hag will diddle me,
For I remember with whom I did it,
When young. Why do you giggle
Like Sheela-na-gig?
(*Casting off the hooded cloak, she appears as a
beautiful young girl, naked but for cusp and* cache-
sexe.)

Who's this,
Nearer than kisses
Or tongue in cheek?
Have I been fooled
Again and cheated,
Tierna of meekness,
Tierna, night-schooled?
Our celibates
Despise and hate you
For the tick pollutes
Their sleep and they wake
Alone. In stews
Of Antioch,
High Rome, in knocking
Shops of Tyre,
You bring confusion,
Strip and tire men.
At the Nun's House
In Clonmacnoise,
You glide by, noiseless,
Squat in the night-time
Below the key-stone,
The carven groyne.
Dark is your groin.
Let niche be shown
To lie-a-lone, cut
By the sculptor's tool.
Wide-open to greet us,
Tierna of meekness,
Tierna, night-schooled.

THE GIRL. Come, Sweeny, let us play a game
Of Hunkers, then, Cut-a-cootcho and Hornio.
(*She cloaks herself, and crouching down, hops
around and out, followed by* SWEENY, *who does
likewise. A pause.* COLGAN *comes in, hurries to door
and shouts.*)

COLGAN. Call the men up.
                              Sound the horn.
The King has forgotten himself again
And run away with the mill-hag
She must have got her jumping fit.
Quick, me, pursue them from hill to haggard
And take them in their doss.
(*Alone, determined.*)
                              Crown fitted
Too narrowly.
                     I'll make him fit
To rule this land, do what is fitting.
(*He hurries out. Sound of men, horn, in distance.*)

Scene II

Morning. Outside the Oratory of St. Moling, which is off stage, left.
WIFE OF MONGAN, *the swineherd, barefoot, lightly clad, enters,*
pours milk into a hollowed cow-pat. Leaves. SWEENY *crawls in on*
hands and knees, laps milk, gets up. She returns.

SWEENY.   Nine
        Succubi all in a blissing night.
        Good Heavens, have I become in age a modern
        Sex-maniac or is it prostatitis?
SWINEHERD'S WIFE. Dampness is on clothes line. The dawn is chill.
        Come closer, wild man, with your shadow.
        I have a story for you. My husband
        Has gone to Tobber with a sow
        That wants the boar. He won't be back
        Till noon. I have a dish of sowans
        Ready. Strike in. First I will tub you
        With lashings of warming water, uncrab you
        Quickly with smearing of lead ointment
        My mother – rest her – gave me.
SWEENY.   You would
        Betray me fast as the one who left me
        In trouble.
SWINEHERD'S WIFE. I have the very cure
        For that.
              Have I not put milk out
        For you before the clover could dry
        At morning?
SWEENY.   Dunting with heel, you made a hole
        In cowdung, filled it that I might know
        Humility.
SWINEHERD'S WIFE. Wild man, I feared
        Your flightiness.
        (*Drawing him close.*)
                See, how I long
        For you.
SWEENY (*puzzled*). Hawthorn in blossom and yet

Two berries.

(*A few harp notes.*)

Pleasant the whiteness of the May.

I smell and pluck it while I may.

Go by it in the twilight, listen

To music coming from rath and liss.

SWINEHERD'S WIFE. Will you not climb the tree?

SWEENY (*withdrawing*).   They sent you

To truss me, pluck and singe my feathers

When I am skewered.

SWINEHERD'S WIFE.   Maybush is yours,

Blossom and haw, another whiteness

That you can guess at.

SWEENY.   Are you a hawthorn

That changes into an airy woman

When touched? At night they rustle my bed

Of bracken. Their lips are half asleep,

Bodies as warm as summer, but frigid

Within. They freeze my courage into

A stalagmite. I fear yet burn

Like a discalced monk.

(MOLING *enters, reading breviary, passes them with
averted eyes. Sound of prayer from Oratory, then
loud slapping, groans, a yell.*)

SWEENY (*alarmed*).   What's that?

SWINEHERD'S WIFE. He's thinking of me, the dirty fellow.

His Fear-go-suck-a-duck-egg left him.

SWEENY (*puzzled, then smiling*). You mean his *Virgo subinducta.*

SWINEHERD'S WIFE. That's it.

He wants me to tempt him o' nights,

Closer, closer, until he has to

Jump into a tub of icy water

Out of his fry-pan.

Come, my Latin

Scholar, your tub will be a hot one

And veil your modesties in rising

Steam.

What is it?

SWEENY.   I left my staff

And scrip within the wood. I'll follow

You.

(*She leaves. Slapping sound and yell from chapel.*)

(*To audience.*)
    It's time to emigrate!
(*He rises into the air.*)

ACT THREE

Scene I

A forest in Britain. Enter, right, left, SWEENY *and* CARADOC.

CARADOC.   Who are
You?
SWEENY.   Sweeny, once King of Dalaradia, Madman
Of Ireland.
                    Who are you?
CARADOC.   Caradoc, once
A Chief, now Madman of Britain.
                                        Why have you left
Your country?
SWEENY.   Not hard to tell.
                                        Wood-spies found out
Nine of my ninety bracken, moss and ivy
Beds.
CARADOC.   How did you quit your mind?
SWEENY.   Scrofulous Saint
Cursed me because I forbade him to rubble, plot,
A church in my best grazing land. He feathered,
Crawed, roosted me.
                    What happened you?
CARADOC.   Aelfric,
My enemy, gave me juice of an Arabic
Root, flavoured with almond. I went into a dump
And cannot wake although I keep knocking my
          noodle
On every oak, big rock, nor can I snooze, for
I must inspect the military camps,
Sneaking by fosse, dug-out, into the bath-house,
Where naked generals lie as if they were
In Rome, while a few lictors play at chuck-stone
Within the porch.
SWEENY.   I talked with Fintan, the Salmon
Under the Falls at Assaroe. His fishy

277

Eye troubled my mind.
                One night, I strode the goat-path
Up Slievenamon. The faery woman drew me
Into her Palace of Quickenberries, red lips,
Around me, bodies warm as summer: inside,
Such chill that I was stalagmited by one
Of them. All disappeared. I crept under
The heather-tops at dawn, to pluck ripe fraughans
For breakfast, wandered, came to a precipice
Above Glen Bolcan. Down below, twin brooks
Shallowed with watercress and in the oakwood,
Sorrel was salad, hazels hung with thicker
Nuts. Droves of wild pigs were unyearing the mast
And there in the ivy-tods I had a dozen
Beds. Dear to me Glen Bolcan.

CARADOC.   I was with Arthur,
Hid under the Round Table, saw certain kneecaps
Touch, fingers creep along the thigh, undo
Chain-mail. I recognised the loving hand
Of Guenivere caressing her Launcelot
Between the meat and the sweet. He spilled brown
      gravy
That Sunday on his surcoat.

SWEENY.   I was with Fionn
MacCumhail, hunting a boar out of his lair.
The pines, red-stemming at dawn, darkened as clouds
Came over the slope of the Slieve Bloom mountains;
              we crossed three fords,
Grounded him in the Glen of Aherlow.
He turned and killed me. I woke in a great light:
Patric, the Son of Calpurn, had raised me from
The dead.
(*Sound of drumming. Scene darkens.*)
        What's that?

CARADOC.   A mighty herd of stallions
Comes at a gallop from the Saxon downs.
For Cerne, the Giant, unchalking himself, big club
In fist, strides up the shadowy dales to shake
The woods.
        Hide here.
(*They crouch beneath a hedge.*)
          – God of fertility.

I pray to loaf and wine.

SWEENY.   And so do I.

CARADOC.   They multiplied their blessings among mankind.

SWEENY.   Before this was hidden beneath
            Monastic frock.
            (*Scene brightens. They get up.*)

CARADOC.   O, by the way, how did
            You travel here?

SWEENY.   By air.

CARADOC (*astonished*).   By air?

SWEENY.   Yes.

            I am an airman.
                           Feel my horse-power wings.
            Ala Spuria.
                        Primaries.
                                    Secondaries,
            Remiges.
            (*Turning.*)
            The Rectrices –
                           tail-feathers.
                                        See. Aristotle –
            Historia Animalium.
                           Daedalus
            Could not have made a better pair.

CARADOC.   Daedalus?

SWEENY.   Inventor.
                    He gave us –
            The wedge, the axe, the wimple –
            (*Explaining.*)
                                            brace and bit.
            Likewise the mainsail, jibber and the spinmaker.

CARADOC.   And wings, you said?

SWEENY.   His keys to Heaven.
            (*He plucks invisible strings. A few harp notes.*)
            (*Recites.*)
            The middle-aged wife of Minos,
            A King of ancient Crete,
            Became so indiscreet.
            She fell in love with a bull.
            Although her husband bullied
            Her, nothing could appease
            That woman but the peazle.

'Great Jove, it must be mine.'
She lay in bed and cried
So much, she was decried
By her own chambermaids.
And even the chamberlain
With whom she had often lain.
To satisfy a vice,
So difficult, Daedalus made
Contraption or device,
Rostrum with step or ramp
As operative base
When she was feeling rampant
In house or temple.

CARADOC. How base!
SWEENY. In anger, the King sent
The royal pimp to prison
For seven years with his son, but
He bribed the sentinels,
Constructed two pairs of wings
From eagle pinions, wax
And stays of wire, to win
Their freedom.
                        Soon the sun
Within the sign of the Bull
Quickly began to wax,
Melting the fine wax
On the wings of Icarus
Who flew too high and dared it.
At the coast near Istanbul,
His father turned in dread
To see the rash youth plunge
Past boatmen diving for sponges,
Sky-suffocated, dead.

Come, let me feel your wings.
(*Raises* CARADOC'S *arms up.*)
                        A handsome
Pair.
        Turn around.
                        Forked swallow-tail.
(*Leads him to higher level.*)
                        Now jump

280

On air, defy the undiscovered law
Of gravity.
(*He catches* CARADOC *as he falls.*)
Come, jump again.
(*Same play.*)
I have it:
That rock a hundred feet above.
We'll glide
Together from it, birdmen of the future.
(*He hurries out.* CARADOC *remains, looks up, shudders, turns and sees* SWEENY *flying in the distance between mountain peaks.*)

CARADOC. Mad Irishman?
Hypnotic trick?
Another
Hallucination?
(*Shrugs.*)

Scene II

SWEENY enters right. CARADOC enters left; he wears a shabby cloak, and carries a green one.

CARADOC.   Who are
                You?
SWEENY.   Sweeny, once King of Dalaradia, Madman
                Of Ireland.
                          Who are you?
CARADOC.   Caradoc, once
                A chief, now Madman of Britain.
                                          Why have you left
                Your country?
SWEENY.   Not hard to tell.
                                          Wood-spies found out
                Nine of my ninety bracken, moss, ivy
                Beds.
CARADOC.   How did you quit your mind?
SWEENY.   Scrofulous Saint
                Cursed me because I forbade him to rubble, plot,
                A church on my best grazing land. He feathered,
                Crawed, roosted me.
                                 What happened to you?
CARADOC.   Aelfric,
                My enemy, gave me juice of an Arabic
                Root, flavoured with almond. I went into a dump
                And cannot wake although I keep knocking my
                    noddle
                On every oak, big rock . . .
                (*He stops, runs and bumps his head against an oak.*)
                                          Good Heavens!
                We're in the wrong century.
                                          Come, try again.
                (CARADOC *gives* SWEENY *the old green cloak. They
                leave, return.*)
CARADOC.   Who are you?
SWEENY.   Cosa Duva of Ireland,

                                             Ex-champion,
Long distance runner.
                             Who are you?
CARADOC.   The Green Man
Of Britain, stone figure from the chapels.
                                             Relate
An exploit.
SWEENY.   Not hard.
(*He signs, sound of waves, seagulls. A blue light
shines on him.*)
                             One day upon Ben Edair,
A day of easterly breeze and eddy,
Fionn and his Fianna were hunting
The deer from brake to heather, a hundred
In number. The brindled hounds were baying
As a trireme came across the bay.
Quick from a shower in the sea-road,
Foreigners in a small boat rowed
And hailed us. Mighty champion from Greece,
His whole appearance disagreeable,
Jumped out. He wore a dirty burlap,
His shoulders, thews, were hairy, burling,
He shambled up to Fionn from the shingle
With knobbled knees and crooked shin,
Challenging by signs a man in Eire
To run a race with him, wherever
He was. Gulping a mug of bragget,
Wide-mouthed, he chuckled, bragged
For he was not the champion runner
Of the eastern world, no runagate,
And he would give a big handicap
Of fifteen miles . . .
(*An IRISH* RUNNER *in shorts has appeared, miming,
in the blue light.*)
RUNNER.   He threw his cap down.
I picked it up. Backers were betting.
And laughing, boasting my form was the better.
Fionn and the Fianna gave a start
As he waddled southward to our starting
Post.
             Next day when the mist was rising,
The pair of us left our camp on a rise

Near Shannon, paced by spruce, fir, elder,
Ribbing together, bicep, elbow.
Bogmen looked up and were afraid of
Lake-dragon or pirates on a raid.
It might have been a Marathon
Until the big fellow broke shoe-lace, thong
And wind, blew nose, belched, spat out, ambled
Into a wood, lay under a bramble
Bush, rolling his body up, all hedgehogged,
Then grunting louder than a hog,
He plucked the blackberries by the grass,
While I was heading for the coast.

CARADOC (*interrupting*). This is a Christian century,
    Such pagan tales are obsolescent.
    (*The* GREEN MAN *appears in green light.*)

GREEN MAN. Stepping lightly from a chapel
    Wall, gaily churching from my nap
    Of ages, I came out, lightly vaulted
    Over the grass, by grave, by vault,
    Before the clerk could pull the bell-rope
    Again, my heels were in the open.
    I ran by field, by copse, by down,
    By dale: the sun was looking down and
    The reapers bending among the sheaves
    Knew by the frightening stir of oak-leaves,
    Green legs were going along the forest
    Pathway, knew by the restlessness
    Of partridge. I was on the Roman
    Road, speeding as bolt from the crossbow.
    Fearing green eye, they crossed themselves
    As I ran on. Two miles from a causeway
    I stole a naggin of ale because
    My track was northward.

RUNNER.   A mile back, I heard him trying to speak
    To bogmen. He scampered, rolled over, hurtled
    From mile to mile without a hurt,
    Ate from his budget, snored for an hour,
    Then washed his face in a Liffey shower.

GREEN MAN. Villagers shouted 'The Green Man, The Green
        Man',
    As they saw me race across the green.
    Doors clapped, key turned. The fox, the badger

              Skulked in the thicket, hiding their badness.

RUNNER.   I'll race you with my story.

                                  Chuckling
The Greek let down his trunks, then chucked
A boulder over a wood, knotted
The bits of his clumsy sandals. Not
A soul was in sight as he darted past
Me, full of food while I was fasting.

GREEN MAN. I came to Hadrian's Wall, ramping
              From tower to buttress along the ramparts
              By fifty look-outs, rubble and ruin
              All overgrown with moss, thrift, rue;
              Counted below a band of Picts
              Riding, a company quickly picked
              By danger, saw the forbidden land
              At darkfall, lit by tow, thin lance.

RUNNER.   That day he won our National Prize,
              Much to the loss and the surprise
              Of Fionn and the betting companies.
              He took his leave, threw back his fee
              Bum-boat came in; the ship still moored
              A mile off shore.

              (*The Runner vanishes.*)

GREEN MAN.   On Rannock Muir
              Ravens were silent, for I brought
              The summer with me. Sudden waters,
              Freshed on the greening hills, new bees
              Came out to clover, centaury,
              To specky orchid, marigold
              And viper's bugloss. Sun was goading
              The Devil's Needle . . .

SWEENY (*interrupting. The* GREEN MAN *looks surprised, vanishes*).
                            Your sheep all baa
              In the wrong field. I sing of Alba.
              Cuchullin drove there. He gave a whoop
              And leaped into Glen Etive where cooking
              Pot smoked and venison was grilling
              That Deirdre, Usnach, might have their fill.

CARADOC.   Schiehallion was misting.

SWEENY.   He came to a sound,
              Crossed to the Isle of Skye: heard sound,
              Of silence. Scathach the Red had hidden

Her strategy.

CARADOC. The Green Man sped.
The summer followed.

SWEENY. Cuchullin sprinted
Along the arches of shadow. Winter
Was sheeting in storm-light the last of the peaks
And, sentinels on crag, gerfalcons peeked
At him.
(*Light dims. In background appear the* HAG OF THE
MILL, *and the* SWINEHERD'S WIFE. *The* HAG
uncloaks and is seen to be Sheela-na-gig.)

CARADOC. Sssh! Don't look.

SWEENY. What is it?

CARADOC. Some of your bad thoughts
Are straying.
(*Clapping his hands.*)
Be off with yourselves.
This is
A Christian century.
(*Figures vanish.*)
(*To Sweeny, puzzled.*)
Why are you here?

SWEENY (*thinking*). I know, I know. The fight for Britain.
God save the . . .
(*Sound of British anthem.*)

CARADOC. I will lead the Irish people
To freedom.
(*Bugle call. Both shoulder invisible rifles, march,
present arms, aim, fire. Sound of volley, off. They
throw away rifles off stage, left, right. Rattle off. As*
CARADOC *is leaving,* SWEENY *rushes at him.*)

SWEENY. Stop, you have stolen the Book of the Dun Cow.

CARADOC. This is an older century, my friend.

SWEENY. The Book of Leinster, the Speckled Book of Leacan,
The Battle Book of Columcille, Book of Howth.

CARADOC. You've robbed from the future, Black Book of
Carmathen, Book of Aneuran, Book of Taleisin,
Red Book of Hengest, the Domesday Book.
(*Britannia appears, back stage.*)

CARADOC (*cutting Sweeny off, right*). Back
To your midland bogs and rain. May Ireland be
conquered,

286

Divided, by Great Britain until the Twentieth
Century.
(*Britannia disappears. Stage-hand in shirt sleeves
carries in a mediaeval chair, places it centre, leaves,
returns, carrying a large invisible book. Places it on
chair and leaves.* CARADOC *returns. Sees book.
Puzzled. Sits down and opens volume.*)

CARADOC.   The Book of Kells!
(*Light dims until he is silhouetted. Rich in hues on the
cyclorama can be seen a page of Celtic illumination;
showing a dragon capital.*)

Scene III

The same. SWEENY, CARADOC, *enter, left, right, both tidier. The latter carries a staff.*

SWEENY. Good morning.

CARADOC.   Good morning, Sweeny.

SWEENY.   You sent for me
By echo?

CARADOC. Yes.

SWEENY (*pointing*). Son of that rock there told me
So.

CARADOC. I am going away –
                    On a journey.

SWEENY.   Where?

CARADOC. First let us talk awhile.

SWEENY.   About the weather?

CARADOC. Why not?

SWEENY.   The winter has been hardy here.
Snow falls in Ireland only for a day
Or two. Wind, rain, soon chase it to the mountain
Tops. Every day the white camps of coldness dwindle,
Beleaguered by cloud, pale sun.

CARADOC.   The mire is firm,
Our ways unfoul.
(*Gets up.*)
                    Look how my little footpath
Is greening. . . .
(*Comes back.*)
                    Twelve months have ringed your ancient oak
And mine. Two perches apart, each in his own
High hermitage, concealed as acorns in leaves,
We have observed the unknown go by, daily
While meditating, have undergone the Nature
Cure, meeting but once a week to argue,
Quarrel and make it up again, share pignut,
Hazelnut, truffle, dip in the spring the broken
Bread left in my bowl by charitable

288

                        Men.
SWEENY.   And the rind of cheese!
CARADOC.   I have some here.
                (*Gives him some.*)
SWEENY.   I eat to your health!
                                Two nights ago, I dreamed
                Again of our national dish.
CARADOC.   What is it?
SWEENY.   Boiled bacon
                And cabbage.
CARADOC.   I dream of roast beef, batter pudding,
                Mercian Hot Pot.
SWEENY.   Despite the tempting of savour
                And sauce, I will remain a vegetarian.
CARADOC (*smiling*). Why, that's more dangerous than the Arian
                Rejection of the Three-in-One.
SWEENY.   Species
                Are food for one another – or the worm.
CARADOC.   Granted, but what of the scholastic species'
                Appearance? Actuality of flesh
                And blood?
SWEENY.   Plain anthropophagy, my friend.
                Have we not learned the gentler lesson of Nature
                From forest and wilderness? The womb and teat
                Are more than mouth, claws.
CARADOC.   Or talon?
SWEENY.   What keeps the nest-egg
                Warm?
CARADOC.   Yes. You're right.
                                Now is our last discussion,
                A couple of sensible men have been saned
                And cured, no longer at their wits' end.
                What have we learned?
SWEENY.   Philosophy of the cave,
                And the higher branches men came down from, after
                They tailored a thicker pelt,
CARADOC.   Discovered the law
                Of friction –
SWEENY.   Learned to master iron,
CARADOC.   Tool
                And spear themselves.
                                When we have reached the end

                            289

Of every proposition, what is left in
The riddle of the world?

SWEENY.   Rattle of wits.

CARADOC.   The ages had no history until
Men notched it on a pillar.

SWEENY.   Or cooked it in
A brick,

CARADOC.   Plucked feather,

SWEENY.   Crushed the oak-gall, made
Sheep entrails readable.

CARADOC.   Lean closer.
                                     What is
Unwritten?

SWEENY.   Secret opinion of mankind
That nothing matters –

CARADOC.   For all is nothing.
                                         In
The Far East, I am told, men build fantastic
Temples to emptiness.

SWEENY.   Across the Irish Sea,
Faith clambers up into round towers, stone-capped,
And belled.

CARADOC.   Here the new glaziers, fetched from Gaul,
Have shown us heavenly light through pane.
                                     In dream
I have hurried to Northumbria, sat down
In class, heard schoolmen arguing over the Eighth
Question that Saint Augustine asked the great
Pope Gregory concerning sex behaviour.
Women, Rome said, must suckle their own babies,
        because
The binding up of the nipples can prevent
Another pregnancy. The ventricles of
The wet nurse trickle in vain. Dutiful husband
After his midnight toil must wash thoroughly
Before he kneels in church on Sunday. Marriage
Is still an inferior state.

SWEENY.   The fault, no doubt,
Of concupiscence?

CARADOC.   Yes. (*They laugh.*)
                                 Monitor read
The holy text.

(*Thinking.*)
                                I have it.
*Behold I was conceived in iniquity, and in sin my
mother brought me forth.*

SWEENY. I disagree.

CARADOC.   I knew an Abbot of Ripon
Called Anselm. How he hated your local church,
Wrong tonsure, date of Easter! He told me
Your Irish saints, from Brigid to Colmcille
Will never be canonised.

SWEENY (*indignant*).   And what of Patric?

CARADOC (*smiling*). A Welshman!
        (SWEENY *clasps his hand to his brow.*)

CARADOC (*alarmed*). What is it?

SWEENY.   A thought has struck me.
                                                That
Assembly of Drumceat convened in five
Hundred and seventy-five. Our colony
In Scotland had demanded independence;
Parley, threat, coming-and-going, every sail,
A spy. Politics day and night, three battles
Fought over again in words. Rathmore, my royal
House, louder than a smithy. Congal Claen
The King of Ulster, conferred with me, camped out
His plans. Churchmen denounced us at the board,
Lit candles, said we were pagans as our poets
Caradoc, at the Battle of Moyra, I
Hated suddenly blow for blow, saw ancient
Heads, bloody, cut-off, heard them talking in
The air. Was it a fit of cowardice or
Curse of a scrofulous saint? How can I tell?

CARADOC. Forget it, man.
                        Recite a parting story.

SWEENY. With pleasure.
        (*He plucks invisible strings. A few harp notes.*)
Here is the story of three hermits
Who went to live in a solitude
Far from wishing-well, termon-stone,
Contention, military feud.
One, after a year of silence, spoke:
'A quiet place.'
                        A year dreamed by.

291

The second considered his reply:
'It is.'
      After another year
Of silence, the third, in a rage,
Exclaiming: 'There's too much blather here',
Got up and, fluttering like a page
Torn out of the Holy Scriptures, left them,
Stamped out to find a mountain cleft
In Connaught where only the clouds rampage.
(*Casts away invisible harp. Discordant arpeggios.*)

CARADOC (*laughing*). A moral tale
                        I must be going now.

SWEENY.   Where to?

CARADOC. My death.
            Constriction in chest, pain in the arms,
Have warned my body. It dreams and fears what is
To come.

SWEENY.   It could be suicidal impulse.

CARADOC. Have we not known the loss of memory
By which we know the self, endured torment
Of ignorance? Better a sudden going
Than years of senile decay, of dirty dotage,
Agony, ignominy of ignorance
Again. Bird, beast, retire into solitude
When feather, claw, are feeble.

SWEENY.   You are wiser
Than I.
      A saying I had forgotten has come
To guide me homeward. 'Death in Ireland'.

CARADOC.   Will you
Fly back?

SWEENY.   For the last time.
                But I'm proud
My country discovered potentialities
In body and mind that future generations
Will use when man is lifted to the sky.

CARADOC. Farewell.
(*Shakes hands, leaves.*)

SWEENY.   Caradoc.

CARADOC (*off*).   Farewell.

ECHO.   Farewell . . .
                    Farewell.

(SWEENY *hesitates, then, sadly, walks towards his oak.*)

CURTAIN

ACT FOUR

Scene I

Bare stage. Darkness. Sound of waves, distant seagulls. In dim light, ST. RONÁN *and monks are seen.*

RONÁN.   Sweeny is cured.
          He hurtles back from Britain.
                                        Fantasies
          And bloody visions of the slain, scatter
          His wits again!
MONKS.   Scatter his wits again,
          Fantasies, bloody visions of the slain.
          (*They leave. In darkness, masklike, distorted faces are
          seen.*)
VOICE.   A curse on the headsman
          From mouths of the dead,
          Earthless we trundle
          Without our trunks,
          Liver and entrails,
          Leave bleeding trails.
          Up, down, on sea-roller
          Our empties are rolled
          And the bump of these balls
          Is loud as our bawling.
          In a game of Twelve Pins
          We bowl down the Twelve Pins
          Of Connaught, bounce, bound,
          Over boundaries
          As rocks cave in,
          Hurry down caves
          Of the river at Cong
          To sport with the conger-
          Eel, hake and dugong.
          (SWEENY *enters. Heads vanish. Voices heard,
          mocking, Sweeny, Sweeny.*)
VOICE.   A curse on the headsman

From mouths of the dead,
Earthless we trundle
Without our trunks,
Liver and entrails,
Leave bleeding trails.
Up, down, on sea-rollers
Our empties are rolled
And the bump of these balls
Is loud as our bawling.
In a game of Twelve Pins
We bowl down the Twelve Pins
Of Connaught, bounce, bound
Over boundaries
As rocks cave in,
Hurry down caves
Of the river at Cong
To sport with the conger-
Eel, hake and dugong.
(*Daylight,* CONAL *enters with heads on a pole.* EMER,
fascinated, yet repelled.)

CONAL.   Emer, sweet of face and in speech,
Good his car in its speed.
Would that your husband, our hero
Cuchullin, had been here.

EMER.   Those heads you carry, bound and withied,
Whose are they, so broad in width
And in size?

CONAL.   A bloody burden
For carrion crow, grave-bird.

EMER.   Whose that huge head, so wry, so wrinkled,
With blood-red jowl, with iron rings
In lobe, you press beneath an elbow,
That head more than an ell?

CONAL.   The son of Cairbre, hairy, rugged.
His trunk lies in the pit I dug.
I trundled it many a league,
His phantom was so eager.

EMER.   Whose that youthful head, all curly,
Those teeth whiter than the curd?
Never was any of its likeness,
Surpassing all.

CONAL.   It's likely.

None fairer.

              Manan, notable champion.
Now let his stable horses champ.
I leapt up gaily as I hewed him
Down. Face kept that healthy hue.

EMER.   Tell of the others, mangled, dun.
The wind enrages with its dust.
They stare into the north, so gruesome
As if their bristles grew.
              Again.

CONAL.   Great Congal, his hair so yellow
And plaited, mouth a silent yell:
Noblest, a golden bush, a burnished
Sheaf that ripens, burns.
Macra the Red. With a sword-stroke,
I baffled him. His head went soaring.
He was the best of them, the greatest.
        See how his teeth still grate.
Cinna of the wars. All mourn him
From Connemara to the Mourne
Mountains.

EMER.   But do they tremble, wail
Follow our lonely way?

CONAL.   Emer, I, too, am desolate
Wandering in a green desert.
Cuchullin, the Hound, has been defeated.
         Unlucky was that feat.

EMER.   O Conal, bury me with my man.
Good his breeding, his war-manners.
For love of him I have sighed.
         Lay me at his side.

CONAL.   Emer, his wife, so modest, fair-necked,
I, too, have become a wayfarer.
No pleasure in tears can I find.
         Our gold has been refined.
(*Black out. In the Mill-house: cloaked hag-figure by
turf fire. As* SWEENY *enters, she reveals herself as a
young girl.*)

SWEENY. Who's this? Who's this,
Nearer than kisses
Or tongue in cheek?
Have I been fooled

> Again and cheated,
> Tierna of meekness,
> Tierna, night-schooled?

GIRL.
> Our celibates
> Despise and hate me
> For the tick pollutes
> Their sleep and they wake
> Alone. In stews
> Of Antioch, in knocking
> Shops of Tyre,
> I bring confusion,
> Strip and tire men.

> At the Nuns' House
> In Clonmacnoise,
> I glide by, noiseless,
> Squat in the night-time
> Below the key-stone,
> The carven groyne.
> Dark is my groin:
> To lie-alone, cut
> By the sculptor's tool –

SWEENY.
> Wide-open to greet me,
> Tierna of meekness,
> Tierna, night-schooled!
> (*She turns, cloaks herself, showing hag mask to audience.*)

GIRL.
> Come, Sweeny, let us play a game
> Of Hunkers, then, Cut-a-cootcho and Hornio,
> The best of all.

SWEENY.
>   I'll try that fall.
> (*She crouches, hops out, followed by* SWEENY *doing likewise. Enter* COLGAN *and* EORANN.)

COLGAN.
> Too late.
>   I saw him, mad-eyed, haggard
> Again. He's away with the Hag o'
> The Mill, to hide in a hedge or mountain haggard.

EORANN.
> The moon is out. Quick, after him, Colgan,
> Into that forest there. Call up
> Your men. My second marriage is void,
> Bigamous. I am in a state
> Of sin. Find him. I know that Nature

Will heal him once more.
(COLGAN *leaves.*)

                      I have avoided,
Yes, disobeyed my second husband,
Got out of the bed, because I husband
Myself for Sweeny, at night, naked,
Lie fallow for his husbandry.

Scene II

Outside the Oratory of St Moling.

MOLING.   Why are you here so early, Madman,
           Before I have had my morning manna?

SWEENY.   Though it seems early to a Cistercian,
           It is an hour in Rome since Terce.

MOLING.   How do you know, bare-footed roamer
           That it's an hour since Terce in Rome?

SWEENY.   Knowledge comes down to me from Heaven
           At daybreak, though my mind is heavy.

MOLING.   How do you recognise me, Madman,
           Whose mind and body have been cast
           Below?

SWEENY (*aside*). Saint Erysipilos of Egypt,
           Protect me: another of them shipped
           To Eire, ungraspable as air.
           Day phantoms have no sense of humour.
           Their substance is so vapid, so humid.
           Ecclesiastics say these spirits sink
           If any mortal gives them a wink.
           I'll test her.
           (*He winks slowly. She winks at audience, nods at him.*)
           (*To audience.*)
                 Willing.
                  I'll molest her.

SWINEHERD'S WIFE. Do you remember . . . a year ago?

SWEENY (*puzzled*).   A year
           Ago?

SWINEHERD'S WIFE. This very day!
           (*Whispers to him.*)
                 See, Man o' the nuts,
           Dampness on clothes-line. Dawn is chill.
           Come closer, wild man with the listening shadow,
           I have a story for you. My husband
           Has gone to Tobber with a sow

That wants the boar. He won't be back
Till noon. I have a dish of sowans
Ready. Strike in. First I will tub you
With lashings of warming water, uncrab you
Quickly with smearing of a lead ointment
My mother – rest her – gave me.

SWEENY. You would
Deceive me, fast as the one who left me
In trouble.

SWINEHERD'S WIFE. Have I not put the new milk out
For you before the clover could dry
At morning?

SWEENY. I saw you dunting with heel. You made
A hole in a cow-pat, filled it that I might know
And drink humility.

SWINEHERD'S WIFE. Wild man, I feared
Your flightiness.
(*She draws him closer.*)
See how I long
For you.

SWEENY (*puzzled*). Hawthorn in blossom, and yet
Two berries on it.
A walking tree.

SWINEHERD'S WIFE. There is another whiteness, you
Can guess at.
Maybush is yours.
Come, climb
My tree.

SWEENY. Leaves might become an airy
Woman.
At night they rustle over my bed
Of bracken. Their lips are half asleep,
Bodies as warm as summer, but frigid
Within. They freeze my courage to
A stalagmite. I fear yet burn in thought
Like a discalced monk.

SWINEHERD'S WIFE. I have the very cure
For that.
Come, Man o' the nuts. Your tub
Is ready.
(*They leave. Long pause. A shriek,* SWINEHERD'S
WIFE *rushes across stage in her nightdress. Pause.*

MOLING *enters from oratory.* MONKS *hurry in, horrified. Whisper to him.*)

MOLING.   Bring him on the litter.

(MOLING *prays.* MONKS *enter, bearing* SWEENY *on litter.*)

SWEENY.   There was a time, I thought more melodious
Than the conversing of my people,
The cooing of the culver in tree-top,
      Murmur of summer in sleep,

A time when I thought more melodious
Than the *glig-glug* of a handbell,
The blackbird on a forest spray,
      The high stag a-belling.

There was a time, I thought more melodious
Than storytelling or the harpstring,
The call of the far-off mountain grouse
      When the heather is rain-dark.

There was a time, I thought more melodious
The yelping of the sleeveen wolves
Than the voices of the clergy,
      A-baaing and bleating.

Though you sit back at a royal banquet
Raising the brew with many a health,
Better to drink this pure cold water
      From your palm at a well-side.

You praise the Latin terms in logic
The Easter gathering of your students,
Better to me the morning muster
      Of the beagles near Slieve Fews.

Although the salted pork, the fresh beef,
Are relished on your frequent feastdays,
Better the firstling of the water-cress,
      When light is in the east.

A rusty blade has gutted me,
Dirt and a wound that will not heal.
O Christ, that I had been roughly slain
      In battle, not shown a heel.

Pleasant the fern-beds I have made up

In the green deserts, the hollows of Eire,
And best the coverts hazelling
      Along Glen Bolcan. Soft air

Comes from the grass of other defiles,
Following itself into the forest,
That warm air, blowing from the Isles
      O' the Blessed. No chill from the North.
(MONGAN *is led in.*)

MOLING.   Although you keep my pigs, Mongan,
With a good hand, your pate is addled.
You have brought down with a strong blade
Our hermit of the forest, our Mad One.

Evil will come from that wicked blow:
The fire below, the testy smoke.
Too late will you repent, moaning.
Body and soul will both be coked.

But Sweeny and I will be enskied,
Be in the high place when my students
Have sung the penitential psalm
And you are damned in a stupor.

He was our King, our royal madman,
Who finds happiness in the grave,
I pity him from my bowels. Sad
      The epitaph to be graven

For him.

MONGAN.   Had I only known the outcome
Of this, I'd shout to the Day of Judgement.
I struck him dumb by the outhouse
      Where a sow littered in mud.

SWEENY.   Although my roving thoughts were tempted,
I made no attempt, unhappy Mongan,
Although you have gutted me and emptied
      My days, I did not wrong you.

MOLING (*to Mongan*). The fire and testy smoke in Hell
Be yours. No book for burial.
Short life and little mercy
      When your sin is heard.

SWEENY.   Though he be punished, Saint Moling,
What holiness can save me now.

The knife that gutted me is cold.
I feel the spirit leave my bones.

MONGAN.   Are you our King?

SWEENY.   Poor skin and bone,
Shadowy ruler.

MONGAN.   Had I guessed at our meeting,
You might have ploughed my furrow till Nones,
Honoured my crop, basted my meat.

SWEENY.   Mongan, believe me, I went unarmed
And never harmed stag-beetle or dace,
Since I was feathered, an old cock-grouse
Asleep on the Rock of Dunamace.

MONGAN.   They said my wife was in the act
Of rounding her back to the Man o' Nuts,
I went to the sty for a rusty blade,
Wiped it with grass-blade, left the muck.

SWEENY.   How could it be right, poor man, to splatter life
Without bad seeing? Your wife had poured
My tilly of milk. She made a platter
Of a cow-pat, heeled a big hole.

Guilty in thought, I bless her soul
And yours. You broke the dish, humbled me
And now I rumble with pain, clay-cold,
Because a swineherd gutted me.
(MOLING *signs to* MONKS. *They carry* SWEENY *into
the Oratory. Sound of prayer. All return.* EORANN
and MAELMORE, *her second husband, enter, right.*)

MOLING.   The Resurrection place of Sweeny,
Our King, is here. I'll think of him
And of his pain, each spot he frequented
      On foot. I sing his hymn.

Dear to me now is Glen Bolcan
That held his folly. Dear the streamlets
That flow there. Dear the green mantling
      Of the cress, white-blossomed, gleamy:

(*Left.*)
I name this spring, Well o' the Madman.
Let that sad name be reverenced.
Dear to me the little sands
      That filter the heaven-sent.

I will remember the lying-in-wait,
When forests were no longer noisy,
His strength despite his feeble weight,
    A hermit far from a cloister.

Dear to me now is every landmark,
Pillar and cromlech that Sweeny visited,
The slope of loose-strife where he basked,
    Branches he used to sit on.

I pray aloud to the King of Pain
In mercy to save myself and this friend
And I will laud the Holy Saviour,
    Accept the fitting end.

Too big a woe. Dear and melodious
Of mouth, our poet of strict measure.
I pray to Him above. O raise us
    From the pit of Your displeasure.

EORANN (*coming forward*). Widow and wife, I weep, I smile.
    Good Saint
    Moling, marry us now that the sacrament
    May bless our union, making our intimacy
    Pure, lawful. Marry us now and you shall have
    A freehold of unparcelled land to build
    A church on, high roof pent as an oak,

MAELMORE.   doorway
    With carven heads of bishops in a row,

EORANN.   Pillars with interknotted serpents,

MAELMORE.   beaded
    Circles and noble champhering.

EORANN.   Book-shrine
    For the illuminated manuscripts within,

MAELMORE. Silver reliquaries and iron handbells,

EORANN.   Bees will bring wax

MAELMORE.   to candle the altar.
                         Each morning

EORANN.   The deer

MAELMORE.   come to that green.

EORANN.   And there in peace,
    Dictate the Life of my first husband, Sweeny,
    The son of Colman Cuar and rightful King
    Of Dalaradia, to your scribe, but not in

Dead Latin, dictate it in the melodious Gaelic
My royal poet, my first husband, loved.

(*She kneels sobbing.* MOLING *signs to* MAELMORE,
*who kneels. She smiles up through her tears at the
groom, as* MOLING *opens his Psalter and begins the
marriage ceremony.*)

CURTAIN

305

Verse-speaking
and Verse Drama

'They have succeeded where we failed', writes Mr. W. G. Fay, describing a performance of Gordon Bottomley's play *Ardvorlich's Wife* by the Falkirk verse-speaking company. However much we may flatter ourselves on the fact that some of the first experiments in verse drama began in this country, we cannot take pride in their ultimate development, since we have not produced even one group of verse-speakers, though such groups are increasing in England, Scotland and elsewhere. It is difficult even to discover what methods were practised by the Fays and their associates in their first experiments. It is impossible, for instance, to gather from Mr. Fay's own book, *The Fays of the Abbey Theatre*, what methods of delivery were used. Here we enter immediately into a world of legend and hearsay. But as Mr. Fay tells us that later on the majority of the audience detested the whole thing and said so, we may suspect that the Yeatsian cult of aestheticism, which has been the bane of the Irish literary movement, was one of the main causes. The failure of verse drama here is linked with the failure of poetry itself to establish contact. The deliberate removal of poetry from the political and moral sphere during the Parnell split undoubtedly improved our art, but it carried with it the implications that poetry is not strong enough to express or analyse the passions of real life. Separated from the vital human drama of good and evil and the exciting historic complications in our life here, our verse drama had a bad start. In destroying the tradition of popular political poetry, a tradition which carried on, however inadequately, the Gaelic practice of the eighteenth century, we narrowed the function of poetry and banished the great ugly emotions which have shaped our national life.

Mr. Fay's reference to immediate lack of sympathy gives us a further clue to the failure – the impatient Renaissance method of demanding unsophisticated minds to accept what is really good for them, whether it be impressionistic pictures of *fin de siècle* plays. This was an artistic method which anticipated the way of the gunmen who were equally impatient in their desire to save our souls politically. There is little doubt but that the specialised method of chanting verse in vogue in the 'nineties was another reason for the lack of success in the experiment of verse drama. This method is entirely limited both in its possibility and effect. The dramatic poetry with which the Irish players were experimenting was itself conditioned by this method, for it emphasises and brings out the hidden monotone basis of verse at the expense of all its other constituents. But in the imaginative and rhythmic prose drama of Synge these players solved the problem of the spoken word and escaped from the abomination of the stereotyped acting of the stage. What was called naturalistic acting was really respect for and recognition of the living word and its power. This is shown by the attitude of the conventional dramatic critics of the period, who dismissed with contempt what they called 'literary drama.' The conventional actor concentrates on histrionics; he treats the words as a medium for displaying a complete range of emotional values and tones. In the flat, trite language of ordinary drama this method is, no doubt, effective. When the hero exclaims, 'I love you. Your face is like a flower. Your eyes are as beautiful as stars', the injection of vociferous passion restores the dead language to some semblance of life. But when words themselves are living, they are promptly suffocated by the weight of elocutionary methods. In their early experiments, with Synge's plays, the Irish players submitted themselves to the imaginative language and allowed it to carry forward the drama on its own plane. Mr. Fay tells us that he worked with Synge himself in the production of the *The Playboy of the Western World*. This collaboration between producer and author resulted in a method which at the time was quite revolutionary. 'He and I soon got together and experimented with the dialogue until, after much hard practice, I got at how the speeches were built up, and could say any of the lines exactly in the way he wanted. They had what I call a balance of their own, and went with a kind of lilt.' The experiment with Synge's plays is not irrelevant to the question of verse drama itself, for Synge's plays depended on their imaginative, rhythmic speech. The whole *Playboy of the Western World* is a tribute to the power of the word. Its real action consists in the kindling of the imagination of the characters themselves through their own excited speech. It develops on the plane of story-telling, and we see the hero himself shaping his story into words as his imagination climbs. These experiments were made thirty years ago, but the knowledge gained then has long since been lost. Recently I listened to a broadcast of *The Playboy of the Western World* by the Abbey Players. It was a triumph of stereotyped acting with all the customary exaggerative tones and violent emphasis. The inherent poetry of the words had vanished and the acrobatics of the acting voice alone remained. Only a few of the players remembered that Synge's vivid idiom does not need an artificial brogue. So far has our taste degenerated in thirty years!

In contrast to our sinking taste, there has been a revival of interest in verse drama in England, Scotland and elsewhere. The movement has been slow but sure and, above all, modest in its demands. Its real strength is due to the gradual finding and preparation of an audience. In this way, a great rift between dramatic tradition and oral sensibility is being closed. The revival of verse drama and the experiments in the speaking of verse drama have not preceded but have followed the cultivation of the art of verse-speaking itself. The speaking of a lyric or sonnet differs from the speaking of dramatic verse. But it follows that people who have become accustomed once more to listen to spoken poetry will inevitably want to hear verse drama. Moreover, they will be familiar with tones and inflections which are beyond the present range of the ordinary actor. They will know, for instance, that a passage of intellectual depth can be spoken as a direct expression of mind and not in the emotional snuffling method to which we have been accustomed.

To revive the art of verse-speaking is incidentally to solve the problem of verse drama, for both involve the contemporary relations between poetry and speech itself. The more we consider the question of spoken poetry of any kind, the more we are faced with a tremendous wall of self-consciousness. For centuries poetry has been confined to the printed page, and this is a contradiction in terms. Poetry is primarily an oral art, though many poets even have forgotten this fact. In reading poetry, we experience vicariously by means of the inner ear the pattern of movement and word music. To reproduce these effects aloud is in itself an art. Like many other obvious facts, however, this has not always been realised. But the fact that most people, if asked to read out a poem, will immediately assume a soulful, mournful or unnatural tone of voice indicates that they are dimly aware that some method is needed. It is not improbably that the discovery of radio precipitated a problem which was already in the minds of some.

309

Unfortunately, the fact that there is a correct method of verse-speaking has not been generally accepted by broadcasting authorities. Performances waver between artificial self-consciousness and soulfulness, mournfulness and the declamatory method of the professional actor. The wall of self-consciousness which builds itself immediately anyone proposes to recite a poem in public is due partly to desuetude and to a dim recognition of the fact that poetry is emotional in its origins. We are ashamed of emotions to which we are no longer accustomed in public. On the other hand, we are not overcome by embarrassment when someone stands up at the piano and performs a song for us. To some extent also we may be influenced by childhood memories of Victorian recitation. The recitation was a substitute for verse-speaking and was, in miniature, a copy or parody of stage method with its archly expressive tones, facial acting and regular system of appropriate gestures.

In recent years there have been several books on the art of verse-speaking. The most recent and the most practical so far is *The Speaking of Poetry* by Wallace B. Nichols. Dr Gordon Bottomley, in a preface, speaks of the work done, notably at the Festivals of Spoken Poetry in Oxford, initiated by the Poet Laureate and afterwards revived by the English Verse-Speaking Association.

So far as I know, the post-War renascence of the speaking of verse came about by the independent action of two or three poets, in different places but almost synchronizing. Yet little might have come of their common impulse if this had not been met with a discerning welcome by some of our most eminent and sound teachers of diction and speech-training experts, who saw in the poets' proposals a possibility of a fresh and more authentic start in a practice of the infinite possibilities which had been too much neglected by lovers of fine poetry.

In these experiments the aim has been to find a perfect balance between the constituent elements of a poem – meaning and emotion, imagery, movement and word-music. Experiments are concerned not only with the technical question of the placing of the speaker's voice, 'but the placing of the mind, the relation of the speaker to her or his material'. The older method of emphasising the metrical basis of poetry as in chanting or monotone, though effective for special types of verse, was too limited and eventually led in our own Yeatsian school to a form of mesmerism. The ideal which has been followed is described by Mr. Nichols.

310

To speak a poem needs the entire subordination of the speaker to the poet. The exploitation of the personality in such a way that it warps a poem's simplicity or meaning, or the undue stressing of any particular natural advantage, such as a voice merely beautiful in itself, is the negation of artistry, because it wraps the poem as in an alien cocoon. Moreover, a good speaker of poetry does not just take from a poem something to give back to it, but gives himself, or herself, to the service of the poet who wrote it, so that his basic purpose in it, the emotion and vision, that is to say, which made him write it, may be given an extended appeal in sound.

Verse-speaking is not a new art: it is a forgotten art. To be reanimated, it needs the same devotion to its practice that a great pianist will give to the conquest of the piano. Lesser service is the mark of insincerity.

Every type of poem, lyric, narrative, satiric, *vers libre*, requires its own treatment and every individual poem is a complete unit in itself and requires inductive treatment. Mr. Nichols deals with recent experiments in unison speech and choral speech. When we consider the slap-dash methods of producers in the immediate past, the inaudible jumble of a hastily rehearsed Greek chorus, the ignorance of volume and rhythm, the exemplary value of these experiments will be perceived. Modern choral speech, however, is a distinct form in itself. As Mr. Nichols points out,

It is unwise, in considering modern choral speech, to think of the Greek chorus. It is unwise because it is inappropriate. The conditions are not the same, neither is the thing itself the same. Modern choral speech is without music and without movement. It is the vocal interpretation of a poem by a group of voices instead of by a single voice.

Choral speaking is of two kinds, unison speech and inter-dependent group speech.

Some poems call for both. It is possible also to set group-speech against a ground of unison speech; it is possible, too, to set a solo voice against a ground of group-speech or unison speech. Imagination in the choir's trainer, or leader, can be productive of the most varied and telling effects in that way. But these effects should always be lyrical in basic tone, and not dramatic.

The effects obtained by the skilful blending of solo and group speech in interpreting certain types of poems can be a revelation. The lyrical use, for instance, of a single voice rising above the tone volume of the entire group, the contrast of varying tone volumes, the effects of distancing, must be heard to be realised.

Unfortunately, the subject of verse drama is outside the range of Mr. Nichols' manual. Verse-speaking is distinct from dramatic verse, since the latter is spoken in character. But the sheer example of mastery of rhythm and voice control, individually or in team work, must eventually have its influence on the production of verse drama. Possible attempts in the immediate past to revive verse drama have, with almost unfailing regularity, been completely stifled by the attitude immediately displayed by the producer and actor. Mr. W. G. Fay, working with Synge, as I have pointed out, first sought to discover how the speeches were built and experimented from within. Until a few years ago, the ordinary producer was content to put a verse drama into rehearsal for the usual week or ten days and then play it according to the dramatic method of an entirely different medium. The metrical and rhythmic basis of verse drama vanished in the process and, unaware of its absence, unaware, too, that action can take place in words, dramatic critics inevitably declared that such-and-such a play did not act. What would we think of a conductor who did not realise that every note in a musical score before him had its own meaning, significance and relation to the whole? What would we think of him if the fiddle parts were played entirely on the trombone or the big drum? The fact that a verse script has to be studied as carefully as a musical score in order to interpret the metrical and rhythmic basis of the speech is quite beyond the perception of the ordinary producer. In other words, the fact that a poet expends labour in expressing ideas in certain rhythms, which are part of the very quality of his thought, is completely ignored. Trained verse-speakers and players, who are willing to submit themselves to the material before them, have shown recently that the medium of verse drama can be realised. Given the attention in detail and delicate sensitiveness of tone which we take as a matter of course in the performance of a sonata or concerto, a one-act verse play can be a self-justified experience. Its basic form becomes expressive and the interdependent rhythms of the various speaking parts seem, as by an invisible conducting, to set up a timing and spacing of their own.

It seems absurd to have to plead for the recognition of verse drama as a distinct medium, considering that it was the oldest form of dramatic art. But the confusion which still exists in the minds of producers is shown in the Romanes Lecture delivered this year by Mr. Granville-Barker entitled *On Poetry in Drama*. Mr. Granville-Barker confuses the entire issue at once by extending the term poetic drama to modern imaginative drama, such as that of Maeterlinck. Critically and abstractly, this may be

312

true, but it is entirely irrelevant to the practical problem of verse. Although Mr. Granville-Barker recognises the existence of modern subjective prose drama and by inference realises that it requires a special type of acting of its own, he is unable to appreciate the fact that verse drama has also been developing. At every point in his lecture he returns inevitably to the Shakespearean model of great speeches, character displayed through violent action with its plots and sub-plots. The actor's cult of Shakespeare is a subject in itself. It affords to actor and producer, in their conservatism, and excuse for histrionics and costumes, ranging from gorgeousness to the simplicity of plus-fours. Owing to the change of vocabulary, idiom and the speech rhythm of everyday language, much of the high-powered verse of Shakespeare is practically incomprehensible in its full detail to the hearing. Textual notes and explanations are required. But this gives the actor a rare chance of displaying his prowess and hurling himself from point to point of meaning. We admire him as we admire the operatic soprano who conveys to us in extravagant vocal flights something quite different from the words which she employs as a means to an end. Even the Shakespearean actor, however, realises dimly that there are certain passages in Shakespeare which have to be brought out for themselves in order to express and carry on the movement of the play. For instance, the famous balcony duet in *Romeo and Juliet*. Mr. Granville-Barker is unable to see that verse drama has developed on similar lines to prose drama and does not necessarily depend on a violent plot of action. The battle for repertory prose drama has long since been won. Audiences can now listen with appreciation to the lengthy arguments and dialectics of Shaw, or enjoy the subtle *laisser-faire* of a Tchekov play. But the battle for new verse drama forms has only really begun. The first problem – that of the correct presentation of dramatic verse – has not even occurred to Mr. Granville-Barker. Among such problems may be mentioned that of tempo and of what may be called psychological inaudibility. Being slaves to the printed word, it requires some practice on our part to regain quick use of the ear. Poetry is more concentrated than prose and involves all the time an unexpectedness or suggestiveness of phrase. In endeavouring to follow speech in a foreign language with which we are not completely acquainted (such as Irish), we suffer from the impression that the speaker is talking at immense speed. This problem has to be faced by the trained verse-speaker and equally applies to verse drama.

The confusion regarding verse drama is due, in a great measure to the peculiarities of its historic place. Verse drama, as a vital art form, had practically disappeared at the close of the last century, and poets were haunted by the colossal dream of restoring the form as in Elizabethan and Restoration times. The dream of capturing a past convention by one or more magnificent plays, the achieving of a veritable *coup d' état*, lingered on. A last bid for power was made, with fatal results, by Stephen Phillips. Meanwhile, like poetry itself, the poetic drama had become a silent art, an art of the closet. Silent poetic drama, with its immensely long speeches, reached an apogee in the plays of Swinburne. The extreme example of the silent poetic drama is, of course, Hardy's epic play, *The Dynasts*, with its nineteen acts and one-hundred-and-thirty scenes. Verse drama only began again when new and more subtle forms were sought; when, too, ambition had become small but intense. The development of a rhythmic prose drama, especially in expressionism, broke down the older hard-and-fast moulds, and showed once more the possibilities of spiritual moods beyond the reach of realism and mere representation. But expressionism is limited, owing to the simple and repetitive rhythmic phrases on which it depends. So far, at least, it can only excite mass emotion and is dependent on types rather than individuals. It brings us back to a rather naïve allegoric form. Only a writer insensitive to the detailed value of words and thoughts, such as Eugene O'Neill, could express himself with satisfaction in this atavistic but certainly exciting form. O'Neill's failure is shown, for instance, in *Lazarus Laughed*, where the vague repetitive rhetoric and windy blather must offend any mind trained to appreciate precise imaginative values. Poets cannot be expected to write entirely for the drum, however big it may be. Rhythmic prose drama, therefore, in its present state of development, is more suggestive in technical possibilities than exemplary.

Recent experimentation in verse drama in England and elsewhere has meant novelty in form. Poets have been encouraged to write plays once more with the knowledge that here and there small groups of players and trained speakers will give to verse notation the same intelligent study which musicians give to an instrumental score. The success of T. S. Eliot's *Murder in the Cathedral* owed much to its production. Lacking the pioneer work in verse and choral speaking, such a production would have been impossible even a couple of decades ago.

The entire cycle of plays in which Gordon Bottomley deals with the historic past of Scotland is written in a new form which requires the combined use of verse-speakers and players. It is difficult to describe these plays in which a complex form is built up before us as rapidly and by as direct means as in the folk ritual of balladry. His poetry abandons the silent page, for it demands to be heard. With its interpreters, characters and chorus, it becomes an interwoven movement of living voices. His plays, in their dramatic inquisitiveness, explore historic motives and emotions. He searches the springs of human cruelty and passion with such persistent sincerity, such necessity, that we are stirred by pity and terror. In Christian eschatology he has found a dramatic form, in which the will replaces the older motif of Fate. One cannot help thinking that if we had had similar dramatic analysis of the emotions which have conditioned our own racial life, when all was favourable at the beginning of this century, our verse drama would have had certain foundations. But we had limited our poetry in its functions. All modern drama uses, as its rhythmic basis, the nervous speech rhythm of to-day. Padraic Colum in his play, *The Miracle of the Corn*, anticipated present-day formalism and the nervous rhythm of living speech. But his play remained an exception.

For various reasons, modern satiric verse drama has lesser problems to face. Thanks to Gilbert and Sullivan, the tradition was carried on by the help of light music. The plays of W. H. Auden and C. Isherwood, with their effective mixture of expressionism and revue, are, therefore, beyond the immediate range of this article. Experiments have also been proceeding for a good number of years in America. *Panic*, by Archibald MacLeish, which was recently produced at Mr. Ashley Dukes' Verse Theatre in London, is an exciting attempt to present modern themes in modern fashion. Its subject is the Wall Street financial crash and the poet attempts to use expressionism in a more subtle way. Believing that American daily speech is trochaic, he uses trochaic stress as the basis of his rhythms. How far he succeeds is another question. But the nature of the experiment indicates the fact that verse drama is developing on many lines, all of which have certain fundamental objects in common.

It is probable that the new verse drama will find increasing use for the effects which have been obtained in choral and experimental group speech and in this way, as an independent art, will not be at the mercy of a purely dramatic tradition. It is mainly a matter of a changed attitude of mind, a willingness to give the care and attention which are a *sine qua non*, for instance, in the art of music. One thing is certain. No poet, who has seen a play of his produced by a trained group of verse-speakers and players, will wish any more to surrender his work to an ordinary repertory company.

Review article, *Dublin Magazine* XII, new series, (October-December 1937), pp. 9–17.

Verse Speaking

Some readers of *This Verse Speaking* in the September number of The Bell may well imagine that the subject itself is as vague, dithering and contradictory as the remarks of Miss Irene Haugh and Mr. Donagh MacDonagh. Far from being so, verse-speaking is a very practical subject, with its own rules and careful definitions. It is now well established and, apart from anything else, its educational value has been generally recognised in England, Scotland and the North of Ireland. There has been, in fact, a quiet 'revolution' among teachers and in all schools of speech training, including those in Dublin. For several generations teachers had followed the old Victorian system of elocution with its dramatic 'recitation', complete with gestures and other attendant horrors. Now lyric poetry had come into its own, and much is due to the enthusiasm of Marjorie Gullan, Elsie Fogerty and others, who worked in consultation with poets. At the annual Festival of Verse Speaking in Oxford many poets acted as adjudicators, including John Masefield, Laurence Binyon, Gordon Bottomley, Walter de la Mere, Victoria Sackville West, Lascelles Abercrombie, Wilfrid Gibson, Richard Church, W. H. Auden, C. Day Lewis. As a member of the Board of Judges for five years before the war, I was able to watch the progress of this movement for the revival of spoken poetry. There are now a number of books which may be recommended to all readers interested in the subject, such as *The Speaking of Poetry* by Wallace B. Nicholls, *Spoken Poetry in the Schools*, and *Choral Speaking*, both by Marjorie Gullan, *Vital Speech* by Harold J. Ripper (all published by Methuen).

Attacks on verse-speaking are always choleric, simply because the experience is still somewhat of a novelty, and any change from conventional habits arouses fury. The plain man avoids verse-speaking because he loathes poetry itself and wants to be allowed to enjoy his game of cards in peace. The reaction of the literary conservative is more complicated. For several centuries poetry, especially in England, has been hidden away in the silence of the printed page despite the fact that the sound is part of its meaning.

Its lonely votaries have murmured poetry to themselves late at night in study or bedroom, fearful of being overheard even by members of their own family. Poetry to Miss Haugh is a communion of souls and she gazes at the printed page in silent ecstasy. Even Mr. MacDonagh, who wants us to think that he is a 'tough guy,' has the same slightly hysterical attitude. A poem to him is so sacred that only the poet himself dare read it. In other words, the poet is endowed, by his mystical profession, with all the skill of voice production. This, in my opinion, a sentimental nonsense. Some of our younger Irish poets, judging by broadcasts, would not be harmed by a three months' course in speech training. After I published my first book of verse, I went to Frank Fay for such a course. This cult of the poet as a sacred being is purely adolescent. What would we think of the composer who shrank from the performance of his songs, who felt that it would be sacrilege if they were interpreted by different singers? The composer trusts the skills, sympathy and intelligence of the trained musician. The sensible poet trusts the skill, sympathy and intelligence of the trained verse-speaker.

Miss Irene Haugh is shocked to think of a delicate personal lyric being spoken by a number of voices in unison. Had she bothered, however, to consult any manual on choral speaking before she rushed into print, she would have learned that the first rule in this art is that only poems of public nature, such as odes, can be interpreted by group speaking. Indeed had she listened-in to choral broadcasts by the Dublin Verse Speaking Society, she would have noticed that the poems chosen expressed general and not private sentiments. For instance, *The Congo* by Vachel Lindsay, *Lepanto* by G. K. Chesterton, *Requiem of Archangels for the World* by Herbert Trench, *The Tower of Marl* by Joseph Campbell. The latter poem was written specially for ensemble speaking, and this shows that poets have been attracted by the possibilities of a new mode.

When reading a poem in print we can hear the word-music with our inner ear, but the fact that we cannot reproduce the same effect with the voice at once means merely that verse-speaking implies skill. Many of us, in the same way, can hear a song in our mind but that does not mean that we can sing it. Verse-speaking is a very delicate and exact compromise between different tendencies, and requires, therefore, perfect control of the voice. The basis of all verse is metre or recurrent pattern, and its direct expression in sound is monotone. If we emphasise this basis element we get sing-song, chanting or intoning. If we break down monotone and emphasise the meaning of the words, the result is elocution or the dramatic method of the actor. Lyrical speaking is a delicate balance between opposites, in which metre, rhythm, meaning are all held in control. It is the art of the miniaturist and it takes a little time before the listener becomes used to the small and delicate range of speech tones used. We are so accustomed to the broader contrasts in tone used by the actor on the stage that it is easy to miss the subtle skill of lyric speaking.

It is an interesting fact that the actual revival of spoken poetry started in this country with the pioneer work of W. B. Yeats. It was, of course, the period of æstheticism, and Yeats went to extremes. He emphasised the monotone and insisted that all verse must be chanted. Intoning, no doubt, suited his own incantatory lyrics and magical spells, but to draw on the hypnotic power of the voice is to annoy many worthy people and Yeats met with furious opposition. In this country intoning is reserved for religious services and family prayers: we believe piously that this limited kind of verse-speaking is liked only in Heaven. But the example shown by Yeats attracted attention elsewhere and, though his extreme methods were abandoned, the correct speaking of poetry, the best ways of rescuing it from the silence of the printed page, became matters for discussion and experiment. The discovery of wireless helped to make the problem a practical one.

In the attempt to set a good standard there has been, needless to say, the inevitable confusion. It is only in recent years that the B.B.C. has discovered the existence of trained verse-speakers. Too often a West End actor or actress has been called in to speak lyrical verse. The results have been deplorable, for the actor, used to the trite language of the modern stage, does not realise that poetry is charged with its own energy and cannot be interpreted by a technique broader than its own. Even the Third Programme shows the same inconsistency and lack of a recognised norm. Over here it has been possible to keep to a consistent policy. The Dublin Verse Speaking Society, founded by Robert Farren and myself, has endeavoured to set a reasonable standard here. In our weekly broadcasts twelve minutes exactly are devoted to verse speaking: these twelve minutes have caused furious controversy and complaints, but after much hard work the fury of the Philistines has abated. At a time when poetry is neglected here and we have few publishers of our own, broadcasting enables us to spread an interest in poetry and particularly to draw attention to the work of the Irish literary revival.

With the increase of interest in spoken poetry, came the opportunity of reviving our tradition in verse drama, which had been abandoned by the Abbey Theatre. The Lyric Theatre Company, the dramatic unit of the Dublin Verse Speaking Society, now hires our National Theatre and gives regular performances of verse plays and has gradually increased its audience. In these programmes of verse plays and poems, we have found that audiences appreciate the poems as much as the plays. *Tomas O Cahan and the Ghost* by Douglas Hyde, an example of ensemble speaking, was a popular success. *Ua Bruaidir* by James Stephens, spoken by Liam Redmond; *The Toy-maker* by Padraic Colum, spoken by Alex Andrews; *The Witches' Ballad* spoken by Marjorie Williams are examples, taken at random, of solo work which won much appreciation.

Mr MacDonagh tells us quite frankly that verse-speaking bores him. That is his own concern. But he overlooks the fact that he owes some of the success of his own verse comedy, *Happy as Larry*, first presented by the Lyric Theatre Co., to these verse-speakers, for whom he has such contempt. Surely he owes something to the skill of George Greene, Ronnie Masterson, Alex Andrews, Ita Little, Oliver Bradley and others, their experience in the difficult art of speaking rhymed and patterned verse, varying it, giving it expressive rhythm. They proved by their skill that a vernacular comedy in verse could attract popular audiences both in the Abbey Theatre and the Gaiety Theatre.

The Bell, XV, 3, December 1947, pp. 52–6.

References
This article responds to remarks by Haugh ('This Poetry Speaking', *The Bell* XV, 1, Oct. 1947, pp. 62–5) and MacDonagh ('Comment on "This Poetry Speaking"', *The Bell* XV, 1, Oct. 1947, pp. 65–6). Haugh wrote that poetry 'should rarely be spoken aloud', and that a 'choir recitation [] distorts the subtle images evoked by poetry: For MacDonagh verse-speaking is a bore, but verse drama 'is of course another man'.

SELECTED CHECKLIST

As the volume of Clarke's publications is great, this checklist enumerates only the first editions of Clarke's books. Details of bibliographies and checklists of his shorter wrings and poems are detailed under the volumes in which they appear.

Plays

The Son of Learning; a Poetic Comedy in Three Acts, Allen & Unwin, London, 1927.

The Flame: a Play in One Act, Allen & Unwin, London, 1930.

Sister Eucharia: a Verse Play in Three Scenes, Orwell Press, Dublin; Williams & Norgate, London, 1939.

Black Fast: a Poetic Farce in One Act, Orwell Press, Dublin, 1941.

As the Crow Flies: a Lyric Play for the Air, Bridge Press, Dublin; Williams & Norgate, London 1943.

The Viscount of Blarney and Other Plays (also contains *The Kiss* and *The Plot is Ready*), Bridge Press, Dublin; William & Norgate, London, 1944.

The Second Kiss: a Light Comedy, Bridge Press, Dublin; Williams & Norgate, London, 1946.

The Plot Succeeds: a Poetic Pantomine, Bridge Press, Dublin; Williams & Norgate, London, 1950.

The Moment Next to Nothing: a Play in Three Acts, Bridge Press, Dublin, 1953.

Collected Plays (containing all the above plays), Dolmen Press, Dublin, 1963.

Two Interludes, Adapted from Cervantes, 'The Student from Salamanca' and 'The Silent Lover', Dolmen Press, Dublin, 1968.

The Impuritans, Dolmen Press, Dublin, 1973.

The Visitation, in *Irish University Review*, IV, 1, Spring 1974, pp. 74–90.

The Third Kiss: a Comedy in One Act, Dolmen Press, Dublin, 1976.

Liberty Lane: a Ballad Play of Dublin in Two Acts with a Prologue, Dolmen Press, Dublin, 1978.

Selected Plays (Chosen and Introduced by Mary Shine Thompson), Colin Smythe, Gerrards Cross, Bucks. 2005.

UNPUBLISHED PLAYS
Bis in Nocte: a Medieval Comedy in Three Scenes.
The Hungry Demon (another version of *The Son of Learning*), performed Gate Theatre, Dublin, 27 September 1930.

Poetry
The Vengeance of Fionn, Maunsel, Dublin & London, 1917.
The Fires of Baal, Maunsel & Roberts, Dublin & London, 1921.
The Sword of the West, Maunsel & Roberts, Dublin & London, 1921.
The Cattledrive in Connaught and Other Poems, Allen & Unwin, London, 1925.
Pilgrimage and Other Poems, Allen & Unwin, 1929; Farrar & Rinehart, New York, 1930.
Collected Poems, Allen & Unwin, London; Macmillan, New York, 1936.
Night and Morning, Orwell Press, Dublin, 1938.
The Straying Student, Gayfield Press, Dublin, 1941.
Ancient Lights, Poems and Satires: First Series, Bridge Press, Dublin, 1955.
Too Great A Vine, Poems and Satires: Second Series, Bridge Press, Dublin, 1957.
The Horse Eaters, Poems and Satires: Third Series, Bridge Press, Dublin, 1960.
Later Poems, Dolmen Press, Dublin, 1961.
Forget-Me-Not, Dolmen Press, Dublin, 1962.
Flight to Africa and Other Poems, Dolmen Press, Dublin, 1963 (with Charles Tomlinson and Tony Connor), *Poems*, Oxford University Press. London, 1964.
Mnemosyne Lay in Dust, Dolmen Press, Dublin; Oxford University Press, London; Dufour Editions, Chester Springs, PA, 1966.
Old-Fashioned Pilgrimage and Other Poems, Dolmen Press, Dublin; Dufour Editions, Chester Springs, PA, 1967.
The Echo at Coole and Other Poems, Dolmen Press, Dublin; Dufour Editions, Chester Springs, PA, 1968.
A Sermon on Swift and Other Poems, Bridge Press, Dublin, 1968.
Orphide and Other Poems, Bridge Press, Dublin, 1970.
Tiresias: A Poem, Bridge Press, Dublin, 1971.

Collected Poems, Dolmen Press, Dublin; Oxford University Press, London & New York, 1974.

Selected Poems (ed. Thomas Kinsella), Dolmen Press, Dublin; Wake Forest University Press, Winston-Salem, NC, 1976.

Selected Poems (ed. Hugh Maxton/W.J. McCormack), Lilliput Press, Dublin; Penguin Books, Harmondsworth, 1991.

RECORDING

Beyond the Pale. A reading, with comentary by Clarke, of his own poetry. Introduction by John Montague, Claddagh Records, Dublin, 1966.

Prose

AUTOBIOGRAPHY

First Visit to England, and Other Memories, Bridge Press, Dublin; Williams & Norgate, London, 1946.

Twice Round the Black Church: Early Memories of England and Ireland, Routledge & Kegan Paul, London, 1962; Moytura Press, Dublin, 1990.

A Penny in the Clouds: More Memories of Ireland and England, Routledge & Kegan Paul, London, 1968; Moytura Press, Dublin, 1990.

FICTION

The Bright Temptation: a Romance, Allen & Unwin, London; William Morrow, New York, 1932; Dublin: Dolmen, 1965.

The Singing Men at Cashel, Allen & Unwin, London, 1936.

The Sun Dances at Easter, Andrew Melrose, London, 1952.

CRITICISM

Foreword to Mervyn Wall's play, *Alarm among the Clerks*, Richview Press, Dublin, 1940.

Poetry in Modern Ireland, Three Candles Press, Dublin, 1951.

Ed. of and Introduction to *The Poems of Joseph Campbell*, Allen Figgis, Dublin, 1963.

Introduction to *The Plays of George Fitzmaurice: I. Dramatic Fantasies*, Dolmen Press, Dublin, 1967.

The Celtic Twilight and the Nineties, Dolmen Press, Dublin; Dufour Editions, Chester Springs, PA, 1969.

Reviews and Essays of Austin Clarke (ed. Gregory Schirmer), Colin Smythe, Gerrards Cross, Bucks., 1995.

Also contains an exhaustive list of Clarke's literary criticism in periodicals (approx. 1,500 reviews, of over 5,000 books), pp. 269–380.

Secondary Biographical and Critical Publications

Rory Brennan (ed.), *Austin Clarke Supplement*, in *Poetry Ireland Review*, nos. 22 & 23, Summer 1988, pp. 93–176.

Susan Halpern, *Austin Clarke, His Life and Works*, Dolmen Press, Dublin; Humanities Press, Atlantic Highlands, NJ, 1974.

Maurice Harmon (ed.), *Irish University Review: Austin Clarke Special Issue*, IV, 1, Spring 1974.
Contains Gerard Lyne's 'Austin Clarke – A Bibliography', pp. 137–155.

Maurice Harmon, *Austin Clarke: A Critical Introduction*, Wolfhound Press, Dublin; Barnes & Noble Books, Totowa, NJ, 1989.
Contains 'Select Bibliography', pp. 267–309.

Maurice Harmon, *Irish Poetry after Yeats: Seven Poets*, Wolfhound Press, Dublin; Little Brown, Boston, PA, 1979, pp. 32–67. Revised ed., Wolfhound, 1997.

Lorraine Ricigliano, *Austin Clarke: A Reference Guide*, G.K. Hall, New York, 1993.

Gregory Schirmer, *The Poetry of Austin Clarke*, Univiersity of Notre Dame Press, Notre Dame, IN; Dolmen Press, Mountrath, Portlaoise, 1983.

G. Craig Tapping, *Austin Clarke, A Study of His Writings*, The Academy Press, Dublin, 1981.
Contains 'A listing of some of Clarke's journalistic writings', pp. 328–355.

FIRST PERFORMANCES

The Son of Learning: Cambridge Festival Theatre, October 1927; Gate Theatre, Dublin, 27 September 1930 under the title *The Hungry Demon (The Son of Learning)*

The Flame: School of Speech Training and Drama, Edinburgh, June 1932.

Sister Eucharia: Gate Theatre, July 1939.

Black Fast: Abbey Theatre, 28 December 1941.

As the Crow Flies: first broadcast on Radio Eireann, 6 February 1942.

The Viscount of Blarney: Abbey Theatre, December 1944.

The Kiss: Abbey Theatre, June 1944.

The Plot is Ready: Peacock Theatre, Dublin, October 1943.

The Second Kiss: Abbey Theatre, June 1946.

The Plot Succeeds: Abbey Theatre, February 1950.

The Moment Next to Nothing: Players' Theatre, Trinity College, Dublin, January 1958.

The Student from Salamanca: Lantern Theatre, Dublin, December 1966.

IRISH DRAMA SELECTIONS

ISSN 0260–7962

1. SELECTED PLAYS OF LENNOX ROBINSON
   Chosen and introduced by Christopher Murray
   Contains *Patriots, The Whiteheaded Boy, Crabbed Youth and Age, The Big House, Drama at Inish, Church Street*, Bibliographical Checklist.
   Hbk ISBN 0-86140-087-9; pbk ISBN 0-86140-088-7

2. SELECTED PLAYS OF DENIS JOHNSTON
   Chosen and introduced by Joseph Ronsley
   Contains *The Old Lady Says 'No!'*, (with Curtis Canfield's list of poems used in the Prologue), *The Moon in the Yellow River, The Golden Cuckoo, The Dreaming Dust, The Scythe and the Sunset*, with Johnston's prose introductions and essays on the plays, Bibliographical Checklist.
   Hbk ISBN 0-86140-123-9; pbk ISBN 0-86140-086-0

3. SELECTED PLAYS OF LADY GREGORY
   Foreword Sean O'Casey
   Chosen and introduced by Mary Fitzgerald
   Contains *The Travelling Man, Spreading the News, Kincora, Hyacinth Halvey, The Doctor In Spite of Himself, The Goal Gate, The Rising of the Moon, Dervorgilla, The Workhouse Ward, Grania, The Golden Apple, The Story Brought by Brigit, Dave*, Lady Gregory on playwriting and her plays, Bibliographical Checklist.
   Hbk ISBN 0-86140-099-2; pbk ISBN 0-86140-100-X

4. SELECTED PLAYS OF DION BOUCICAULT
   Chosen and introduced by Andrew Parkin
   Contains *London Assurance, The Corsican Brothers, The Octoroon, The Colleen Bawn, The Shaughraun, Robert Emmet*, Bibliographical Checklist.
   Hbk ISBN 0-86140-150-6; pbk ISBN 0-86140-151-4

5. SELECTED PLAYS OF ST JOHN ERVINE
   Chosen and introduced by John Cronin
   Contains *Mixed Marriage, Jane Clegg, John Ferguson, Boyd's Shop*,

Friends and Relations, prose extracts, Bibliographical Checklist.
Hbk ISBN 0-86140-101-8; pbk ISBN 0-86140-102-6

6. SELECTED PLAYS OF BRIAN FRIEL
   Chosen and introduced by Seamus Deane
   Contains *Philadelphia, Here I Come*, *Translations*, *The Freedom of the City*, *Living Quarters*, *Faith Healer*, *Aristocrats*, Bibliographical Checklist.
   This title is only for sale in North America, where it is published by the Catholic University of America Press. It is not a Colin Smythe publication.

7. SELECTED PLAYS OF DOUGLAS HYDE
   Chosen and introduced by Janet Egleson Dunleavy and Gareth Dunleavy
   Contains *The Twisting of the Rope*, *The Marriage*, *The Lost Saint*, *The Nativity*, *King James*, *The Bursting of the Bubble*, *The Tinker and the Sheeog*, *The Matchmaking*, *The Schoolmaster*, Bibliographical Checklist. This volume publishes the original Irish language texts with Lady Gregory's translations.
   Hbk ISBN 0-86140-095-X; pbk ISBN 0-86140-096-8

8. SELECTED PLAYS OF GEORGE MOORE
   AND EDWARD MARTYN
   Chosen and introduced by David B. Eakin and Michael Case
   Contains Moore's *The Strike at Arlingford*, *The Bending of the Bough*, *The Coming of Gabrielle*, *The Passing of the Essenes;* and Martyn's *The Heather Field*, *Maeve*, *The Tale of a Town*. Bibliographical Checklist.
   Hbk ISBN 0-86140-144-1; pbk ISBN 0-86140-145-X

9. SELECTED PLAYS OF HUGH LEONARD
   Chosen and introduced by S. F. Gallagher
   Contains *The Au Pair Man*, *The Patrick Pearse Motel*, *Da*, *Summer*, *A Life*, *Kill*. Bibliographical Checklist.
   Hbk ISBN 0-86140-140-9; pbk ISBN 0-86140-141-7

10. SELECTED PLAYS OF T. C. MURRAY
    Chosen and introduced by Richard Allen Cave
    Contains *Sovereign Love*, *Birthright*, *Maurice Harte*, *The Briery Gap*, *Autumn Fire*, *The Pipe in the Fields*, the hitherto unpublished *Illumination*, and his essay 'George Shiels, Brinsley MacNamara, Etc.'

Bibliographical Checklist.
Hbk ISBN 0-86140-142-5; pbk ISBN 0-86140-143-3

11. SELECTED PLAYS OF MICHEÁL mac LIAMMÓIR
Chosen and introduced by John Barrett
Contains *Where Stars Walk, Ill Met by Moonlight, The Mountains Look Different, The Liar, Prelude in Kazbek Street*, selected writings on plays and players, Bibliographical Checklist.
Hbk ISBN 0-86140-154-9; pbk ISBN 0-86140-155-7

12. SELECTED PLAYS OF M. J. MOLLOY
Chosen and introduced by Robert O'Driscoll
Contains *The King of Friday's Men, The Paddy Pedlar, The Wood of the Whispering, Daughter from Over the Water, Petticoat Loose*, and the previously unpublished *The Bachelor's Daughter*. Bibliographical Checklist.
Hbk ISBN 0-86140-148-4; pbk ISBN 0-86140-149-2

13. SELECTED PLAYS OF RUTHERFORD MAYNE
Chosen and introduced by Wolfgang Zach
Contains *The Turn of the Road, The Drone, Red Turf, The Troth, Phantoms, Bridge Head, Peter*, Bibliographical Checklist.
Although the two articles 'The Ulster Literary Theatre' and 'Meet Rutherford Mayne' were announced as being part of this collection they were, for reasons the publisher is unable to explain, omitted from the published book. They can now be read and downloaded from the relevant page of our website: *www.colinsmythe.co.uk*.
Hbk ISBN 0-86140-292-8; pbk ISBN 0-86140-293-6

14. SELECTED PLAYS OF AUSTIN CLARKE
Chosen and introduced by Mary Shine Thompson
Includes *The Son of Learning, The Flame, Black Fast, The Kiss, As the Crow Flies, The Viscount of Blarney, The Second Kiss, Liberty Lane*, and the hitherto unpublished *The Frenzy of Sweeney*, and *St Patrick's Purgatory* (a translation of Calderón's play), 'Verse Speaking and Verse Drama', Bibliographical Checklist.
Hbk ISBN 0-86140-208-1; there is no paperback edition.